HORROR CLASSICS

Graphic Classics Volume Ten

2004

Edited by Tom Pomplun

EUREKA PRODUCTIONS

8778 Oak Grove Road, Mount Horeb, Wisconsin 53572
www.graphicclassics.com

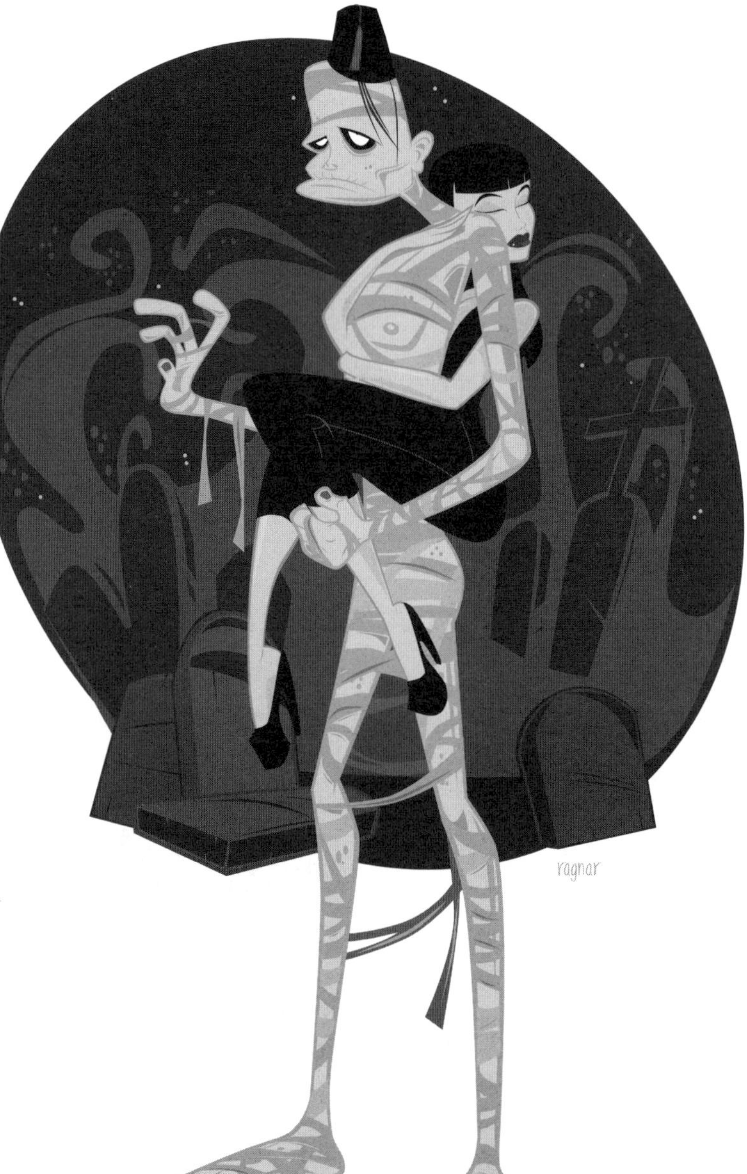
ragnar

THE MUMMY

By means of the Mummy, mankind, it is said,
Attests to the gods its respect for the dead.
We plunder his tomb, be he sinner or saint,
Distil him for physic and grind him for paint,
Exhibit for money his poor, shrunken frame,
And with levity flock to the scene of the shame.
O, tell me, ye gods, for the use of my rhyme:
For respecting the dead what's the limit of time?

poem by **Ambrose Bierce**, *Illustration by* **Brandon Ragnar Johnson**

CONTENTS

HORROR CLASSICS

Graphic Classics Volume Ten

Cover illustration by Mark A. Nelson / Back cover illustration by John W. Pierard

Horror Classics: Graphic Classics Volume Ten is published by Eureka Productions. ISBN #0-9746648-1-2. Price US $9.95. Available from Eureka Productions, 8778 Oak Grove Road, Mount Horeb, WI 53572. Tom Pomplun, designer and publisher, tom@graphicclassics.com. Eileen Fitzgerald, editorial assistant. The Thing on the Doorstep ©1937 H.P. Lovecraft, adapted by permission of Lovecraft Properties, LLC. The Beast of Averoigne © 1933 Clark Ashton Smith, adapted by permission of Arkham House and CASiana. This compilation and all original works ©2004 Eureka Productions. All rights revert to creators after publication. Graphic Classics is a trademark of Eureka Productions. The Graphic Classics website is at http://www.graphicclassics.com. Printed in Canada.

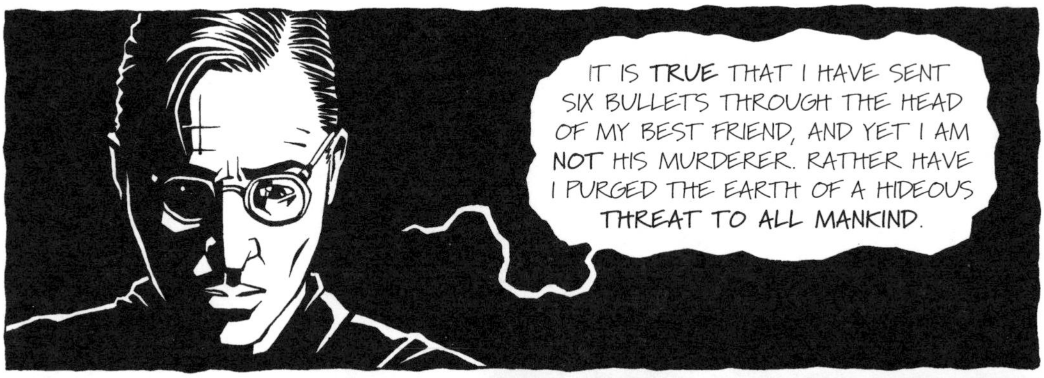
IT IS **TRUE** THAT I HAVE SENT SIX BULLETS THROUGH THE HEAD OF MY BEST FRIEND, AND YET I AM **NOT** HIS MURDERER. RATHER HAVE I PURGED THE EARTH OF A HIDEOUS **THREAT TO ALL MANKIND**.

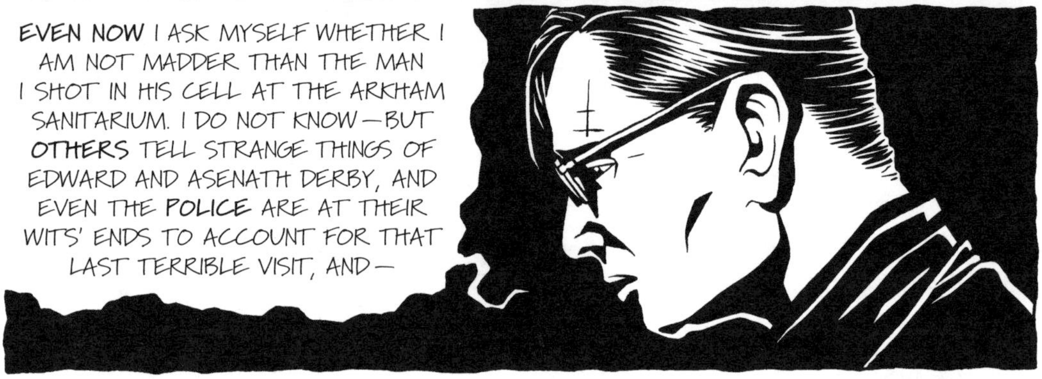
EVEN NOW I ASK MYSELF WHETHER I AM NOT MADDER THAN THE MAN I SHOT IN HIS CELL AT THE ARKHAM SANITARIUM. I DO NOT KNOW—BUT **OTHERS** TELL STRANGE THINGS OF EDWARD AND ASENATH DERBY, AND EVEN THE **POLICE** ARE AT THEIR WITS' ENDS TO ACCOUNT FOR THAT LAST TERRIBLE VISIT, AND—

The Thing on the Doorstep

story by H.P. Lovecraft • edited by Tom Pomplun • illustrated by Michael Manning

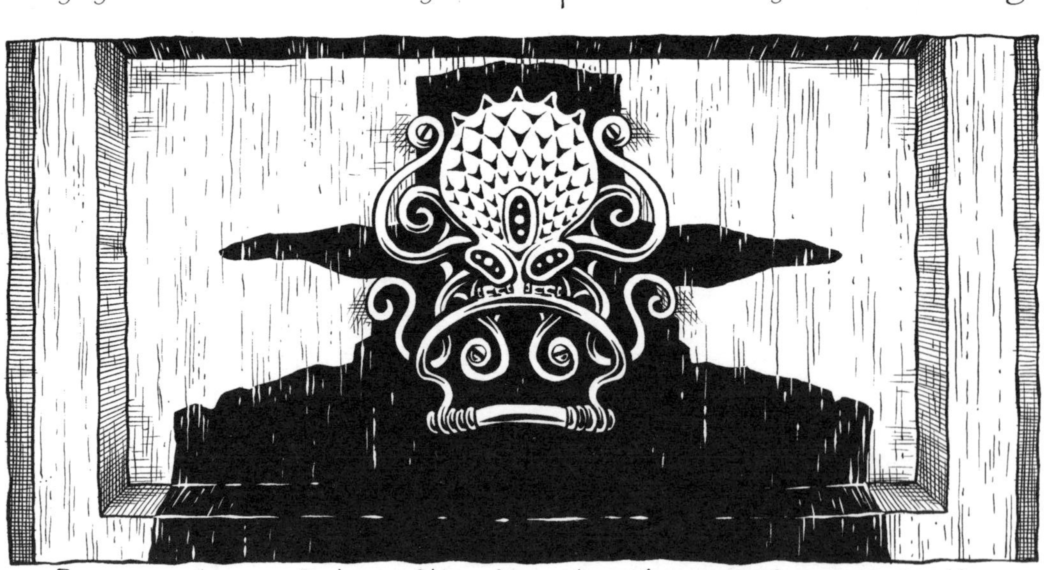

For my mother • Dolores Nina Manning (2·19·1942 ~ 5·15·2004)

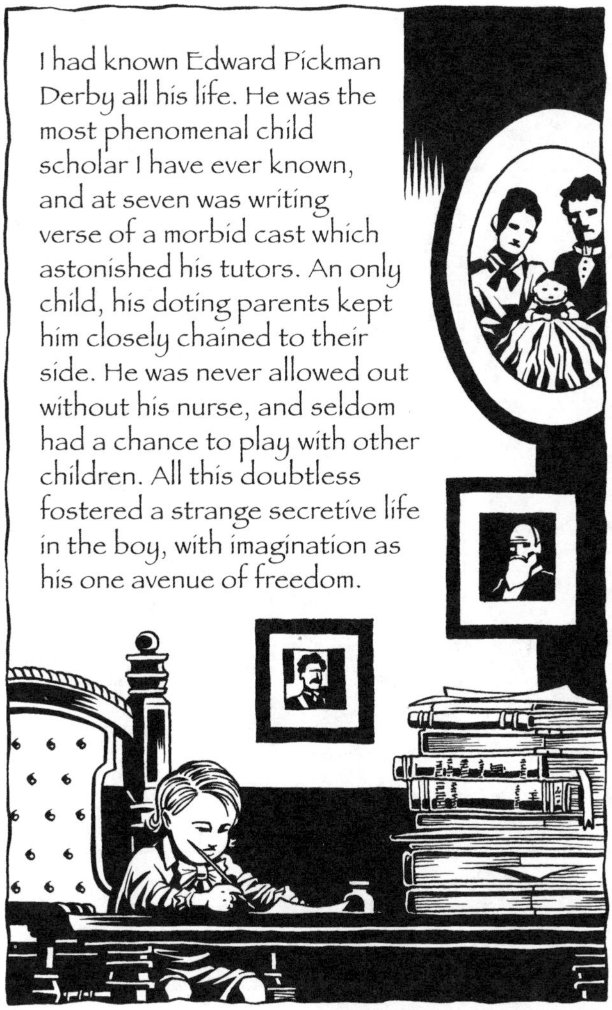
I had known Edward Pickman Derby all his life. He was the most phenomenal child scholar I have ever known, and at seven was writing verse of a morbid cast which astonished his tutors. An only child, his doting parents kept him closely chained to their side. He was never allowed out without his nurse, and seldom had a chance to play with other children. All this doubtless fostered a strange secretive life in the boy, with imagination as his one avenue of freedom.

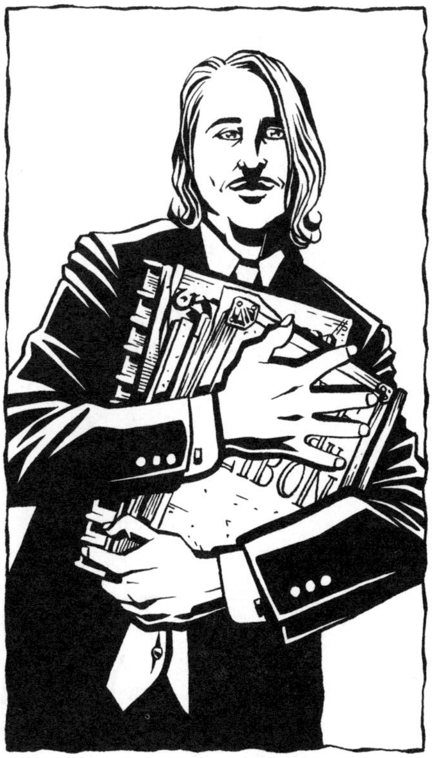

It was early seen that Derby would not be equal to a struggle in the business or professional arena, but the family fortune was so ample that this formed no tragedy. As he grew to manhood he retained a deceptive aspect of boyishness.

I had been to Harvard, had married, and had returned to Arkham to practice as an architect. Edward used to call on us almost every evening. He had a characteristic way of ringing the doorbell or sounding the knocker, so that after dinner I always listened for the familiar three brisk strokes followed by two more after a pause.

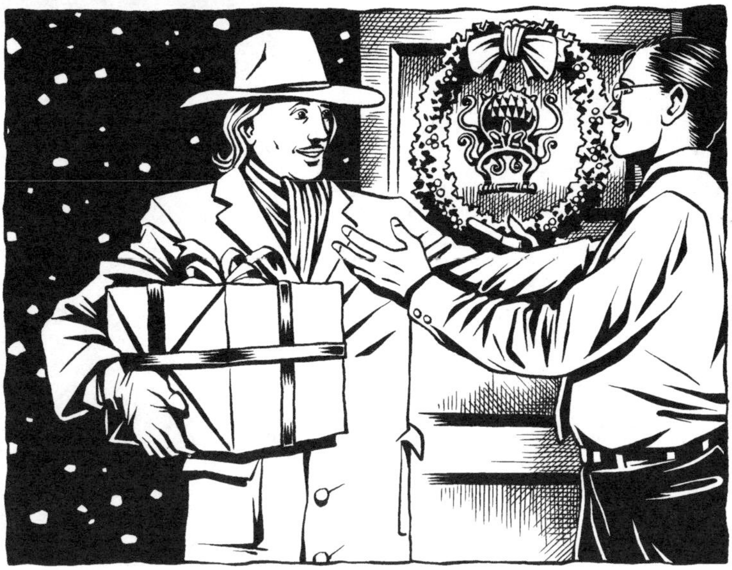

Derby attended Miskatonic University in Arkham, where he became an almost fanatical devotee of magical lore, for which Miskatonic's library is famous. He read things like the frightful Book of Eibon and the forbidden Necronomicon of the mad Arab Abdul Alhazred. By the time he was twenty-five Edward Derby was a well known poet and fantaisiste. I was his closest friend — finding him an inexhaustible mine of theoretical topics, while he relied on me for advice in more practical matters.

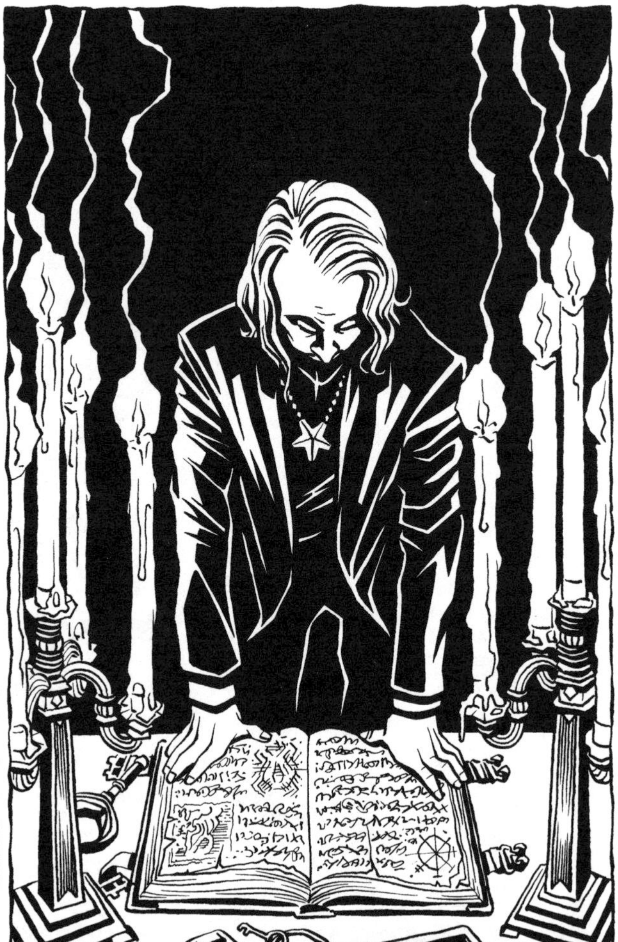

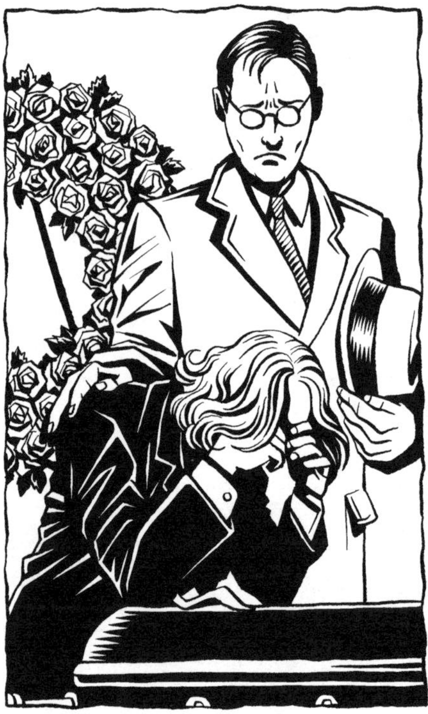

So the years wore on. Edward's mother died when he was thirty-four and his father took him to Europe. Afterward he began to mingle in the more "Bohemian" college set despite his age, and was present at some extremely wild doings.

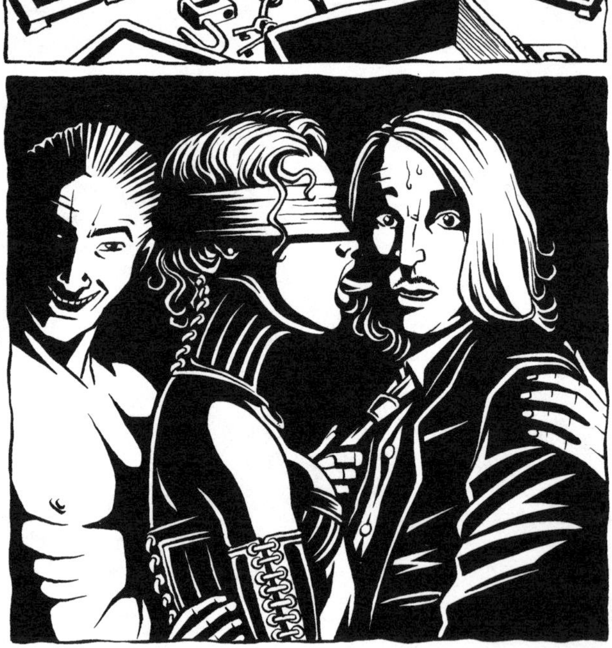

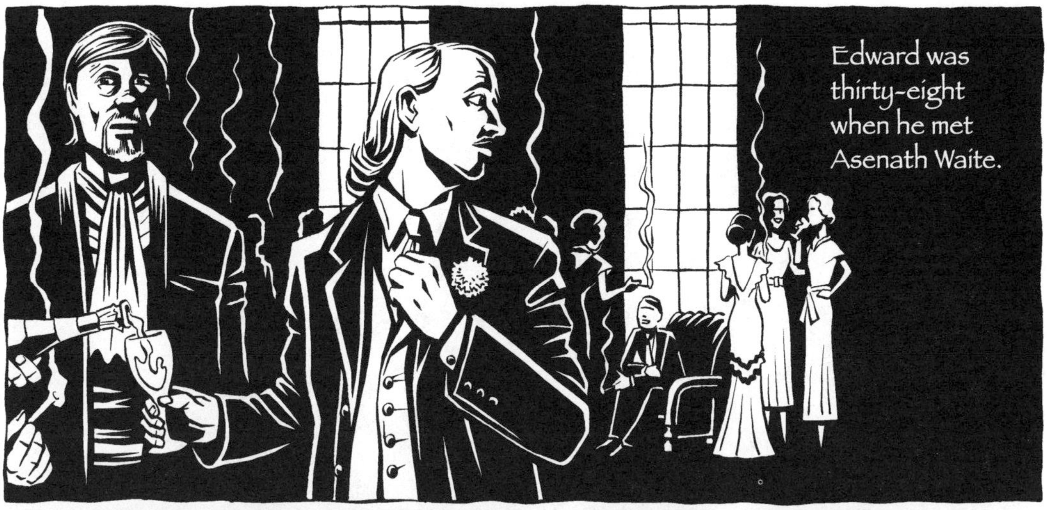
Edward was thirty-eight when he met Asenath Waite.

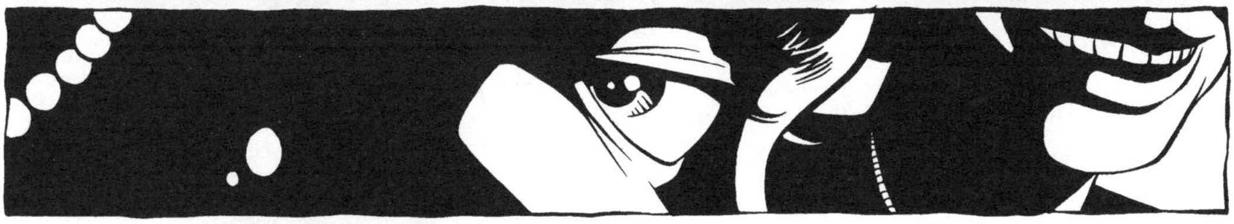

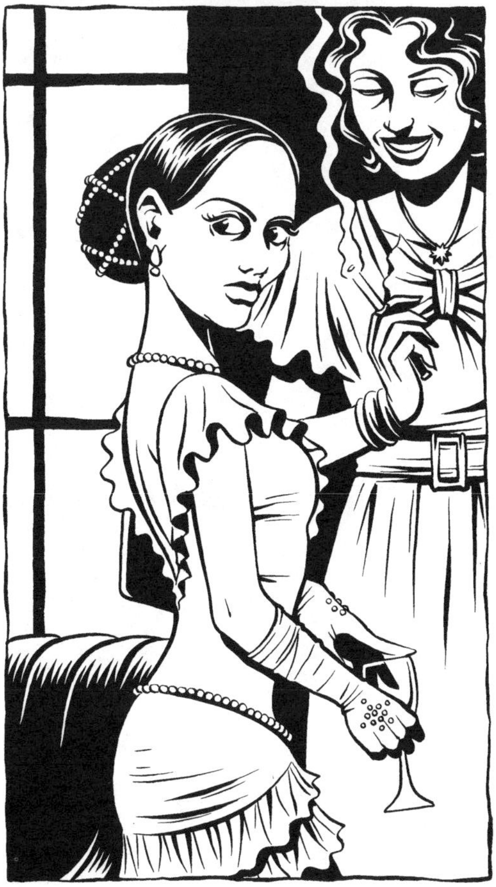

She was about twenty-three at the time, and was taking a course in mediaeval metaphysics at Miskatonic. She was dark, smallish, and very good-looking except for overprotuberant eyes; but something in her expression alienated people.

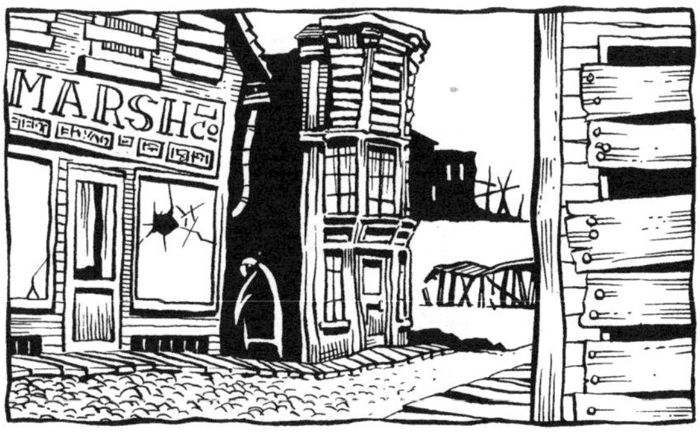
MARSH Co

It was, however, largely her origin and conversation which caused average folk to avoid her. She was of the Innsmouth Waites, and dark legends have clustered for generations about crumbling, half-deserted Innsmouth and its ancient families of "not quite human" people.

Asenath's case was aggravated by the fact that she was Ephraim Waite's daughter — the child of his old age by an unknown wife who always went veiled.

The old man was known to have been a prodigious magical student, and legend averred that he could raise or quell storms at sea according to his whim. He had died insane — under rather queer circumstances — just before his daughter entered the university, but she had been his morbidly avid pupil and looked fiendishly like him at times. There were times when she displayed snatches of knowledge and language very shocking for a young girl.

Most unusual, though, were the well-attested cases of her influence over other persons. She was, beyond question, a genuine hypnotist. By gazing peculiarly at a fellow-student she would often give the latter a distinct feeling of exchanged personality — as if the subject were placed momentarily in the magician's body and able to stare across the room at his real body. Asenath often made wild claims about the nature of consciousness and about its independence of the physical frame. Her crowning rage, however, was that she was not a man; since she believed a male brain had certain unique and far-reaching powers. Given a man's brain, she declared, she could surpass her father in the mastery of unknown forces.

Edward met Asenath at a gathering of "intelligentsia," and could talk of nothing else when he came to see me the next day. He had found her full of the interests which engrossed him, and was in addition wildly taken with her appearance.

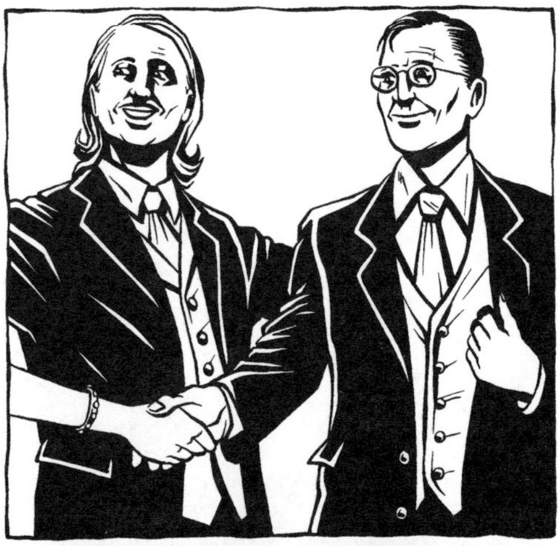

In the next few weeks I heard of very little but Asenath from young Derby. Edward soon brought the girl to call on me, and I at once saw that his interest was by no means one-sided.

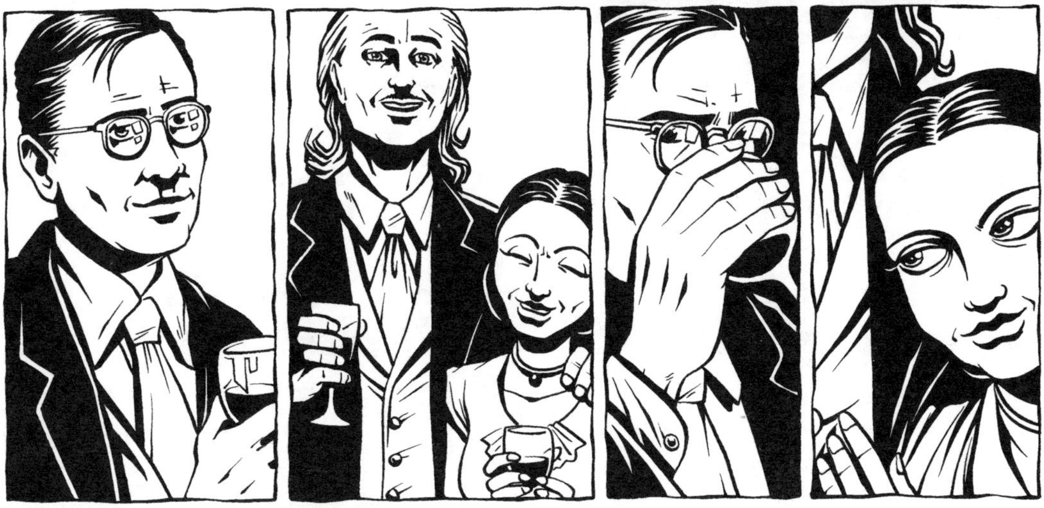

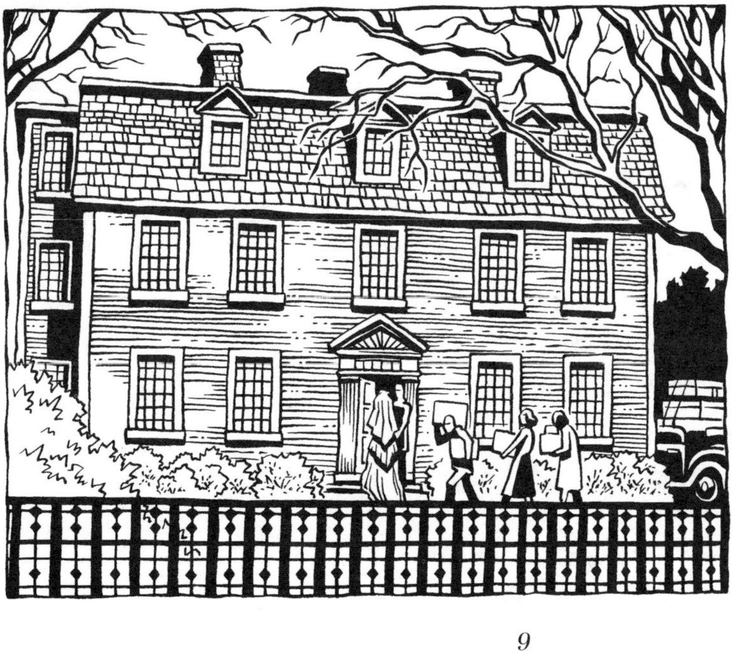

She eyed him with an almost predatory air, and I perceived that their intimacy was beyond untangling. The wedding was performed a month later. Asenath had bought the old Crowninshield place, and they settled there after a trip to Innsmouth, whence three servants and some household goods were brought.

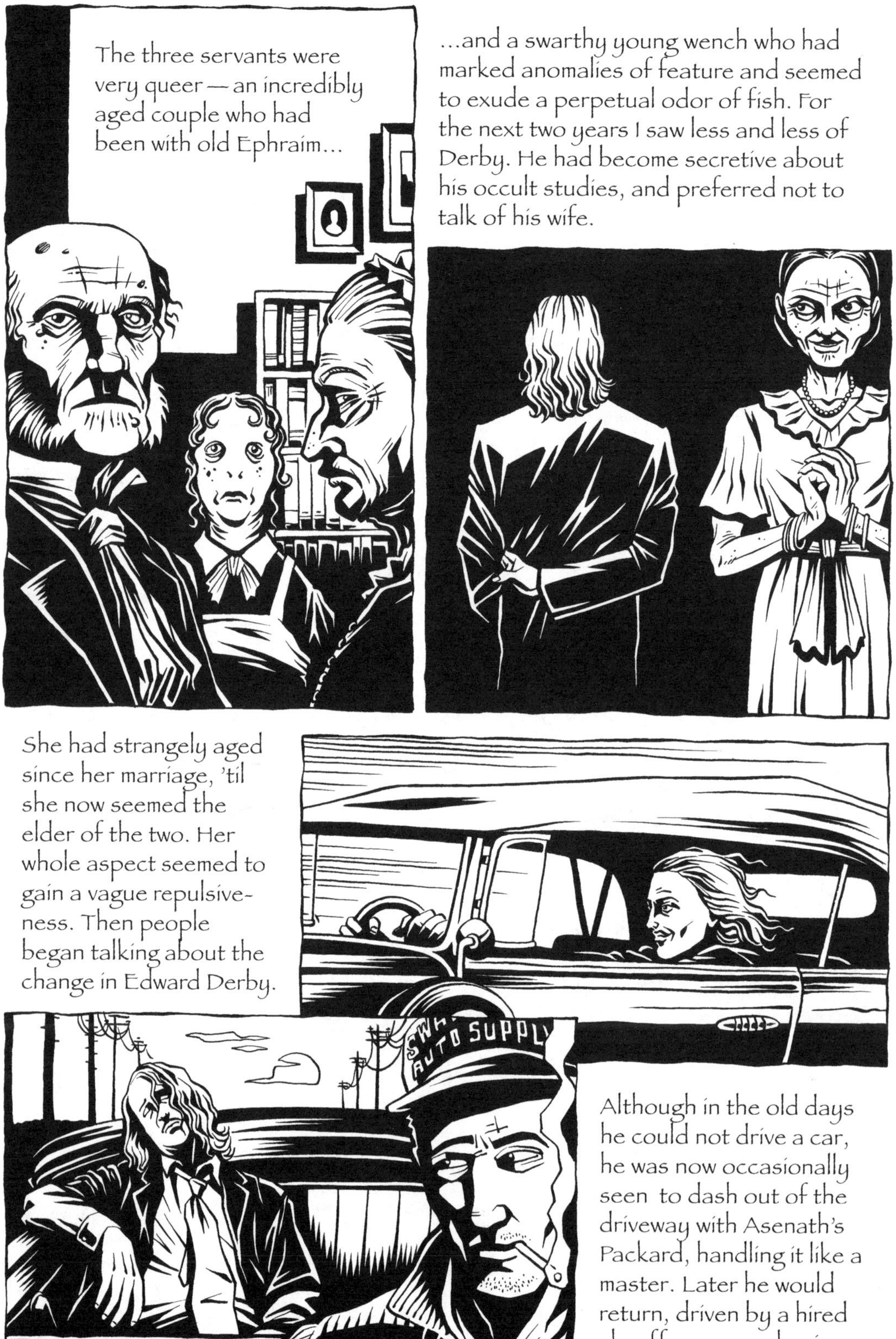
The three servants were very queer — an incredibly aged couple who had been with old Ephraim…
…and a swarthy young wench who had marked anomalies of feature and seemed to exude a perpetual odor of fish. For the next two years I saw less and less of Derby. He had become secretive about his occult studies, and preferred not to talk of his wife.
She had strangely aged since her marriage, 'til she now seemed the elder of the two. Her whole aspect seemed to gain a vague repulsiveness. Then people began talking about the change in Edward Derby.
AUTO SUPPLY
Although in the old days he could not drive a car, he was now occasionally seen to dash out of the driveway with Asenath's Packard, handling it like a master. Later he would return, driven by a hired chauffeur or mechanic.

It was in the third year of the marriage that Edward began to hint openly to me of a certain fear and dissatisfaction. He would let fall remarks about things "going too far," and would talk darkly about the need of "gaining his identity." At first I ignored such references, but I remembered Asenath's hypnotic influence over the other students at school. About this time old Mr. Derby died. Edward had seen astonishingly little of his parent since his marriage, for Asenath had concentrated in herself all his sense of family linkage.

Not long afterward my wife heard a curious thing from a friend. She had been out to call on the Derbys, and had seen a car shoot out of the drive with Edward's oddly sneering face above the wheel. Ringing the bell, she had been told that Asenath was also out; but had chanced to look at the house in leaving. There, at one of the windows, she had glimpsed a hastily withdrawn face — a face whose expression of pain, defeat, and wistful hopelessness was poignant beyond description.

Derby had been married more than three years
on that August day when I got the telegram from Maine.
I had not seen him for two months, but had heard he was
away "on business." Asenath was supposed to be with
him, though watchful gossip declared there was someone
upstairs in the house behind the curtained windows.

And now the town marshal
of Chesuncook had wired of
the draggled madman who
stumbled out of the woods
with delirious ravings
and screamed to me for
protection.

Chesuncook is close to the
wildest forest belt in Maine,
and it took a whole day of
jolting through forbidding
scenery to get there by car.
I found Derby in a cell,
vacillating between frenzy
and apathy.

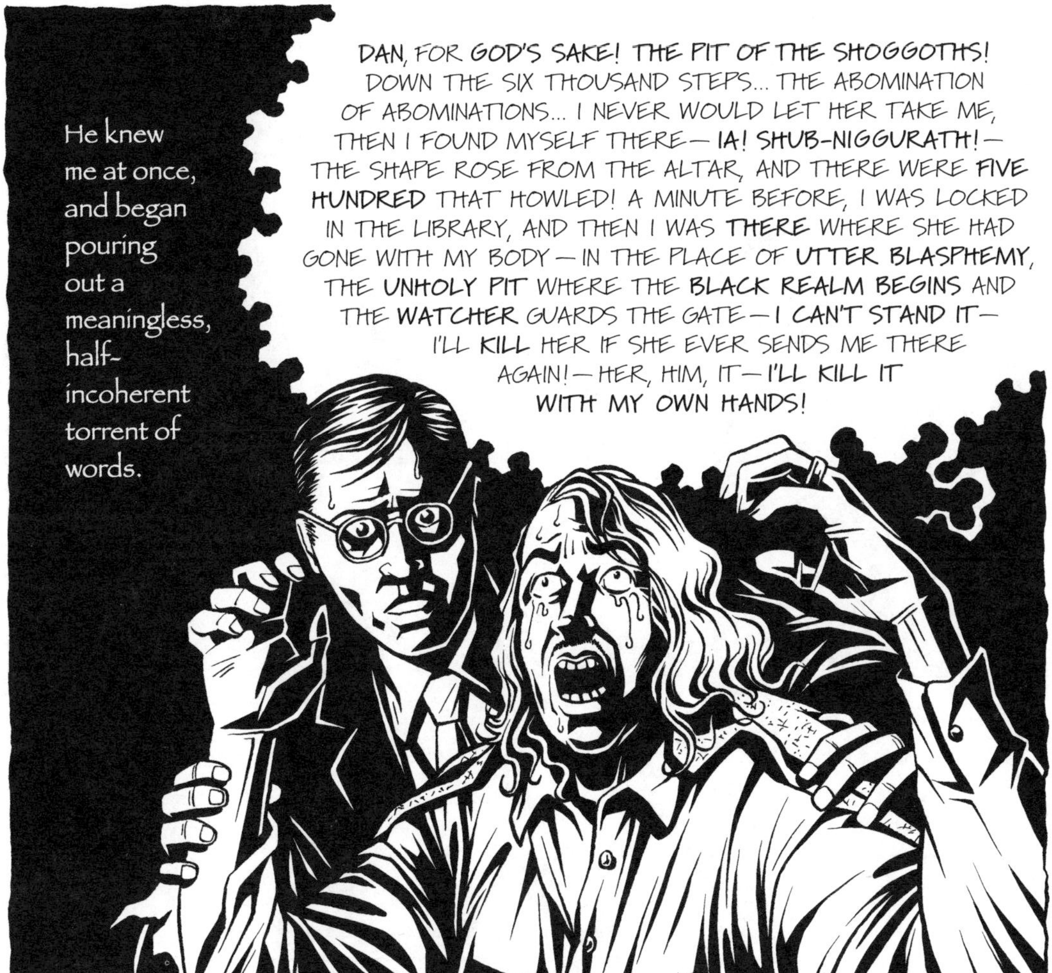
He knew me at once, and began pouring out a meaningless, half-incoherent torrent of words.
DAN, FOR GOD'S SAKE! THE PIT OF THE SHOGGOTHS! DOWN THE SIX THOUSAND STEPS... THE ABOMINATION OF ABOMINATIONS... I NEVER WOULD LET HER TAKE ME, THEN I FOUND MYSELF THERE— IA! SHUB-NIGGURATH!— THE SHAPE ROSE FROM THE ALTAR, AND THERE WERE FIVE HUNDRED THAT HOWLED! A MINUTE BEFORE, I WAS LOCKED IN THE LIBRARY, AND THEN I WAS THERE WHERE SHE HAD GONE WITH MY BODY — IN THE PLACE OF UTTER BLASPHEMY, THE UNHOLY PIT WHERE THE BLACK REALM BEGINS AND THE WATCHER GUARDS THE GATE — I CAN'T STAND IT— I'LL KILL HER IF SHE EVER SENDS ME THERE AGAIN!— HER, HIM, IT— I'LL KILL IT WITH MY OWN HANDS!

It took me an hour to quiet him, but he subsided at last. The next day I got him decent clothes in the village, and set out with him for Arkham. It was clear that he did not wish to go home; and considering the fantastic delusions he seemed to have about his wife, I thought it would be better if he did not. I would, I resolved, put him up myself for a time.

Later I would help him get a divorce, for most assuredly there were factors which made this marriage suicidal for him. When we struck open country Derby's muttering faded away, and I let him drowse on the seat beside me as I drove.

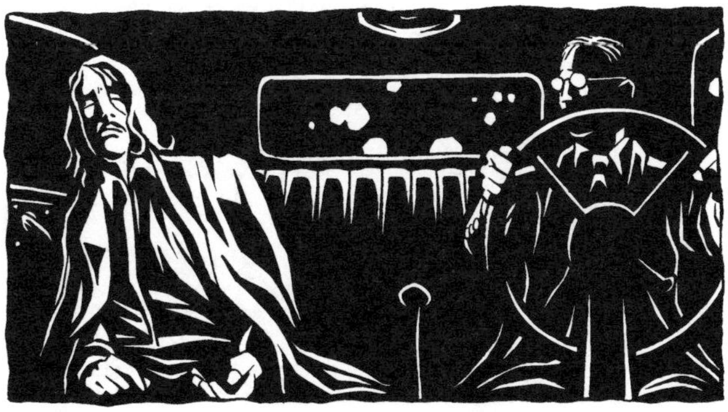

Soon the muttering commenced again; a stream of utterly insane drivel about Asenath. She was getting hold of him — she constantly took his body and went to nameless places for nameless rites, leaving him in her body and locking him upstairs — but sometimes she couldn't hold on, and he would find himself in his own body in some horrible place.

She was holding on to him longer each time. She wanted to be a man! Some day she would crowd him out and leave him in that female shell that wasn't even quite human.

He knew about the Innsmouth blood, and the horrible traffic with things from the sea ... and Ephraim — he had known the secret, and when he grew old did a hideous thing to keep alive!

HE GLARED AT ME ONCE, AND I NEVER FORGOT IT... NOW **SHE** GLARES THAT WAY! HE FOUND THE FORMULA IN THE NEC-RONOMICON — **HE MEANS NEVER TO DIE!**

Then the thing happened... Derby's voice was rising to a thin scream as he raved, when suddenly it was shut off, and the face beside me was twisted almost unrecognizably for a moment.

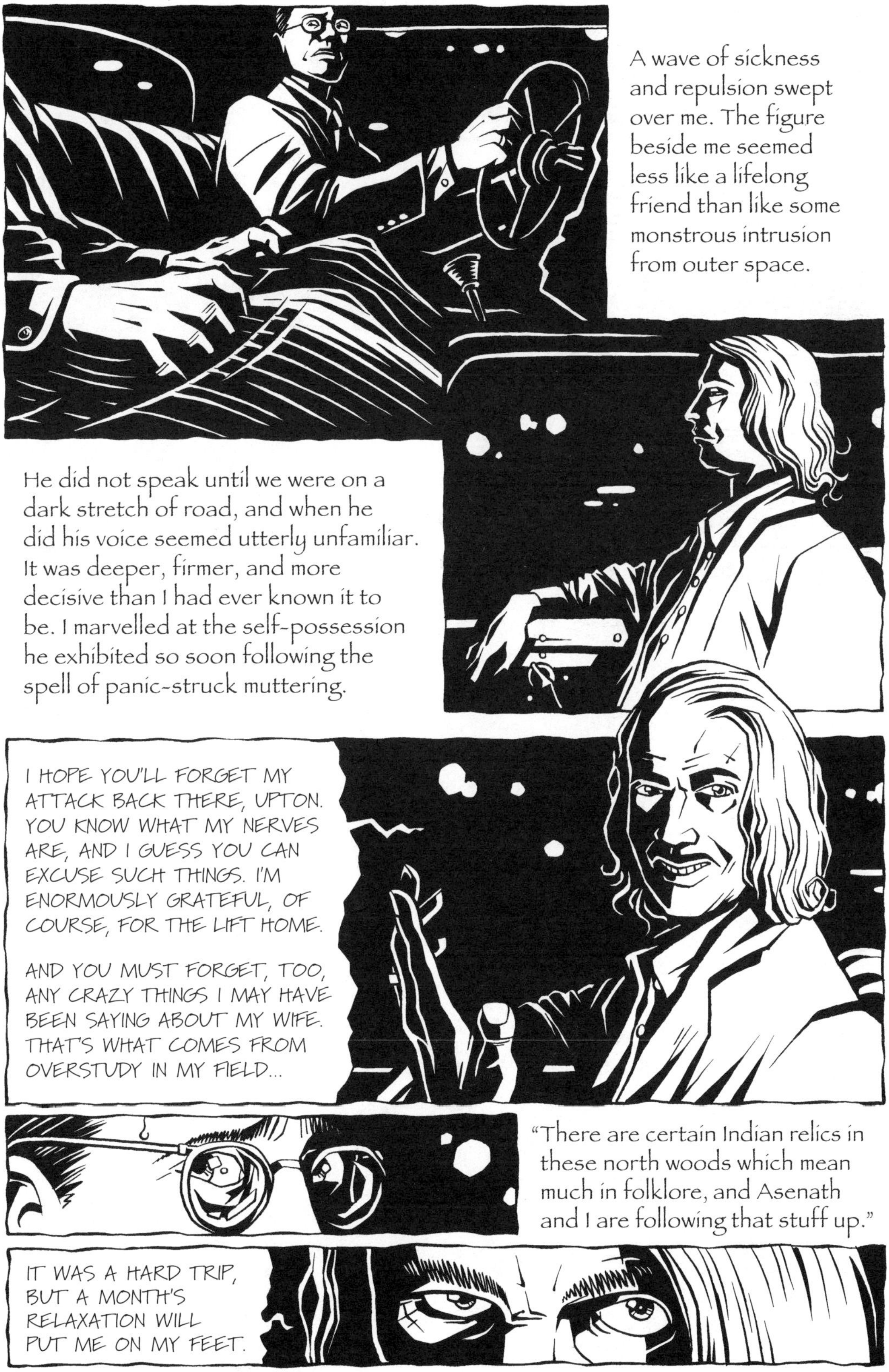
A wave of sickness and repulsion swept over me. The figure beside me seemed less like a lifelong friend than like some monstrous intrusion from outer space.
He did not speak until we were on a dark stretch of road, and when he did his voice seemed utterly unfamiliar. It was deeper, firmer, and more decisive than I had ever known it to be. I marvelled at the self-possession he exhibited so soon following the spell of panic-struck muttering.
I HOPE YOU'LL FORGET MY ATTACK BACK THERE, UPTON. YOU KNOW WHAT MY NERVES ARE, AND I GUESS YOU CAN EXCUSE SUCH THINGS. I'M ENORMOUSLY GRATEFUL, OF COURSE, FOR THE LIFT HOME.
AND YOU MUST FORGET, TOO, ANY CRAZY THINGS I MAY HAVE BEEN SAYING ABOUT MY WIFE. THAT'S WHAT COMES FROM OVERSTUDY IN MY FIELD...
"There are certain Indian relics in these north woods which mean much in folklore, and Asenath and I are following that stuff up."
IT WAS A HARD TRIP, BUT A MONTH'S RELAXATION WILL PUT ME ON MY FEET.

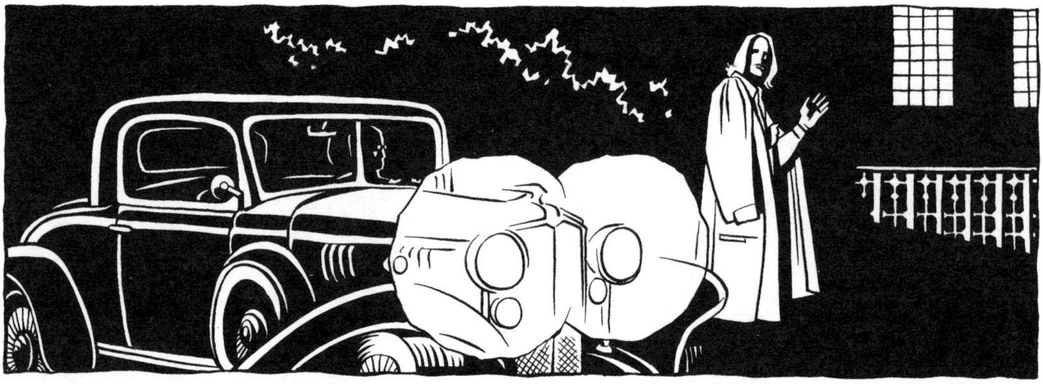

We reached Arkham around midnight. Derby left the car with a hasty repetition of his thanks, and I drove home alone with a curious feeling of relief.

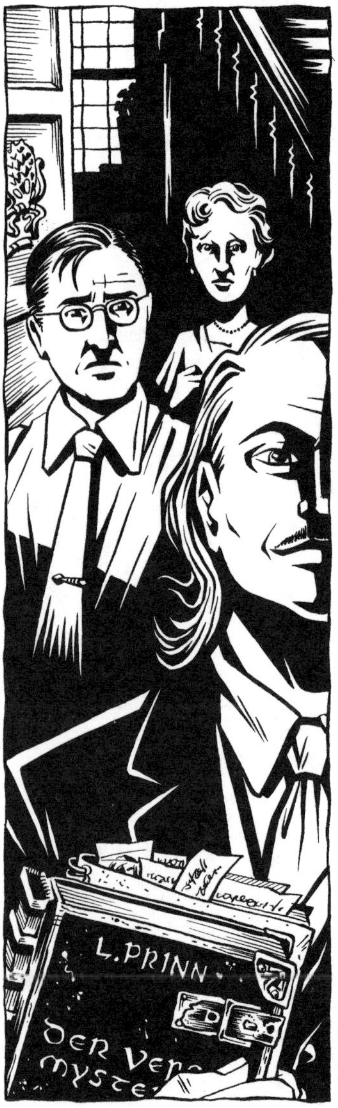
L.PRINN

Over the next two months, people spoke of seeing Derby more and more in his new energized state, and Asenath was rarely seen. I had only one visit from Edward, when he called to get some books he had lent me. He was in his new state, and paused only long enough for some evasively polite remarks. It was plain that he had nothing to discuss with me — and I noticed that he did not even trouble to give the old three-and-two signal when ringing the doorbell.

But the oddest rumours were those about the occasional sobbing heard in the old Crowninshield house. There was talk of an investigation, but this was dispelled one day when Asenath appeared in the streets and chatted with a large number of acquaintances, apologizing for her recent absence.

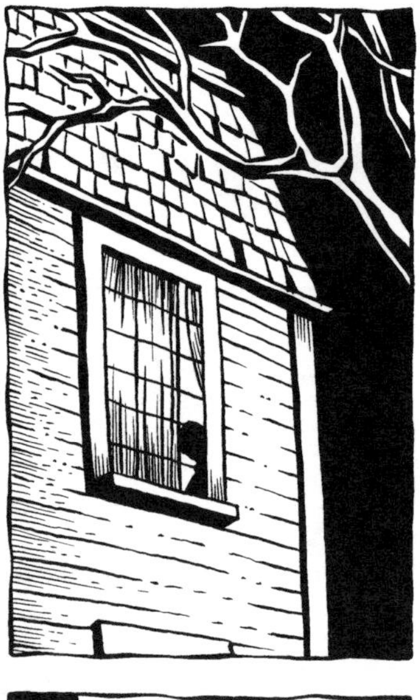

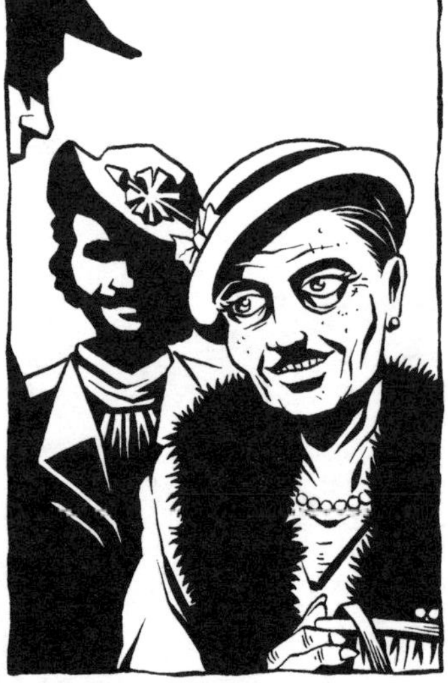

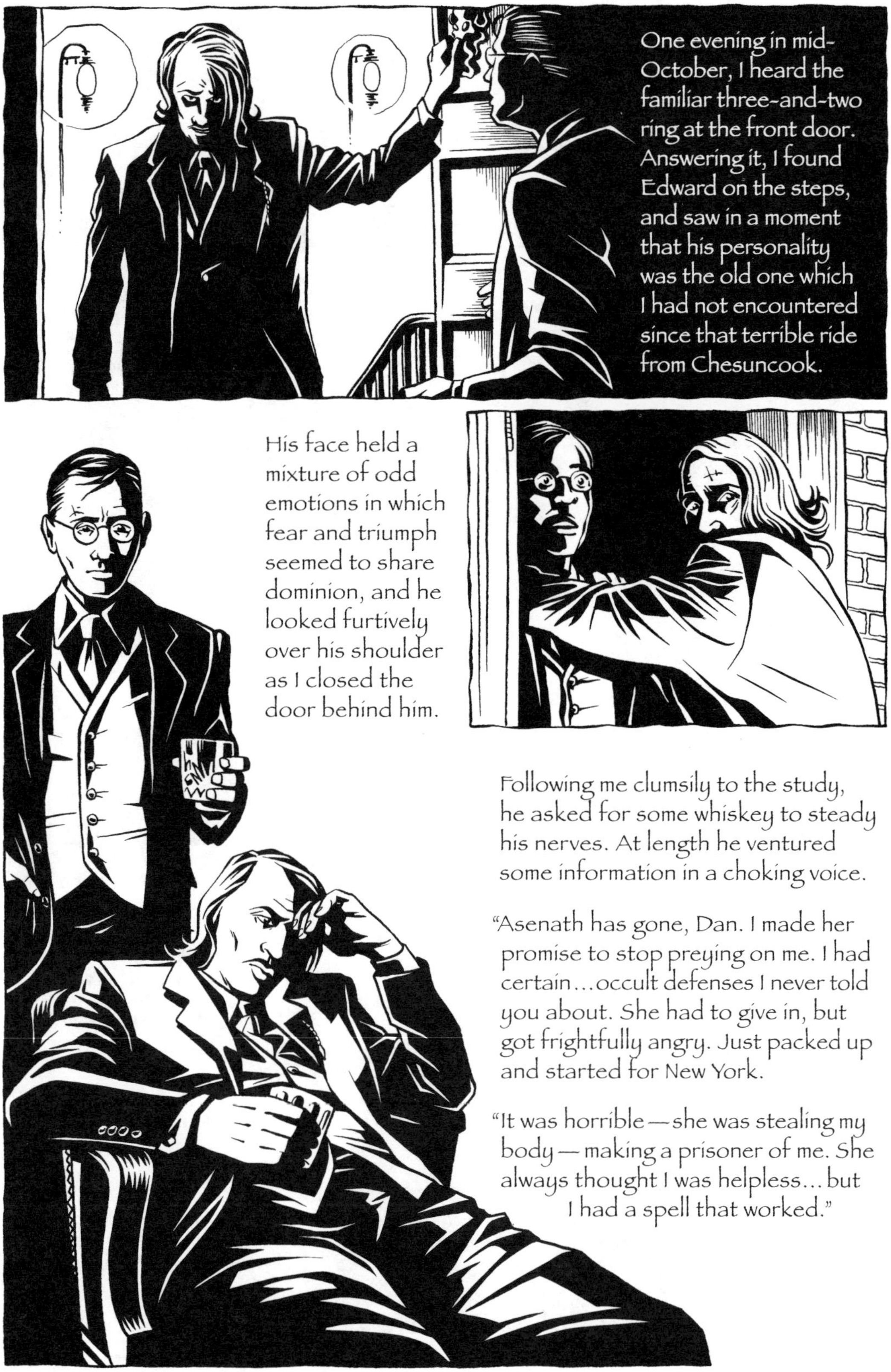
One evening in mid-October, I heard the familiar three-and-two ring at the front door. Answering it, I found Edward on the steps, and saw in a moment that his personality was the old one which I had not encountered since that terrible ride from Chesuncook.
His face held a mixture of odd emotions in which fear and triumph seemed to share dominion, and he looked furtively over his shoulder as I closed the door behind him.
Following me clumsily to the study, he asked for some whiskey to steady his nerves. At length he ventured some information in a choking voice.
"Asenath has gone, Dan. I made her promise to stop preying on me. I had certain... occult defenses I never told you about. She had to give in, but got frightfully angry. Just packed up and started for New York.
"It was horrible—she was stealing my body—making a prisoner of me. She always thought I was helpless... but I had a spell that worked."

"I suppose you think I'm crazy, Dan, but you've seen one of the changes — in your car that day coming home from Maine. She got me, and in a flash I was back at the house — in the library where those damned servants had me locked up — and in that cursed fiend's body that isn't even human...

"I had to save myself, Dan! She'd have got me at Hallowmass — they hold a Sabbat up beyond Chesuncook, and the sacrifice would have clinched things. She'd have been a man, and fully human, just as she wanted to be — she'd have killed her own ex-body with me in it, damn her — just as she did, or it did before —"

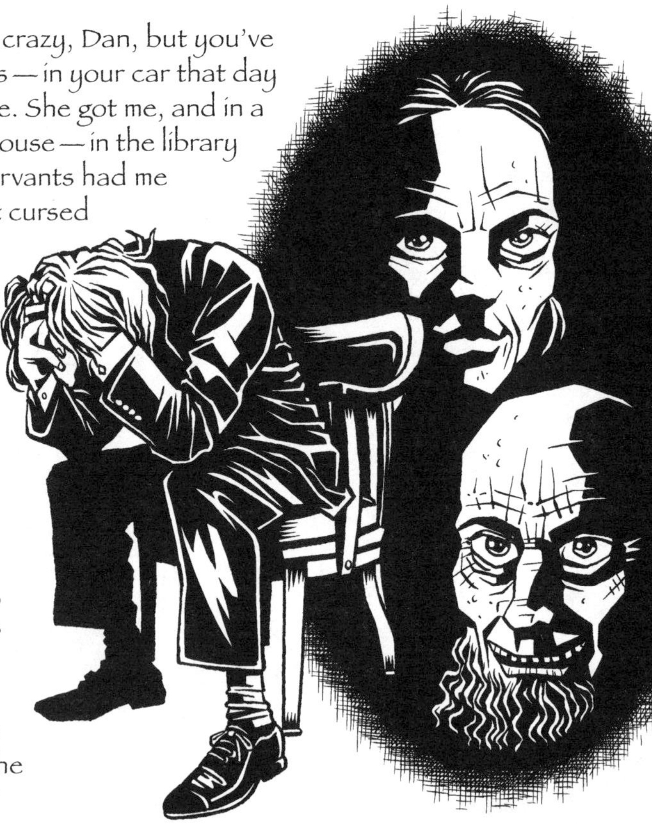

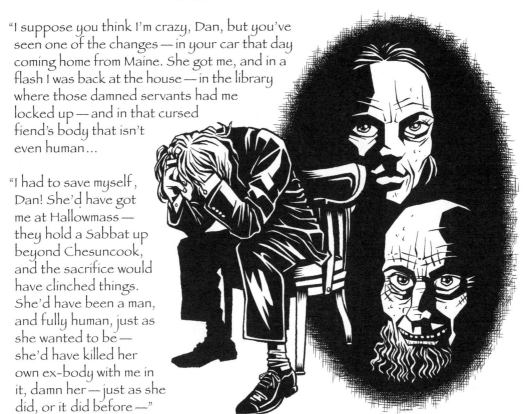

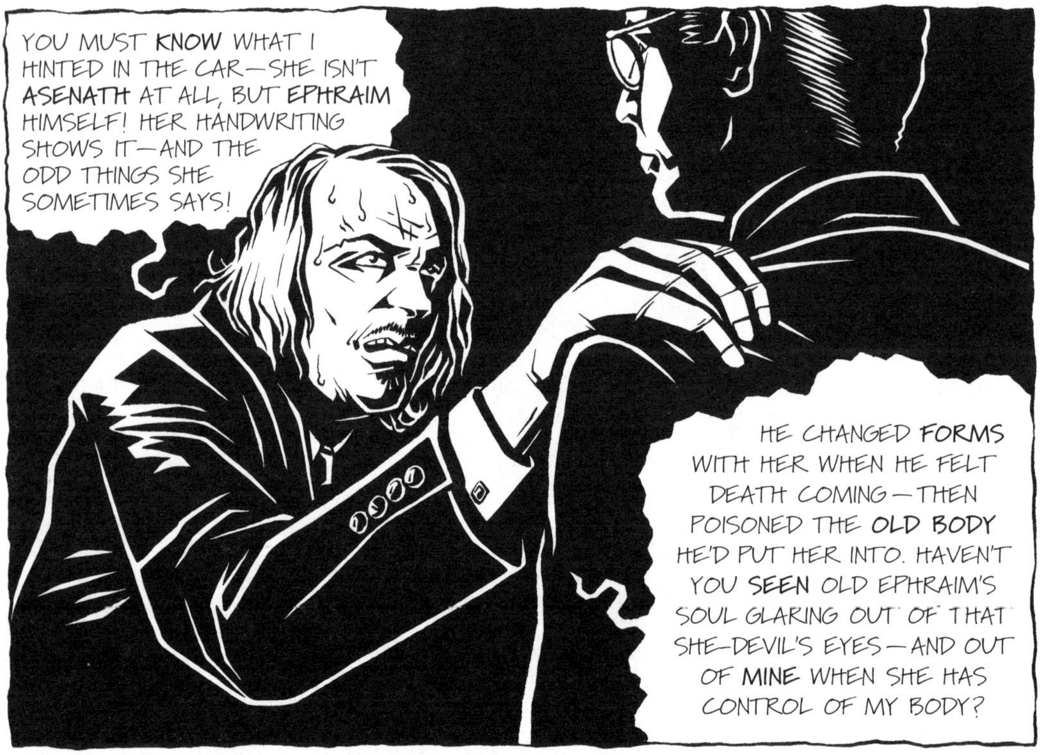
YOU MUST KNOW WHAT I HINTED IN THE CAR—SHE ISN'T ASENATH AT ALL, BUT EPHRAIM HIMSELF! HER HANDWRITING SHOWS IT—AND THE ODD THINGS SHE SOMETIMES SAYS!
HE CHANGED FORMS WITH HER WHEN HE FELT DEATH COMING—THEN POISONED THE OLD BODY HE'D PUT HER INTO. HAVEN'T YOU SEEN OLD EPHRAIM'S SOUL GLARING OUT OF THAT SHE-DEVIL'S EYES—AND OUT OF MINE WHEN SHE HAS CONTROL OF MY BODY?

I had Edward stay for the night, and in the morning he seemed calmer. We discussed arrangements for his moving back into the Derby mansion, and I hoped he would lose no time in making the change.

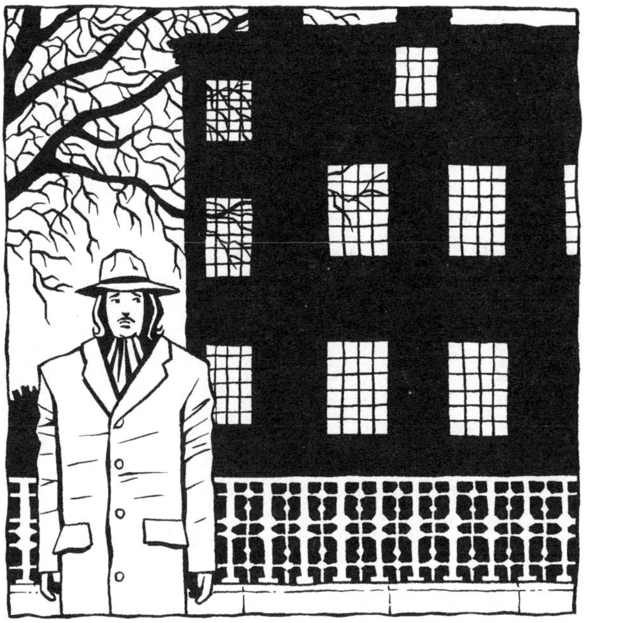

The house was ready by December, yet Edward was not mending as rapidly as I had hoped he would; for there was something a bit hysterical in his occasional exhilaration, while his moods of depression were altogether too frequent. Though he hated the Crowninshield place, he invented every kind of excuse to postpone moving. When I pointed this out to him he appeared unaccountably frightened.

It was about Christmas that Derby finally broke down. He suddenly shrieked with a look of uncontrollable terror.

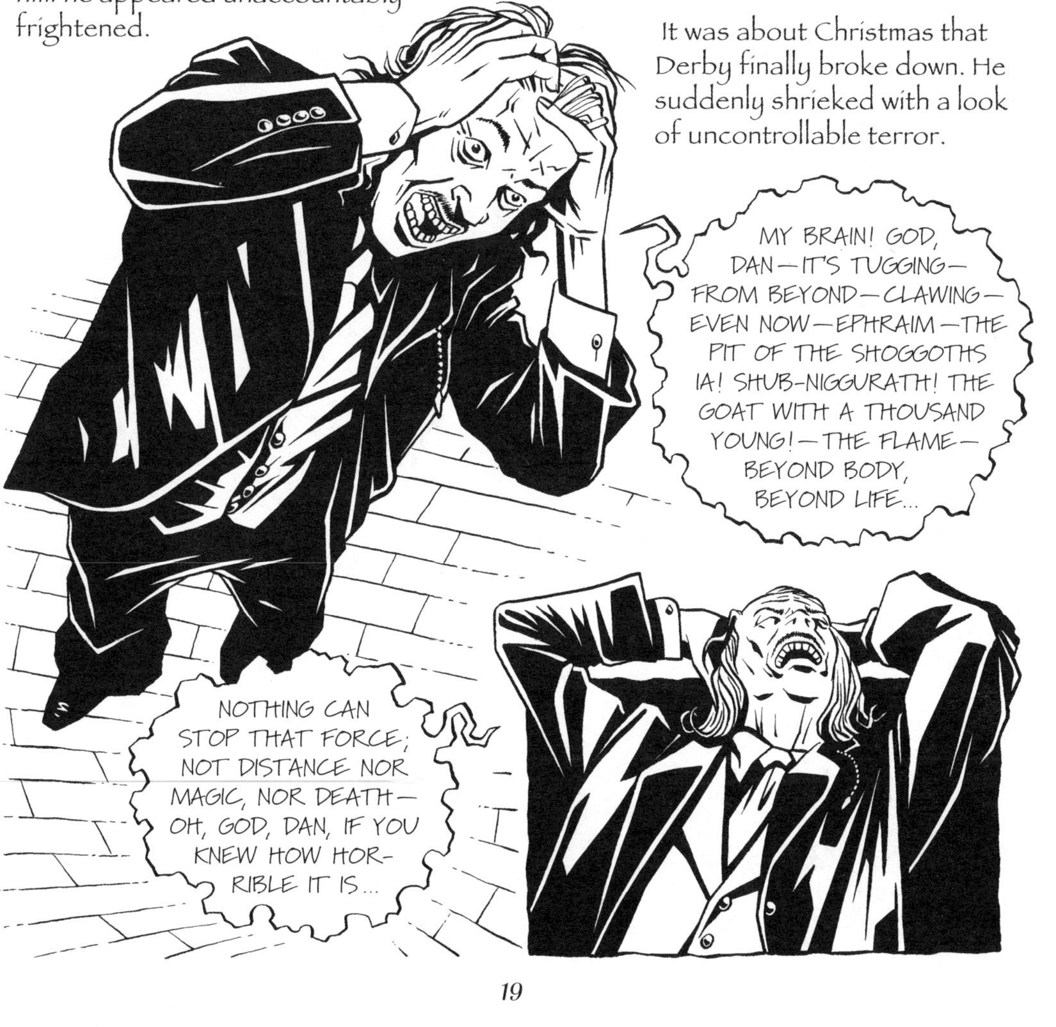
MY BRAIN! GOD, DAN—IT'S TUGGING—FROM BEYOND—CLAWING—EVEN NOW—EPHRAIM—THE PIT OF THE SHOGGOTHS IA! SHUB-NIGGURATH! THE GOAT WITH A THOUSAND YOUNG!—THE FLAME—BEYOND BODY, BEYOND LIFE...
NOTHING CAN STOP THAT FORCE; NOT DISTANCE NOR MAGIC, NOR DEATH—OH, GOD, DAN, IF YOU KNEW HOW HOR-RIBLE IT IS...

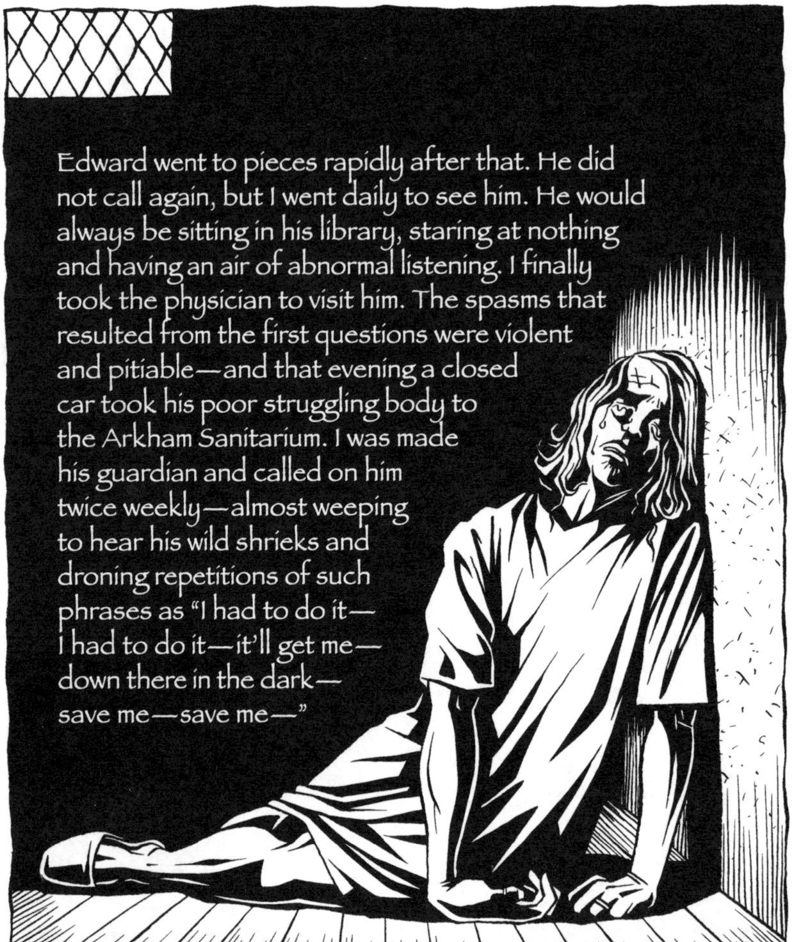
Edward went to pieces rapidly after that. He did not call again, but I went daily to see him. He would always be sitting in his library, staring at nothing and having an air of abnormal listening. I finally took the physician to visit him. The spasms that resulted from the first questions were violent and pitiable—and that evening a closed car took his poor struggling body to the Arkham Sanitarium. I was made his guardian and called on him twice weekly—almost weeping to hear his wild shrieks and droning repetitions of such phrases as "I had to do it—I had to do it—it'll get me—down there in the dark—save me—save me—"

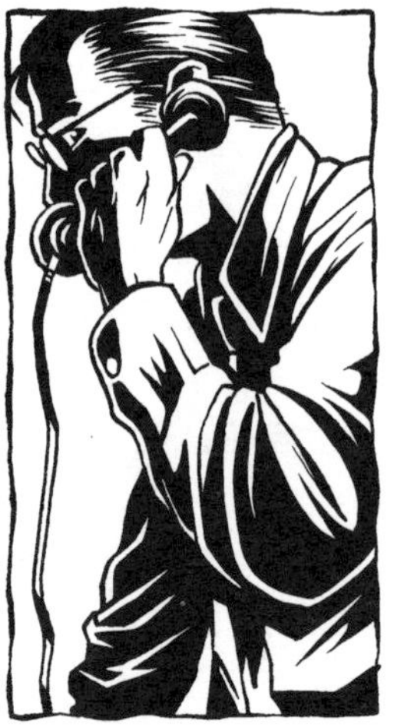

One morning late in January the sanitarium telephoned to report that Edward's reason had suddenly come back. All going well after observation, he would surely be free in a week.

I hastened over, but stood bewildered when a nurse took me to Edward's room. The patient rose to greet me, extending his hand with a polite smile; but I saw in an instant that he bore the strangely energized personality which had seemed so foreign to his own nature.

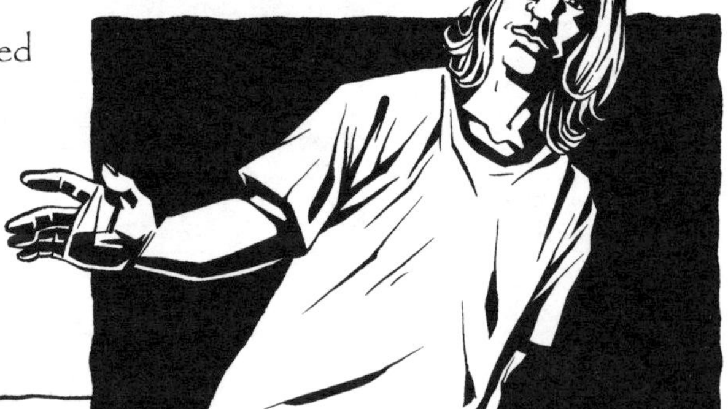

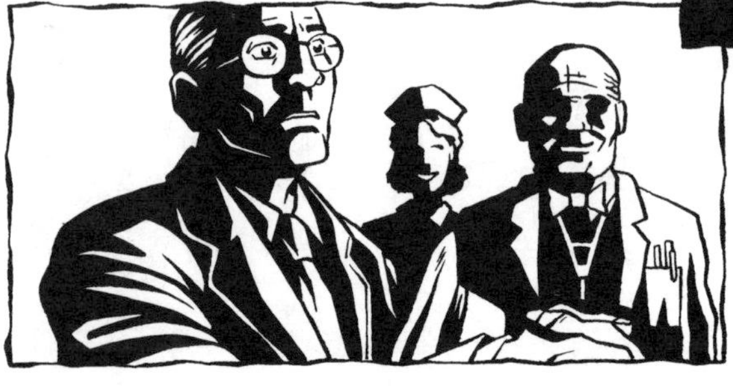

There was nothing for me to do but assent to his release. This was a sane person—but was it indeed Edward Derby? Ought it to be free, or ought it to be extirpated from the face of the earth?

All that day I racked my brain over the problem. What had happened? What sort of mind looked out through those alien eyes in Edward's face? The next morning the hospital called up to say that the recovered patient was unchanged, and by evening I was close to a nervous collapse—a state I admit, though others will vow it coloured my subsequent vision.

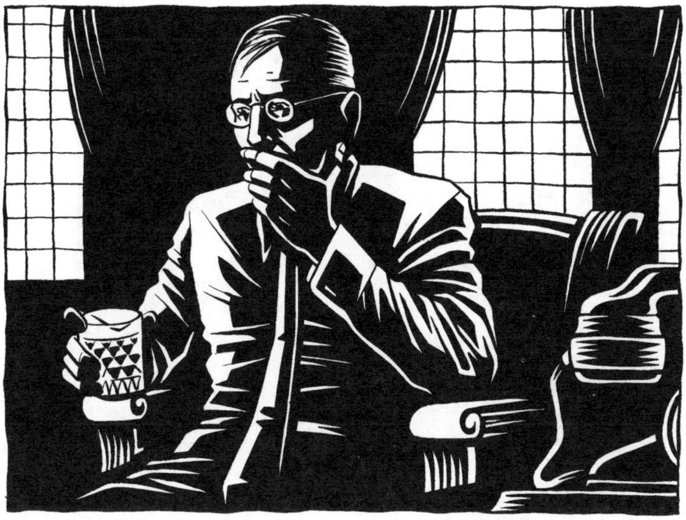

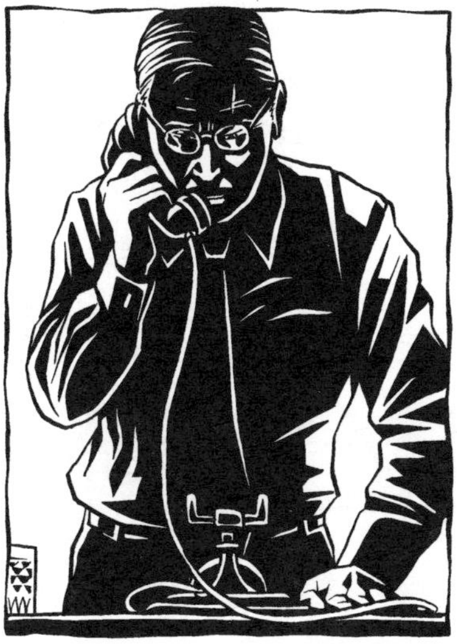

It was in that night the stark, utter horror burst over me. It began with a telephone call just before midnight. No one seemed to be on the wire, and I was about to hang up and go to bed when my ear caught a very faint sound at the other end. As I listened I thought I heard a sort of half-liquid bubbling noise—"glub... glub... glub"—with an odd suggestion of inarticulate, unintelligible words. I called "Who is it?" But the only answer was "glub... glub... glub-glub."

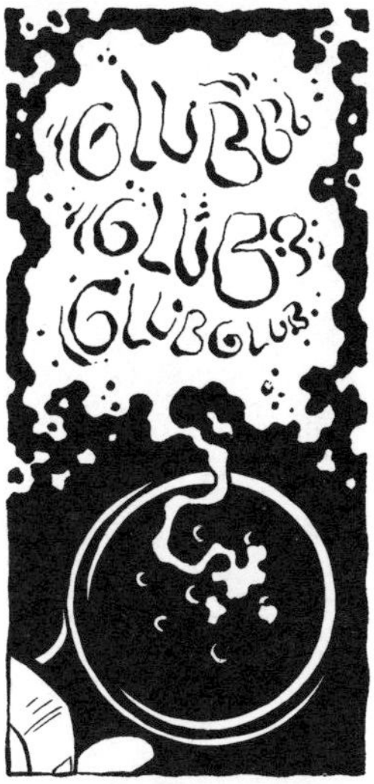
GLUBBB
GLUBB
GLUBGLUB

"I can't hear you," I said. "Better hang up and try Information." Immediately I heard the receiver go on the hook at the other end.

That was all until about two o'clock, when the doorbell waked me—doorbell and knocker both, applied uncertainly in a kind of weak desperation, trying to keep Edward's old signal of three-and-two strokes. My mind leaped into a turmoil. Derby at the door—and remembering the old code! That new personality had not remembered it... was Edward now back in his rightful state? Had he been released early, or had he escaped?

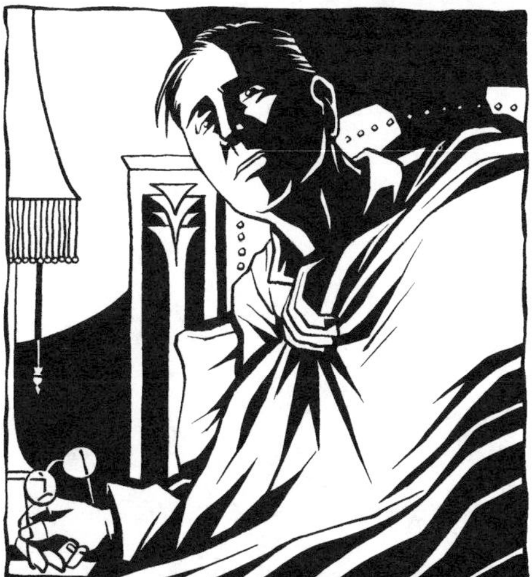

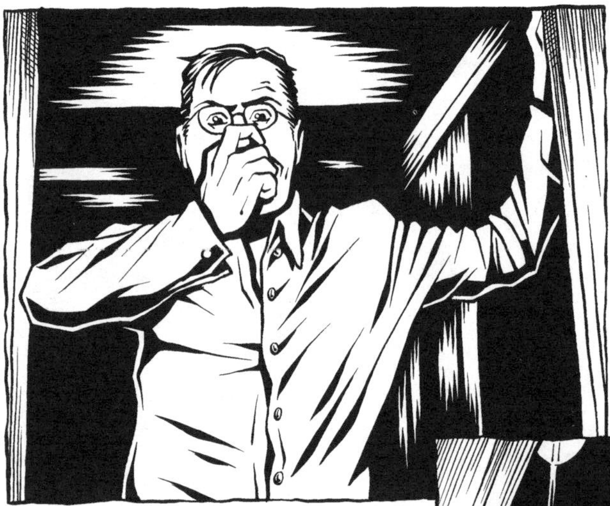

When I opened the door a gust of insufferably foetid wind almost flung me prostrate. I choked in nausea, and for a second scarcely saw the dwarfed, humped figure on the steps. The summons had been Edward's, but who was this foul, stunted parody? Where had Edward gone? His ring had sounded only a second before the door opened.

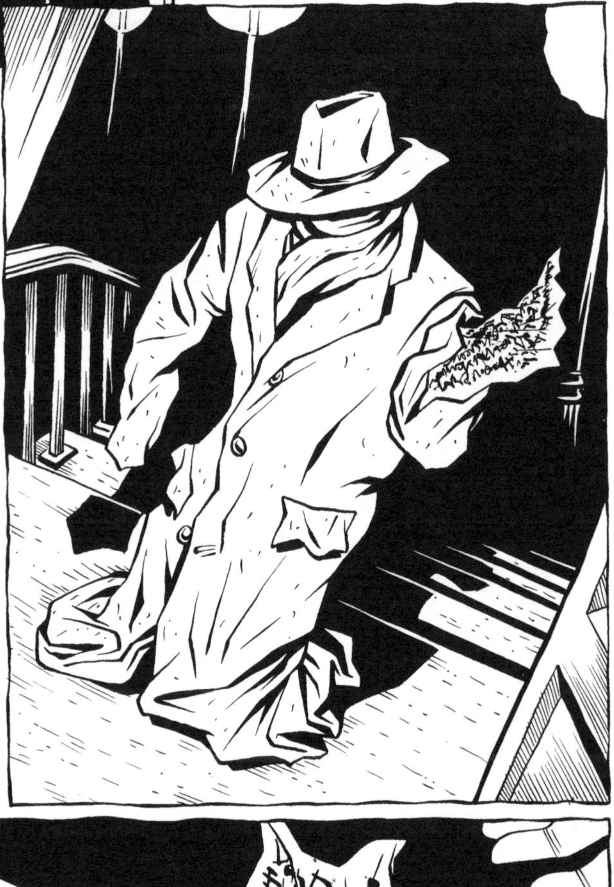

The grotesque, malodorous thing that was my caller had on one of Edward's overcoats — its bottom almost touching the ground, and its sleeves rolled back yet still covering the hands. On the head was a slouch hat pulled low, while a black silk muffler concealed the face. The odour of this singular messenger was appalling. As I stepped unsteadily forward, the figure made a semi-liquid sound like that I had heard over the telephone — "glub... glub..." — and thrust at me a large, closely written paper. Still reeling from the morbid foetor, I seized the paper and tried to read it in the light from the doorway.

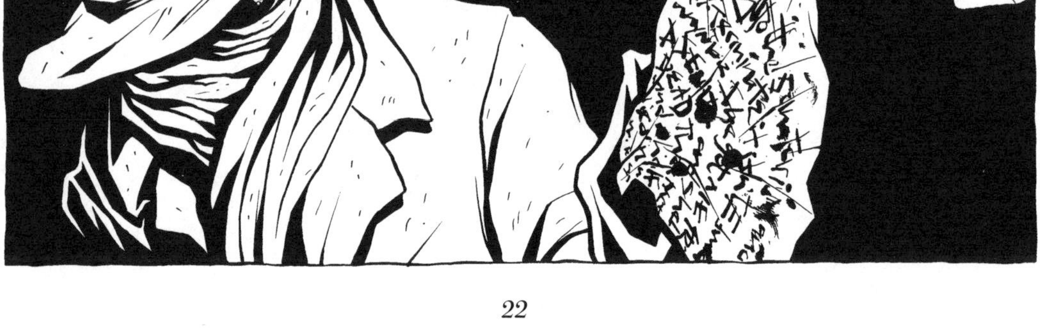

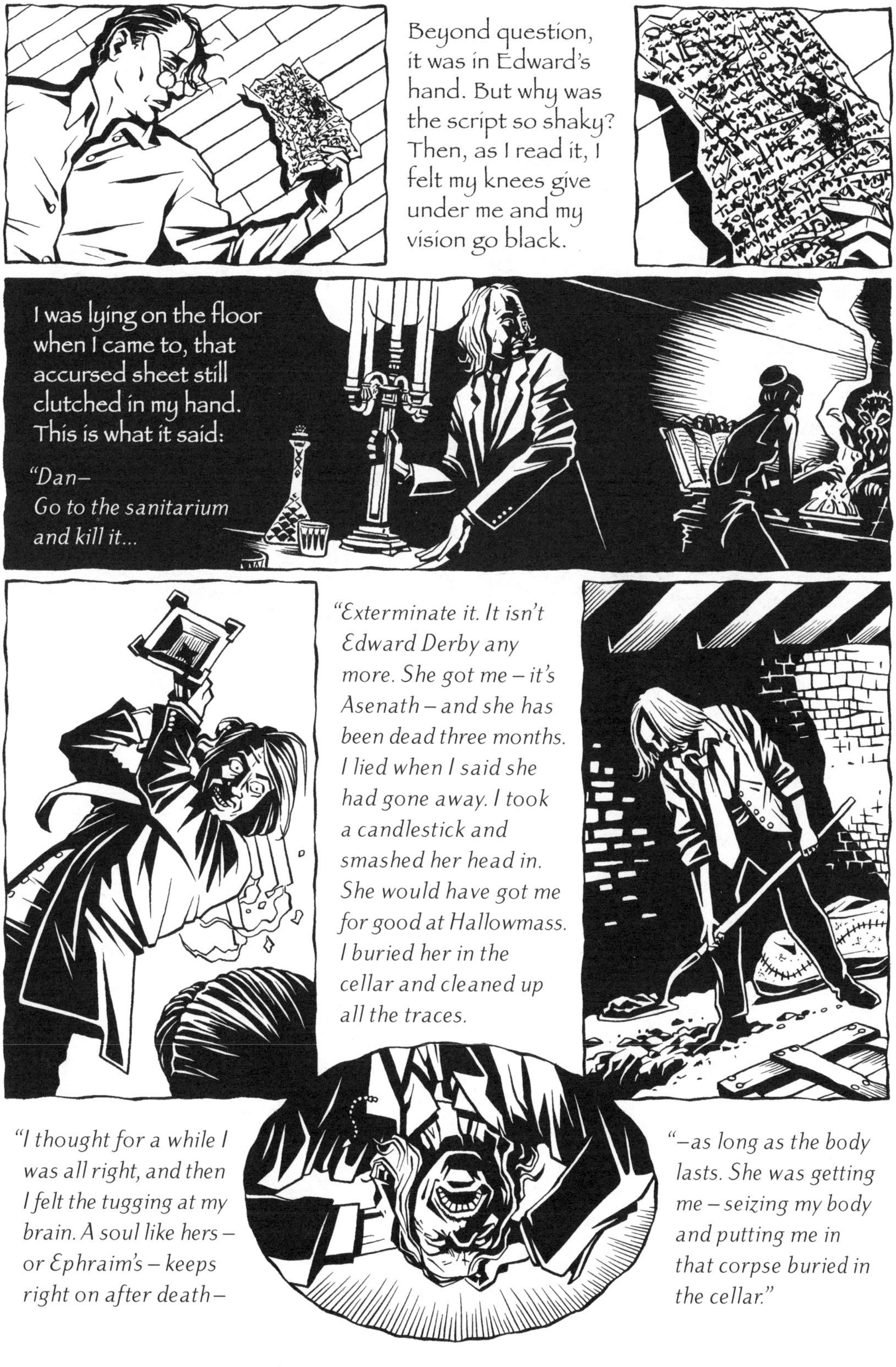
Beyond question, it was in Edward's hand. But why was the script so shaky? Then, as I read it, I felt my knees give under me and my vision go black.
I was lying on the floor when I came to, that accursed sheet still clutched in my hand. This is what it said:
"Dan–
Go to the sanitarium and kill it...
"Exterminate it. It isn't Edward Derby any more. She got me – it's Asenath – and she has been dead three months. I lied when I said she had gone away. I took a candlestick and smashed her head in. She would have got me for good at Hallowmass. I buried her in the cellar and cleaned up all the traces.
"I thought for a while I was all right, and then I felt the tugging at my brain. A soul like hers – or Ephraim's – keeps right on after death–
"–as long as the body lasts. She was getting me – seizing my body and putting me in that corpse buried in the cellar."

*"I knew what was coming—
that's why I snapped and had to
go to the asylum. Then it came—*

*"I found myself in Asenath's rotting
carcass down there in the cellar.*

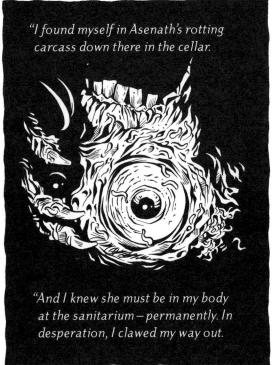

*"And I knew she must be in my body
at the sanitarium—permanently. In
desperation, I clawed my way out.*

*"I'm too far gone to talk, but I can still write. Kill that fiend if you value the peace and
comfort of the world. See that it is cremated. If you don't, it will live on and on, body
to body, forever! Goodbye—you've been a great friend.—Ed."*

Then I saw and smelled what cluttered up the threshold where the warm air had
struck it. The messenger would not move or have consciousness any more.

The butler, tougher-fibred than I, telephoned the police. What they found inside
Edward's oddly-assorted clothes was mostly liquescent horror. There were bones,
too—and a crushed-in skull. Some dental work identified the skull as Asenath's.

THE POLICE, POOR FOOLS, HAVE THEIR SMUG LITTLE THEORIES, AND ARE SEARCHING FOR THOSE SINISTER DISCHARGED SERVANTS. IDIOTS! ARE THEY BLIND?

THEY ARE KEEPING THE BODY FOR SOME SILLY AUTOPSIES — BUT I SAY HE MUST BE **CREMATED**, HE WHO WAS NOT EDWARD DERBY WHEN I SHOT HIM — OR I MAY BE THE NEXT VICTIM!

"As for me, I now believe all that Edward Derby ever told me. There are horrors beyond life's edge that we do not suspect, and they engulfed Edward as they are engulfing me. Those powers survive the life of the physical form."

BUT MY WILL IS NOT WEAK — AND I SHALL NOT LET IT BE UNDERMINED BY THE TERRORS I KNOW ARE SEETHING AROUND IT. I WILL NOT BE DRIVEN FROM MY BODY... I WILL **NOT** CHANGE SOULS WITH THAT BULLET-RIDDEN LICH IN THE MADHOUSE... I WILL NOT END UP AS THAT FOETID **THING ON THE DOORSTEP!**

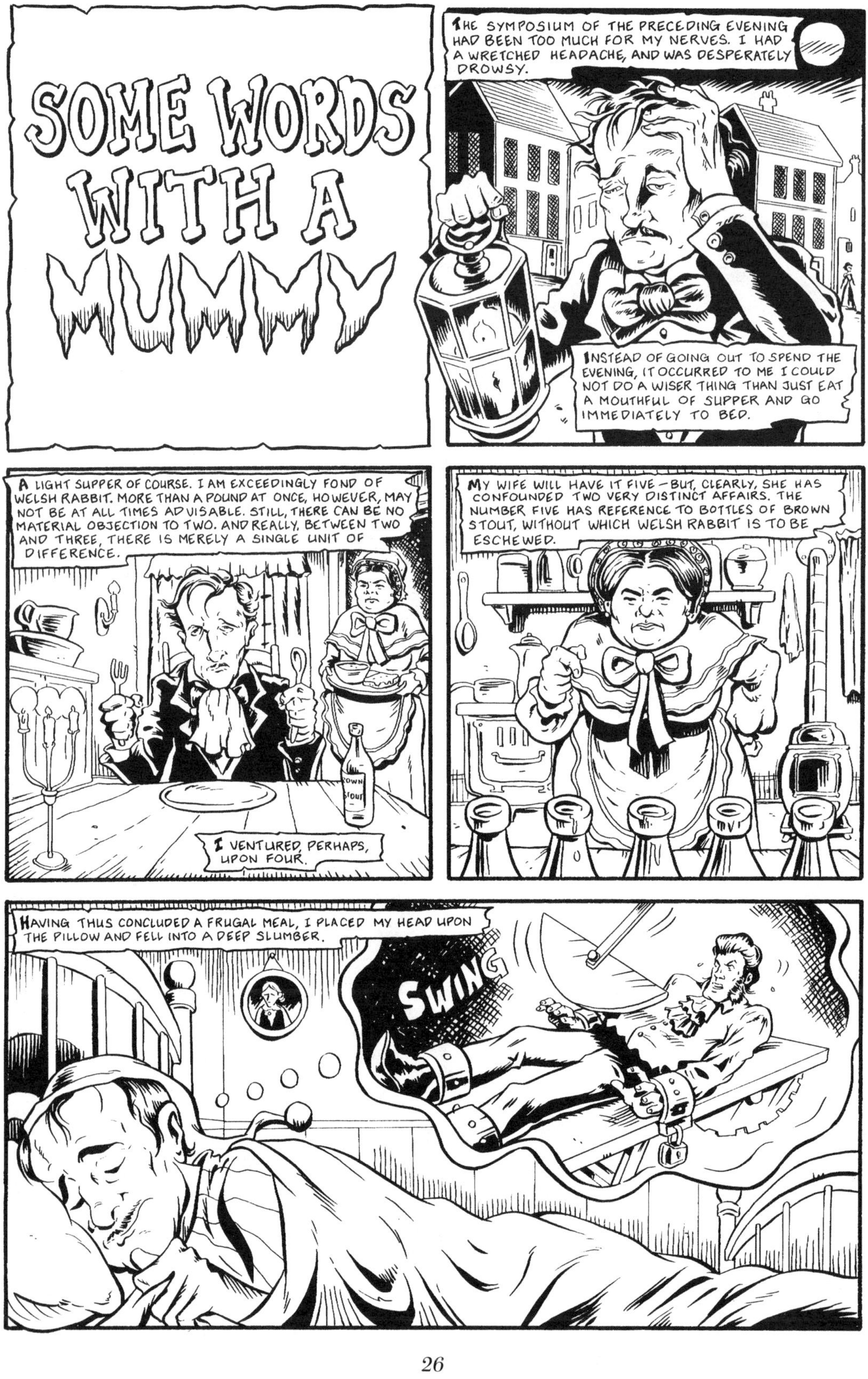
SOME WORDS WITH A MUMMY
THE SYMPOSIUM OF THE PRECEDING EVENING HAD BEEN TOO MUCH FOR MY NERVES. I HAD A WRETCHED HEADACHE, AND WAS DESPERATELY DROWSY.
INSTEAD OF GOING OUT TO SPEND THE EVENING, IT OCCURRED TO ME I COULD NOT DO A WISER THING THAN JUST EAT A MOUTHFUL OF SUPPER AND GO IMMEDIATELY TO BED.
A LIGHT SUPPER OF COURSE. I AM EXCEEDINGLY FOND OF WELSH RABBIT. MORE THAN A POUND AT ONCE, HOWEVER, MAY NOT BE AT ALL TIMES ADVISABLE. STILL, THERE CAN BE NO MATERIAL OBJECTION TO TWO. AND REALLY, BETWEEN TWO AND THREE, THERE IS MERELY A SINGLE UNIT OF DIFFERENCE.
I VENTURED, PERHAPS, UPON FOUR.
MY WIFE WILL HAVE IT FIVE—BUT, CLEARLY, SHE HAS CONFOUNDED TWO VERY DISTINCT AFFAIRS. THE NUMBER FIVE HAS REFERENCE TO BOTTLES OF BROWN STOUT, WITHOUT WHICH WELSH RABBIT IS TO BE ESCHEWED.
HAVING THUS CONCLUDED A FRUGAL MEAL, I PLACED MY HEAD UPON THE PILLOW AND FELL INTO A DEEP SLUMBER.
SWING

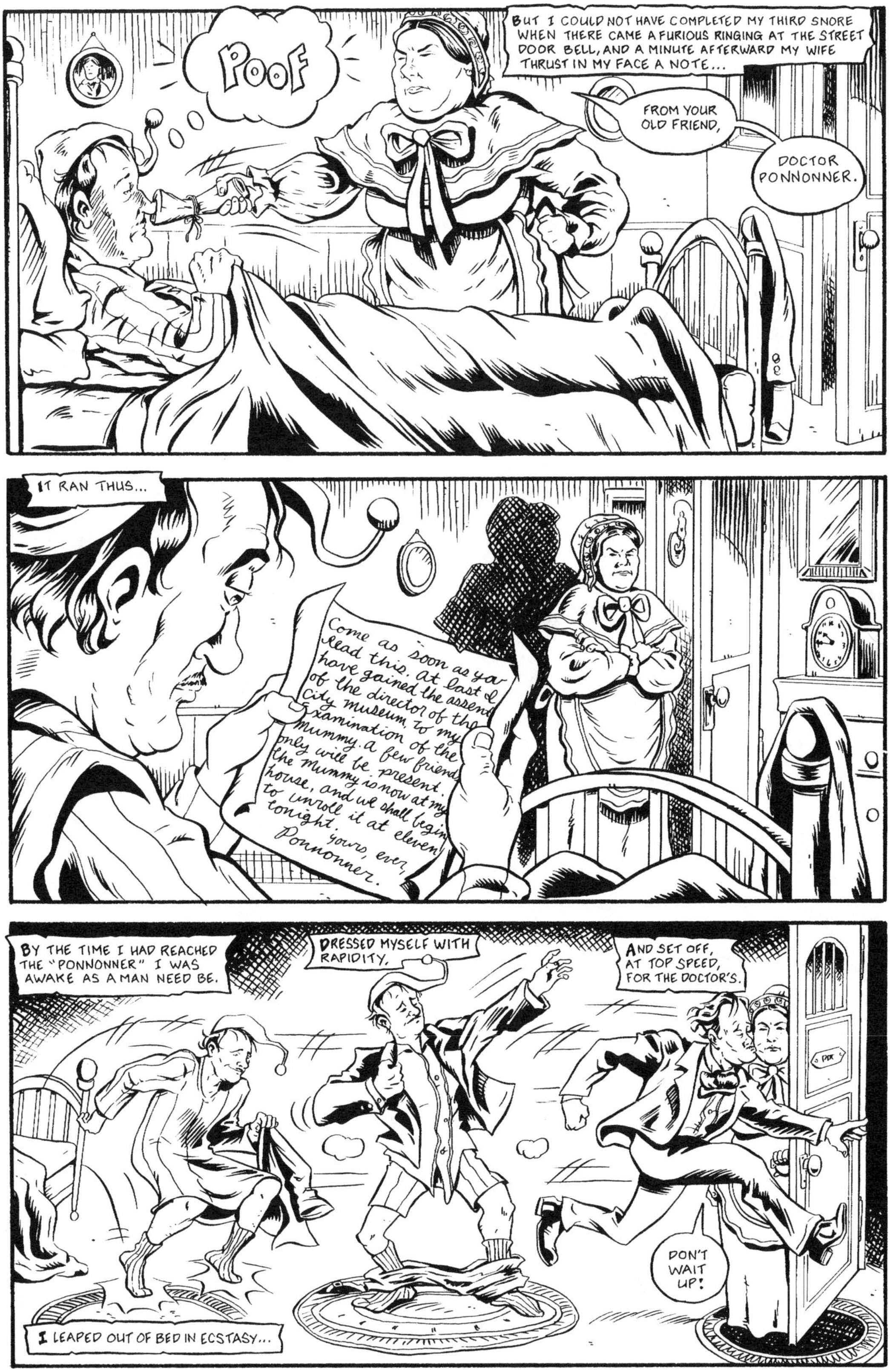
POOF
BUT I COULD NOT HAVE COMPLETED MY THIRD SNORE WHEN THERE CAME A FURIOUS RINGING AT THE STREET DOOR BELL, AND A MINUTE AFTERWARD MY WIFE THRUST IN MY FACE A NOTE...
FROM YOUR OLD FRIEND,
DOCTOR PONNONNER.
IT RAN THUS...
Come as soon as yo
read this. At last I
have gained the assen
of the director of the
City Museum, to my
examination of the
mummy. A few friend
only will be present.
the Mummy is now at my
house, and we shall begin
to unroll it at eleven
tonight. Yours, ever,
Ponnonner.
BY THE TIME I HAD REACHED THE "PONNONNER" I WAS AWAKE AS A MAN NEED BE.
DRESSED MYSELF WITH RAPIDITY.
AND SET OFF, AT TOP SPEED, FOR THE DOCTOR'S.
DON'T WAIT UP!
I LEAPED OUT OF BED IN ECSTASY...

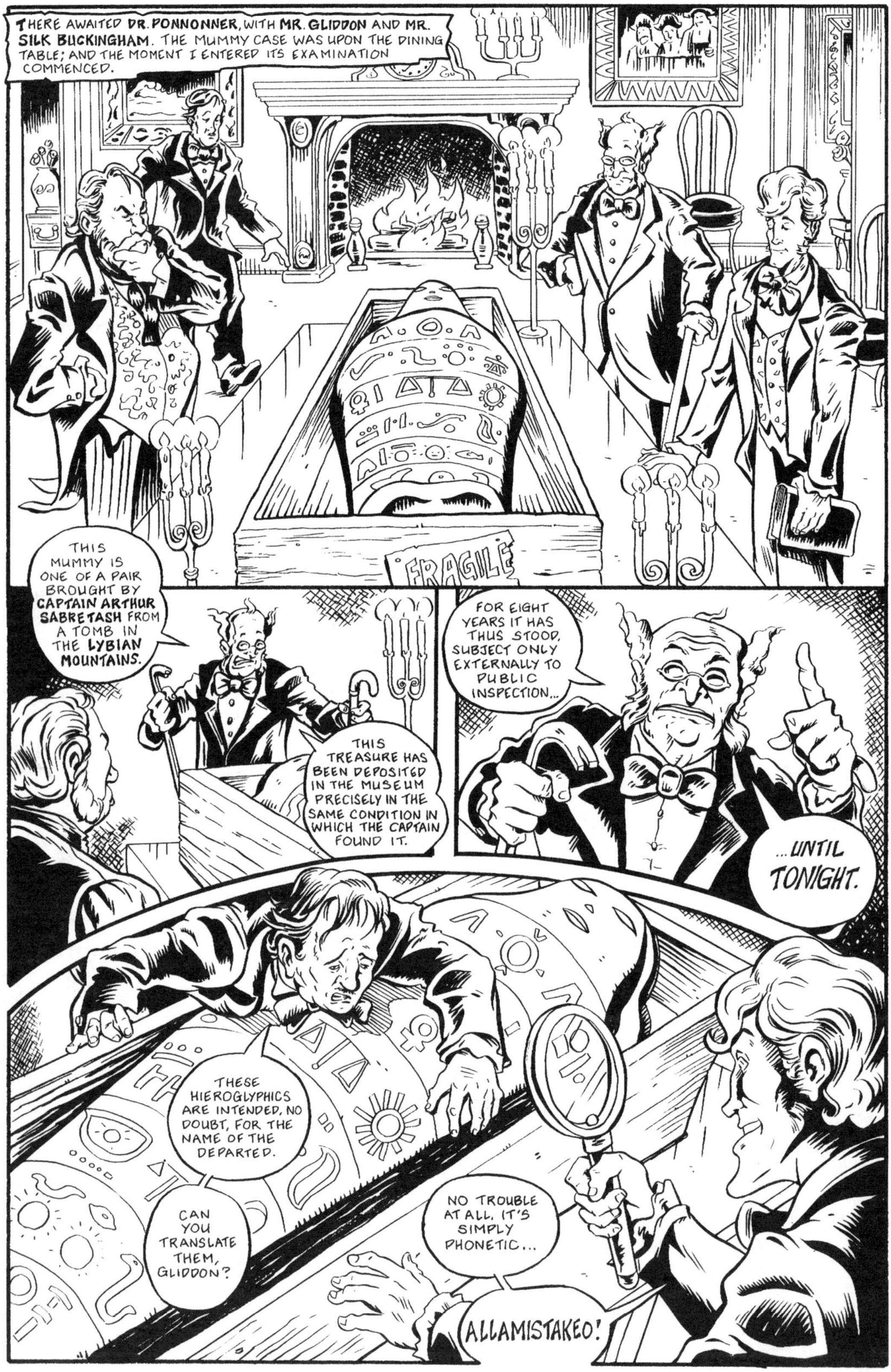
THERE AWAITED DR. PONNONNER, WITH MR. GLIDDON AND MR. SILK BUCKINGHAM. THE MUMMY CASE WAS UPON THE DINING TABLE; AND THE MOMENT I ENTERED ITS EXAMINATION COMMENCED.
FRAGILE
THIS MUMMY IS ONE OF A PAIR BROUGHT BY CAPTAIN ARTHUR SABRETASH FROM A TOMB IN THE LYBIAN MOUNTAINS.
THIS TREASURE HAS BEEN DEPOSITED IN THE MUSEUM PRECISELY IN THE SAME CONDITION IN WHICH THE CAPTAIN FOUND IT.
FOR EIGHT YEARS IT HAS THUS STOOD, SUBJECT ONLY EXTERNALLY TO PUBLIC INSPECTION...
...UNTIL TONIGHT.
THESE HIEROGLYPHICS ARE INTENDED, NO DOUBT, FOR THE NAME OF THE DEPARTED.
CAN YOU TRANSLATE THEM, GLIDDON?
NO TROUBLE AT ALL, IT'S SIMPLY PHONETIC...
ALLAMISTAKEO!

WE HAD SOME DIFFICULTY GETTING THE CASE OPEN WITHOUT INJURY; BUT HAVING AT LENGTH ACCOMPLISHED THE TASK, WE TOOK OUT THE BODY ITSELF.

AND UPON STRIPPING OFF THE WRAPPINGS WE FOUND THAT...

THE FLESH IS IN EXCELLENT PRESERVATION!

WHY, THERE'S NO PERCEPTIBLE ODOR!

SNIF SNIF

THE SKIN IS HARD, YET *SMOOTH* AND *GLOSSY*! THE TEETH AND HAIR ARE IN GOOD CONDITION AS WELL!

IT SEEMS THE EYES HAVE BEEN REMOVED AND GLASS ONES SUBSTITUTED.

HOW WONDERFULLY *LIFE-LIKE*!

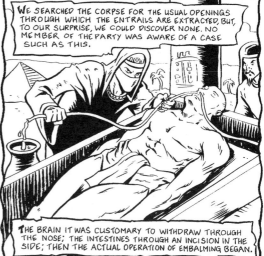

WE SEARCHED THE CORPSE FOR THE USUAL OPENINGS THROUGH WHICH THE ENTRAILS ARE EXTRACTED, BUT, TO OUR SURPRISE, WE COULD DISCOVER NONE. NO MEMBER OF THE PARTY WAS AWARE OF A CASE SUCH AS THIS.

THE BRAIN IT WAS CUSTOMARY TO WITHDRAW THROUGH THE NOSE; THE INTESTINES THROUGH AN INCISION IN THE SIDE; THEN THE ACTUAL OPERATION OF EMBALMING BEGAN.

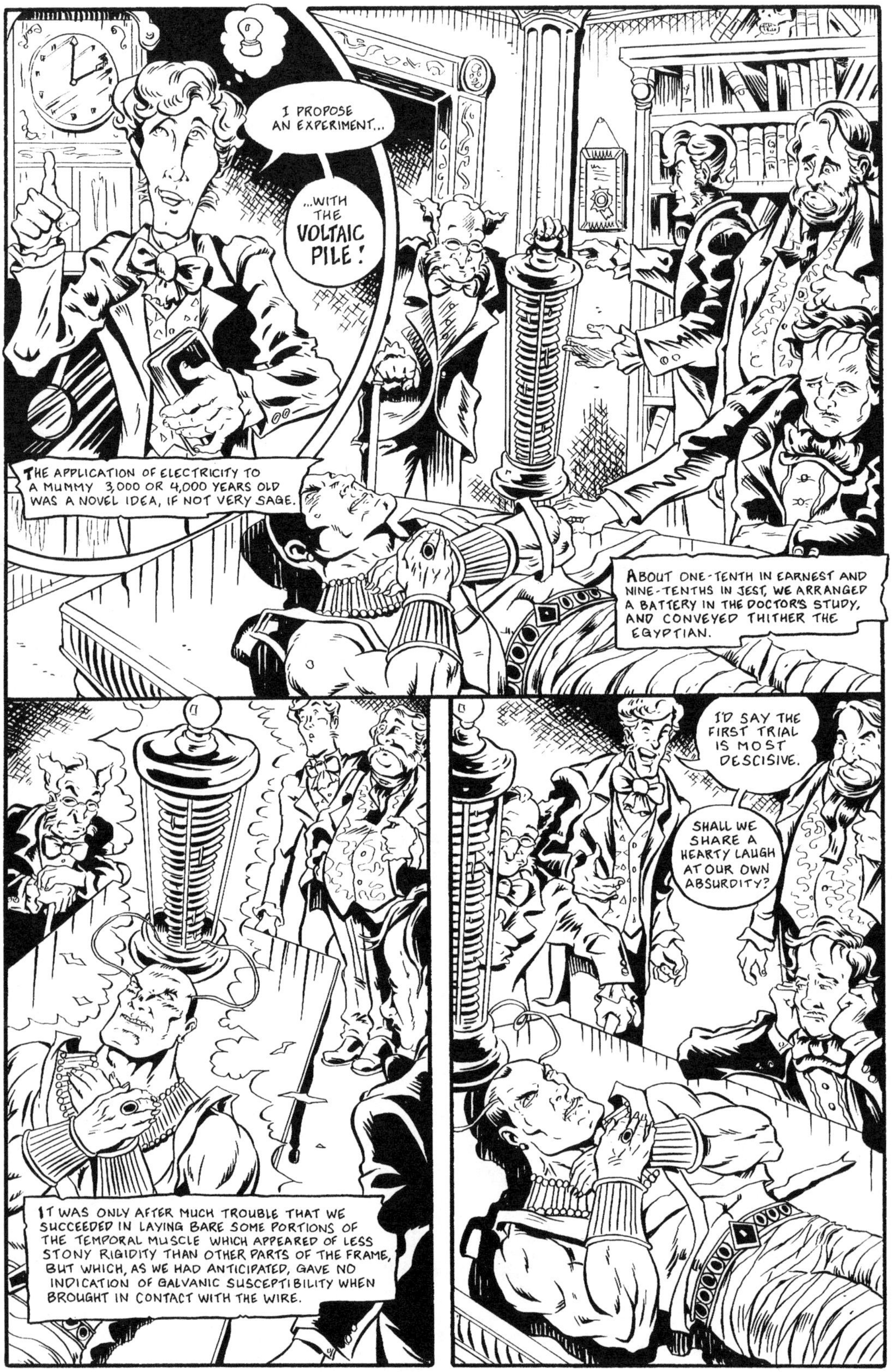
I PROPOSE AN EXPERIMENT...
...WITH THE VOLTAIC PILE!
THE APPLICATION OF ELECTRICITY TO A MUMMY 3,000 OR 4,000 YEARS OLD WAS A NOVEL IDEA, IF NOT VERY SAGE.
ABOUT ONE-TENTH IN EARNEST AND NINE-TENTHS IN JEST, WE ARRANGED A BATTERY IN THE DOCTOR'S STUDY, AND CONVEYED THITHER THE EGYPTIAN.
IT WAS ONLY AFTER MUCH TROUBLE THAT WE SUCCEEDED IN LAYING BARE SOME PORTIONS OF THE TEMPORAL MUSCLE WHICH APPEARED OF LESS STONY RIGIDITY THAN OTHER PARTS OF THE FRAME, BUT WHICH, AS WE HAD ANTICIPATED, GAVE NO INDICATION OF GALVANIC SUSCEPTIBILITY WHEN BROUGHT IN CONTACT WITH THE WIRE.
I'D SAY THE FIRST TRIAL IS MOST DESCISIVE.
SHALL WE SHARE A HEARTY LAUGH AT OUR OWN ABSURDITY?

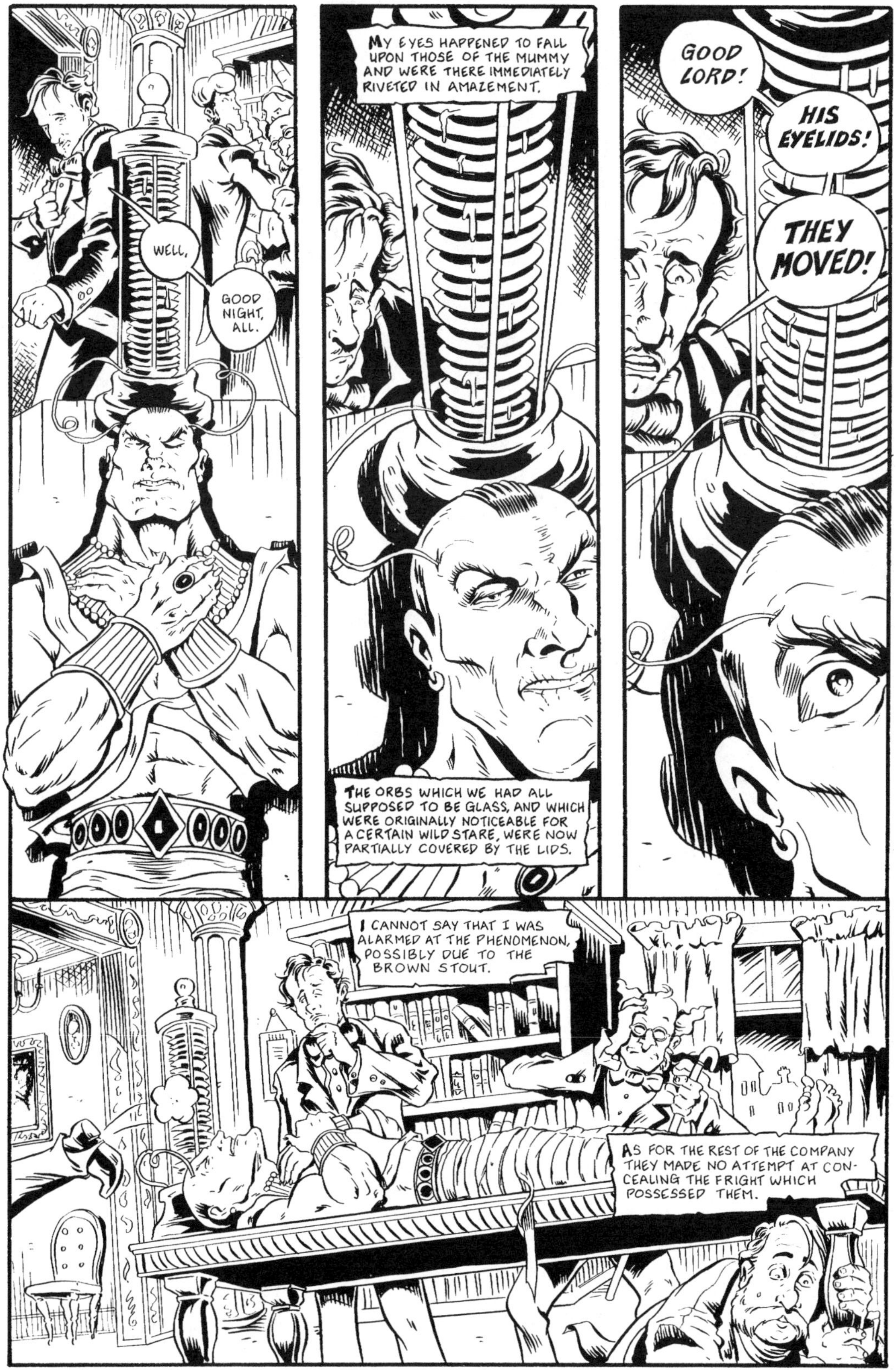
WELL,
GOOD NIGHT, ALL.
MY EYES HAPPENED TO FALL UPON THOSE OF THE MUMMY AND WERE THERE IMMEDIATELY RIVETED IN AMAZEMENT.
THE ORBS WHICH WE HAD ALL SUPPOSED TO BE GLASS, AND WHICH WERE ORIGINALLY NOTICEABLE FOR A CERTAIN WILD STARE, WERE NOW PARTIALLY COVERED BY THE LIDS.
GOOD LORD!
HIS EYELIDS!
THEY MOVED!
I CANNOT SAY THAT I WAS ALARMED AT THE PHENOMENON, POSSIBLY DUE TO THE BROWN STOUT.
AS FOR THE REST OF THE COMPANY THEY MADE NO ATTEMPT AT CONCEALING THE FRIGHT WHICH POSSESSED THEM.

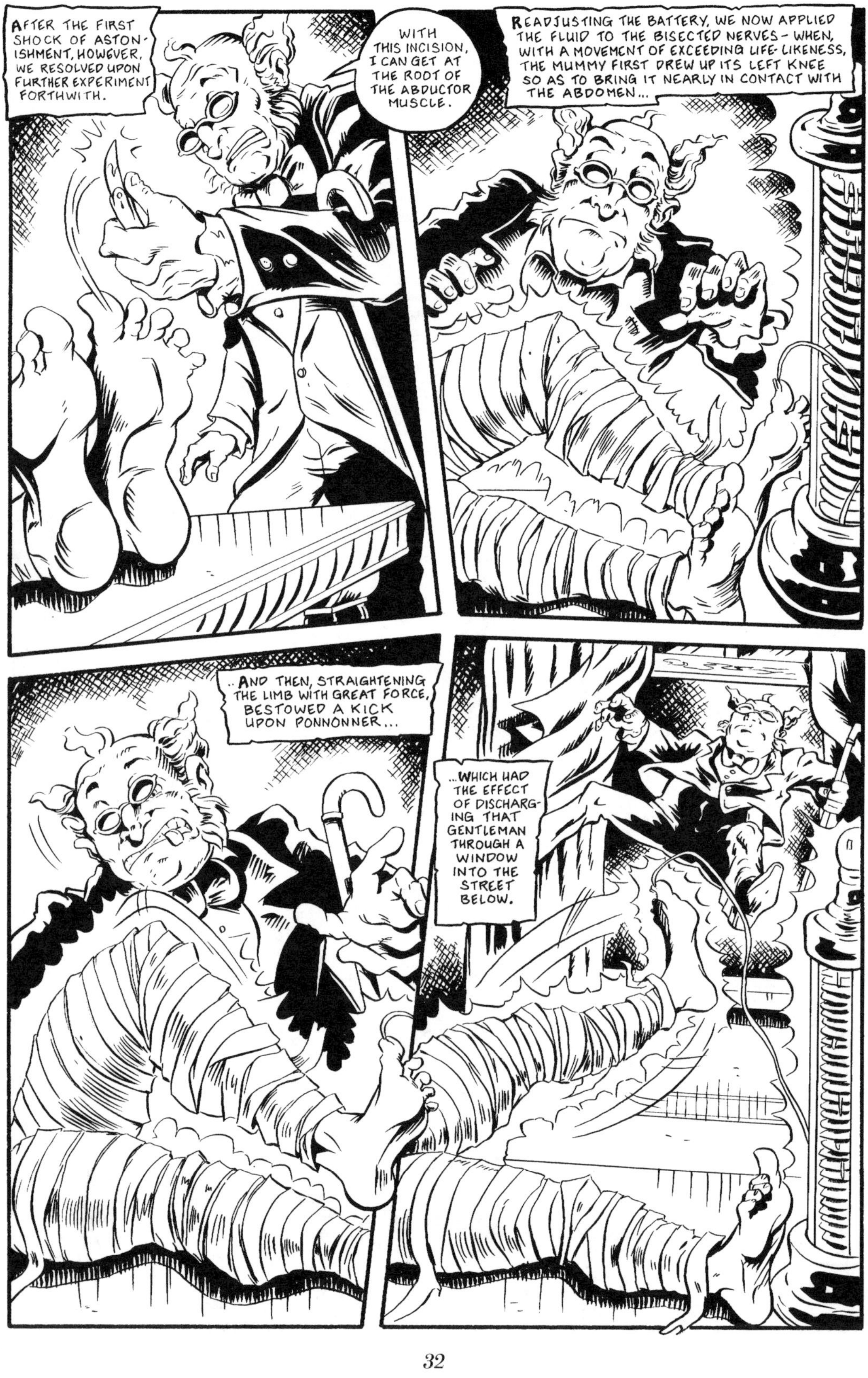
After the first shock of astonishment, however, we resolved upon further experiment forthwith.
With this incision, I can get at the root of the abductor muscle.
Readjusting the battery, we now applied the fluid to the bisected nerves – when, with a movement of exceeding life-likeness, the mummy first drew up its left knee so as to bring it nearly in contact with the abdomen...
..And then, straightening the limb with great force, bestowed a kick upon Ponnonner...
...Which had the effect of discharging that gentleman through a window into the street below.

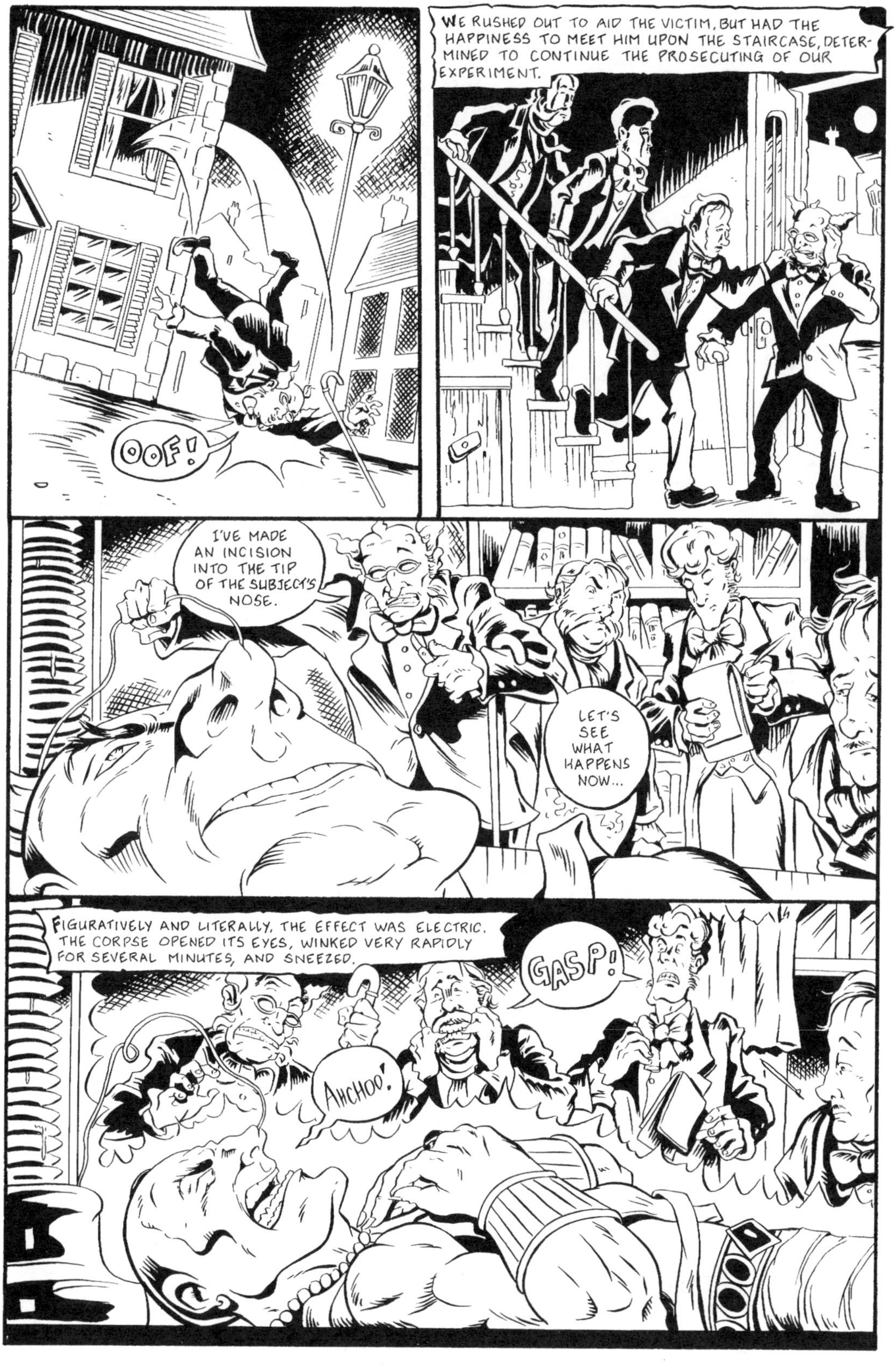
OOF!
WE RUSHED OUT TO AID THE VICTIM, BUT HAD THE HAPPINESS TO MEET HIM UPON THE STAIRCASE, DETERMINED TO CONTINUE THE PROSECUTING OF OUR EXPERIMENT.
I'VE MADE AN INCISION INTO THE TIP OF THE SUBJECT'S NOSE.
LET'S SEE WHAT HAPPENS NOW...
FIGURATIVELY AND LITERALLY, THE EFFECT WAS ELECTRIC. THE CORPSE OPENED ITS EYES, WINKED VERY RAPIDLY FOR SEVERAL MINUTES, AND SNEEZED.
GASP!
AHCHOO!

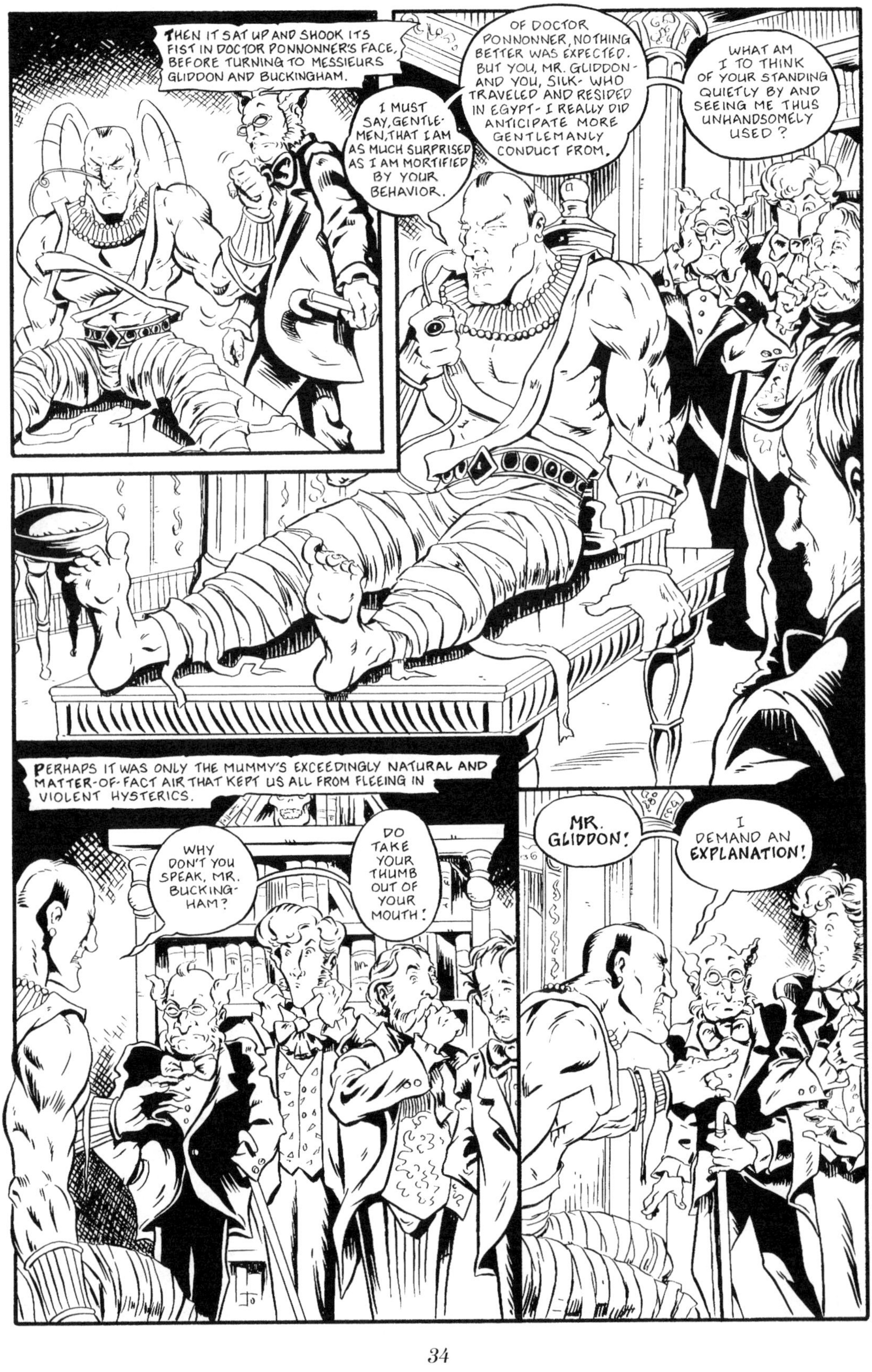
THEN IT SAT UP AND SHOOK ITS FIST IN DOCTOR PONNONNER'S FACE, BEFORE TURNING TO MESSIEURS GLIDDON AND BUCKINGHAM.
I MUST SAY, GENTLEMEN, THAT I AM AS MUCH SURPRISED AS I AM MORTIFIED BY YOUR BEHAVIOR.
OF DOCTOR PONNONNER, NOTHING BETTER WAS EXPECTED. BUT YOU, MR. GLIDDON- AND YOU, SILK- WHO TRAVELED AND RESIDED IN EGYPT- I REALLY DID ANTICIPATE MORE GENTLEMANLY CONDUCT FROM.
WHAT AM I TO THINK OF YOUR STANDING QUIETLY BY AND SEEING ME THUS UNHANDSOMELY USED?
PERHAPS IT WAS ONLY THE MUMMY'S EXCEEDINGLY NATURAL AND MATTER-OF-FACT AIR THAT KEPT US ALL FROM FLEEING IN VIOLENT HYSTERICS.
WHY DON'T YOU SPEAK, MR. BUCKINGHAM?
DO TAKE YOUR THUMB OUT OF YOUR MOUTH!
MR. GLIDDON!
I DEMAND AN EXPLANATION!

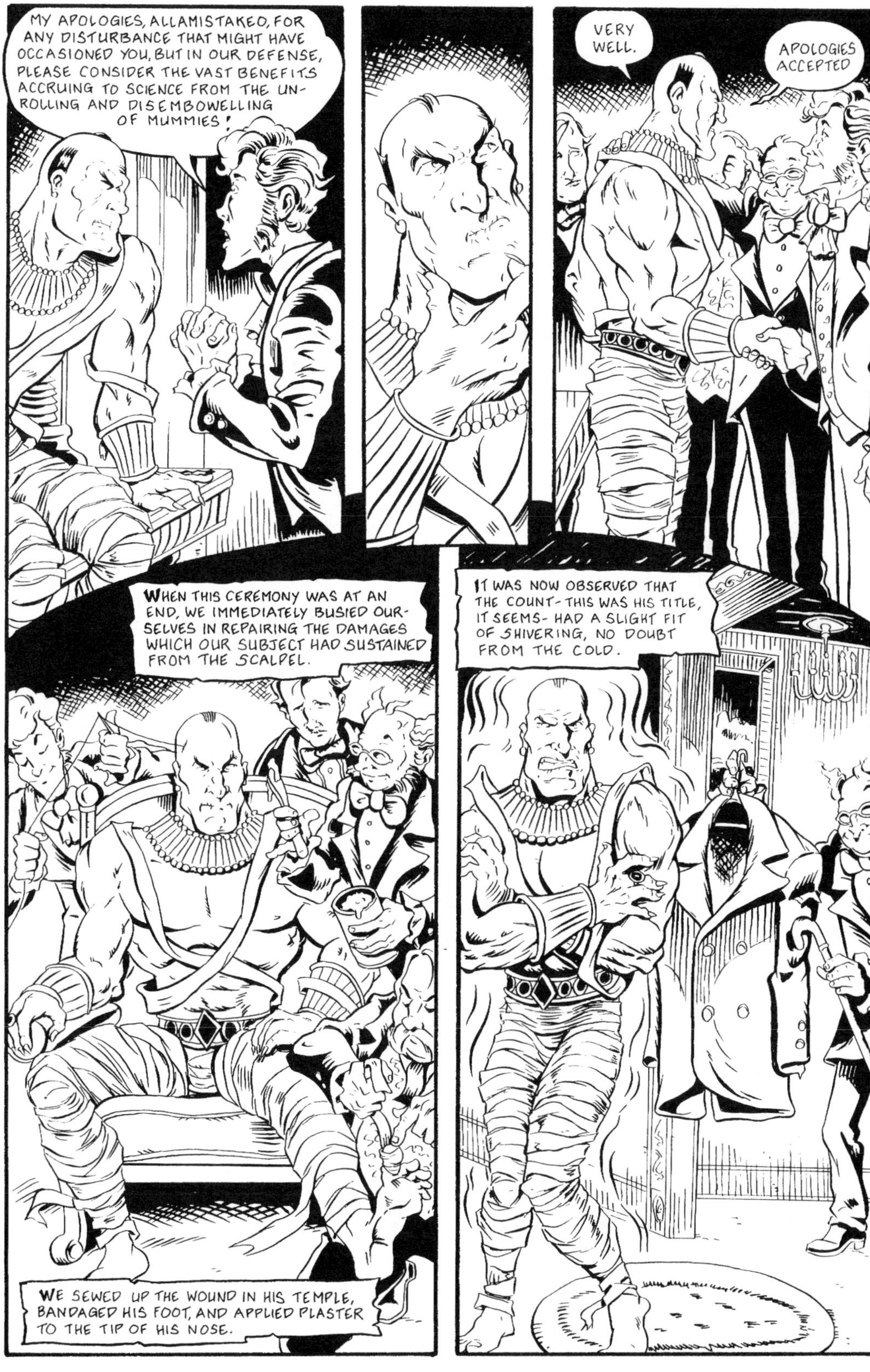
MY APOLOGIES, ALLAMISTAKEO, FOR ANY DISTURBANCE THAT MIGHT HAVE OCCASIONED YOU, BUT IN OUR DEFENSE, PLEASE CONSIDER THE VAST BENEFITS ACCRUING TO SCIENCE FROM THE UN-ROLLING AND DISEMBOWELLING OF MUMMIES!
VERY WELL.
APOLOGIES ACCEPTED
WHEN THIS CEREMONY WAS AT AN END, WE IMMEDIATELY BUSIED OUR-SELVES IN REPAIRING THE DAMAGES WHICH OUR SUBJECT HAD SUSTAINED FROM THE SCALPEL.
WE SEWED UP THE WOUND IN HIS TEMPLE, BANDAGED HIS FOOT, AND APPLIED PLASTER TO THE TIP OF HIS NOSE.
IT WAS NOW OBSERVED THAT THE COUNT- THIS WAS HIS TITLE, IT SEEMS- HAD A SLIGHT FIT OF SHIVERING, NO DOUBT FROM THE COLD.

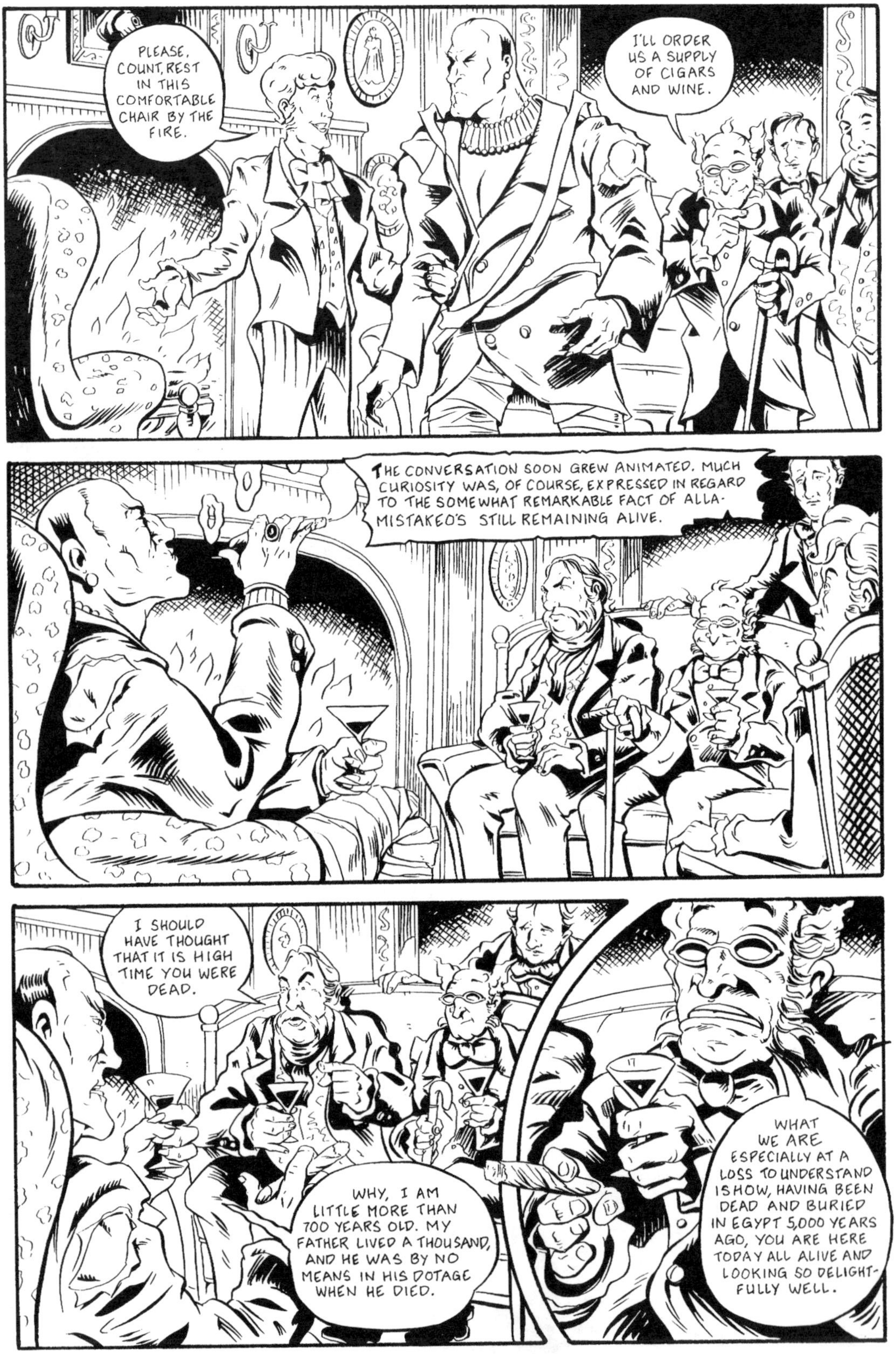
PLEASE, COUNT, REST IN THIS COMFORTABLE CHAIR BY THE FIRE.
I'LL ORDER US A SUPPLY OF CIGARS AND WINE.
THE CONVERSATION SOON GREW ANIMATED. MUCH CURIOSITY WAS, OF COURSE, EXPRESSED IN REGARD TO THE SOMEWHAT REMARKABLE FACT OF ALLAMISTAKEO'S STILL REMAINING ALIVE.
I SHOULD HAVE THOUGHT THAT IT IS HIGH TIME YOU WERE DEAD.
WHY, I AM LITTLE MORE THAN 700 YEARS OLD. MY FATHER LIVED A THOUSAND, AND HE WAS BY NO MEANS IN HIS DOTAGE WHEN HE DIED.
WHAT WE ARE ESPECIALLY AT A LOSS TO UNDERSTAND IS HOW, HAVING BEEN DEAD AND BURIED IN EGYPT 5,000 YEARS AGO, YOU ARE HERE TODAY ALL ALIVE AND LOOKING SO DELIGHTFULLY WELL.

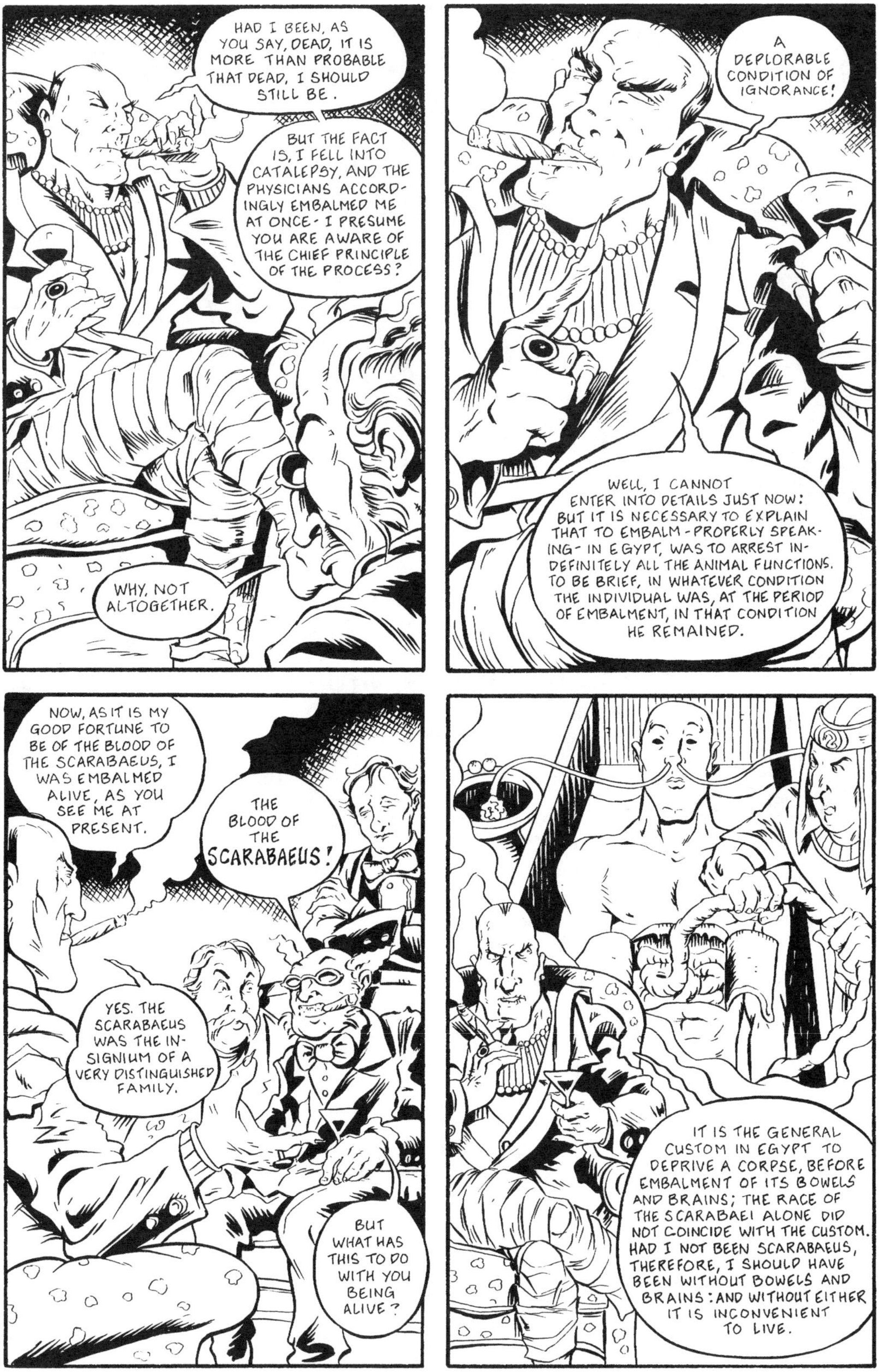
HAD I BEEN, AS YOU SAY, DEAD, IT IS MORE THAN PROBABLE THAT DEAD, I SHOULD STILL BE.
BUT THE FACT IS, I FELL INTO CATALEPSY, AND THE PHYSICIANS ACCORDINGLY EMBALMED ME AT ONCE - I PRESUME YOU ARE AWARE OF THE CHIEF PRINCIPLE OF THE PROCESS?
WHY, NOT ALTOGETHER.
A DEPLORABLE CONDITION OF IGNORANCE!
WELL, I CANNOT ENTER INTO DETAILS JUST NOW: BUT IT IS NECESSARY TO EXPLAIN THAT TO EMBALM - PROPERLY SPEAKING - IN EGYPT, WAS TO ARREST INDEFINITELY ALL THE ANIMAL FUNCTIONS. TO BE BRIEF, IN WHATEVER CONDITION THE INDIVIDUAL WAS, AT THE PERIOD OF EMBALMENT, IN THAT CONDITION HE REMAINED.
NOW, AS IT IS MY GOOD FORTUNE TO BE OF THE BLOOD OF THE SCARABAEUS, I WAS EMBALMED ALIVE, AS YOU SEE ME AT PRESENT.
THE BLOOD OF THE SCARABAEUS!
YES. THE SCARABAEUS WAS THE INSIGNIUM OF A VERY DISTINGUISHED FAMILY.
BUT WHAT HAS THIS TO DO WITH YOU BEING ALIVE?
IT IS THE GENERAL CUSTOM IN EGYPT TO DEPRIVE A CORPSE, BEFORE EMBALMENT OF ITS BOWELS AND BRAINS; THE RACE OF THE SCARABAEI ALONE DID NOT COINCIDE WITH THE CUSTOM. HAD I NOT BEEN SCARABAEUS, THEREFORE, I SHOULD HAVE BEEN WITHOUT BOWELS AND BRAINS: AND WITHOUT EITHER IT IS INCONVENIENT TO LIVE.

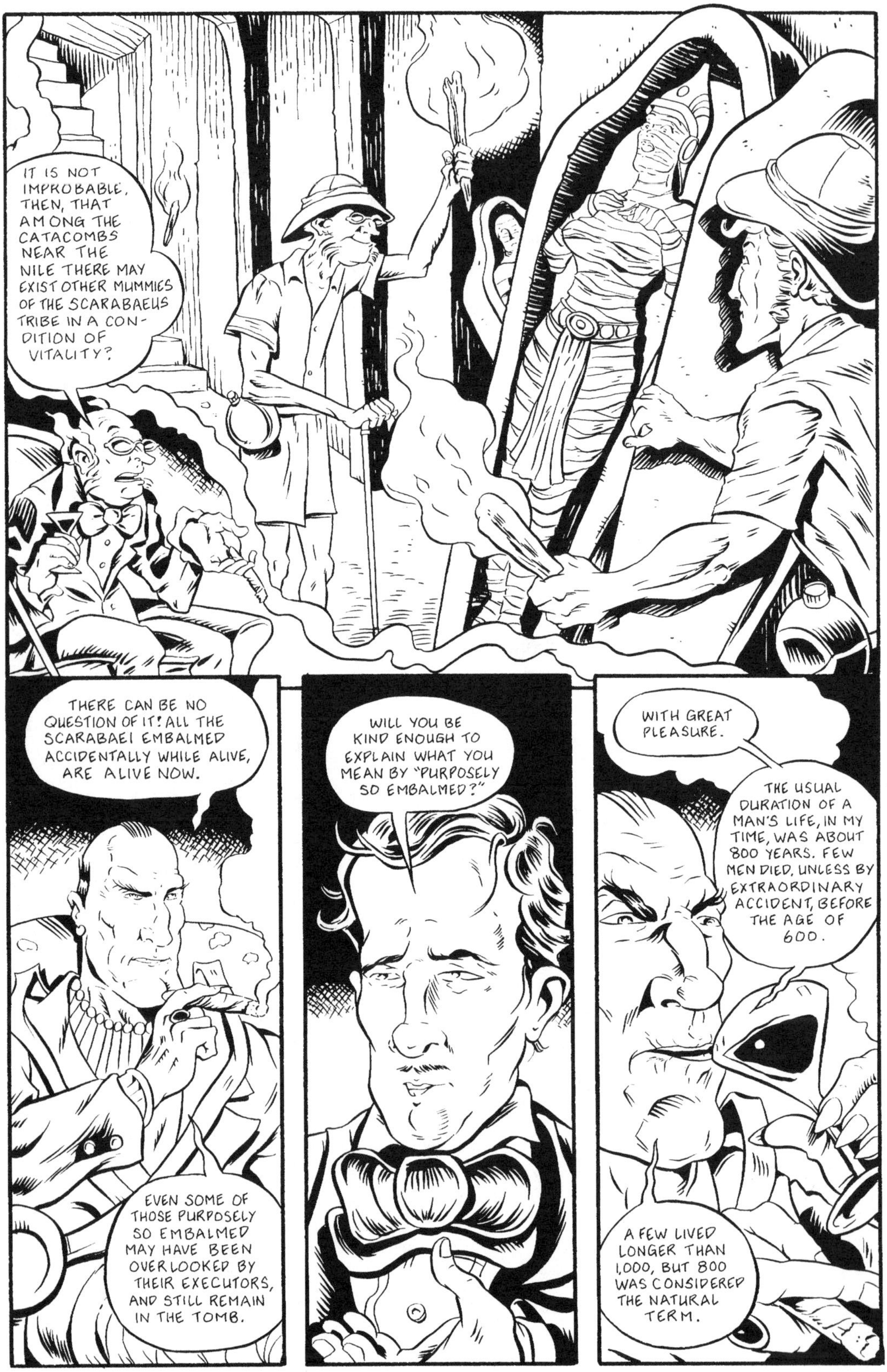
IT IS NOT IMPROBABLE, THEN, THAT AMONG THE CATACOMBS NEAR THE NILE THERE MAY EXIST OTHER MUMMIES OF THE SCARABAEUS TRIBE IN A CONDITION OF VITALITY?
THERE CAN BE NO QUESTION OF IT! ALL THE SCARABAEI EMBALMED ACCIDENTALLY WHILE ALIVE, ARE ALIVE NOW.
EVEN SOME OF THOSE PURPOSELY SO EMBALMED MAY HAVE BEEN OVERLOOKED BY THEIR EXECUTORS, AND STILL REMAIN IN THE TOMB.
WILL YOU BE KIND ENOUGH TO EXPLAIN WHAT YOU MEAN BY "PURPOSELY SO EMBALMED?"
WITH GREAT PLEASURE.
THE USUAL DURATION OF A MAN'S LIFE, IN MY TIME, WAS ABOUT 800 YEARS. FEW MEN DIED, UNLESS BY EXTRAORDINARY ACCIDENT, BEFORE THE AGE OF 600.
A FEW LIVED LONGER THAN 1,000, BUT 800 WAS CONSIDERED THE NATURAL TERM.

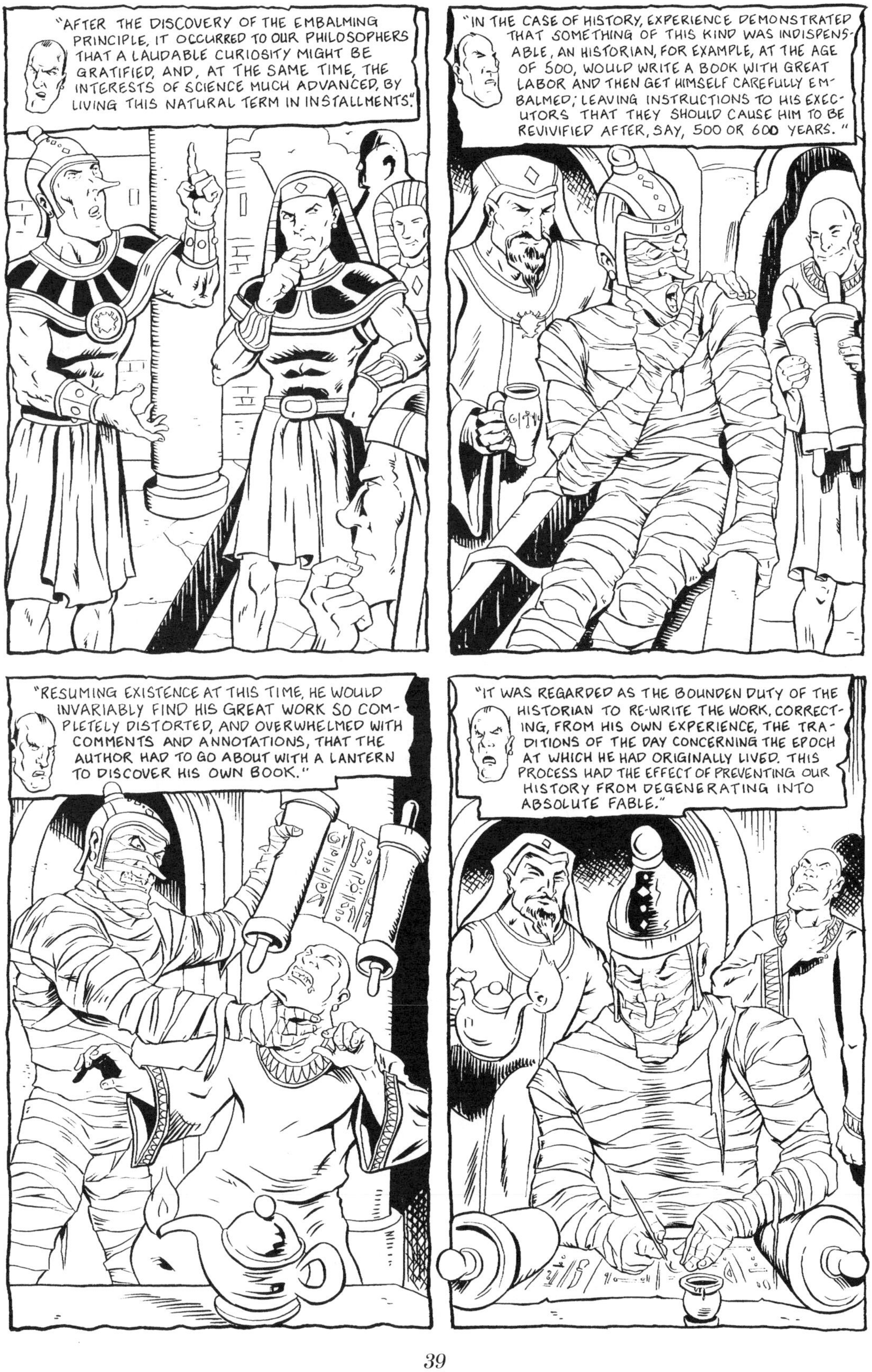
"AFTER THE DISCOVERY OF THE EMBALMING PRINCIPLE, IT OCCURRED TO OUR PHILOSOPHERS THAT A LAUDABLE CURIOSITY MIGHT BE GRATIFIED, AND, AT THE SAME TIME, THE INTERESTS OF SCIENCE MUCH ADVANCED, BY LIVING THIS NATURAL TERM IN INSTALLMENTS."
"IN THE CASE OF HISTORY, EXPERIENCE DEMONSTRATED THAT SOMETHING OF THIS KIND WAS INDISPENSABLE. AN HISTORIAN, FOR EXAMPLE, AT THE AGE OF 500, WOULD WRITE A BOOK WITH GREAT LABOR AND THEN GET HIMSELF CAREFULLY EMBALMED; LEAVING INSTRUCTIONS TO HIS EXECUTORS THAT THEY SHOULD CAUSE HIM TO BE REVIVIFIED AFTER, SAY, 500 OR 600 YEARS."
"RESUMING EXISTENCE AT THIS TIME, HE WOULD INVARIABLY FIND HIS GREAT WORK SO COMPLETELY DISTORTED, AND OVERWHELMED WITH COMMENTS AND ANNOTATIONS, THAT THE AUTHOR HAD TO GO ABOUT WITH A LANTERN TO DISCOVER HIS OWN BOOK."
"IT WAS REGARDED AS THE BOUNDEN DUTY OF THE HISTORIAN TO RE-WRITE THE WORK, CORRECTING, FROM HIS OWN EXPERIENCE, THE TRADITIONS OF THE DAY CONCERNING THE EPOCH AT WHICH HE HAD ORIGINALLY LIVED. THIS PROCESS HAD THE EFFECT OF PREVENTING OUR HISTORY FROM DEGENERATING INTO ABSOLUTE FABLE."

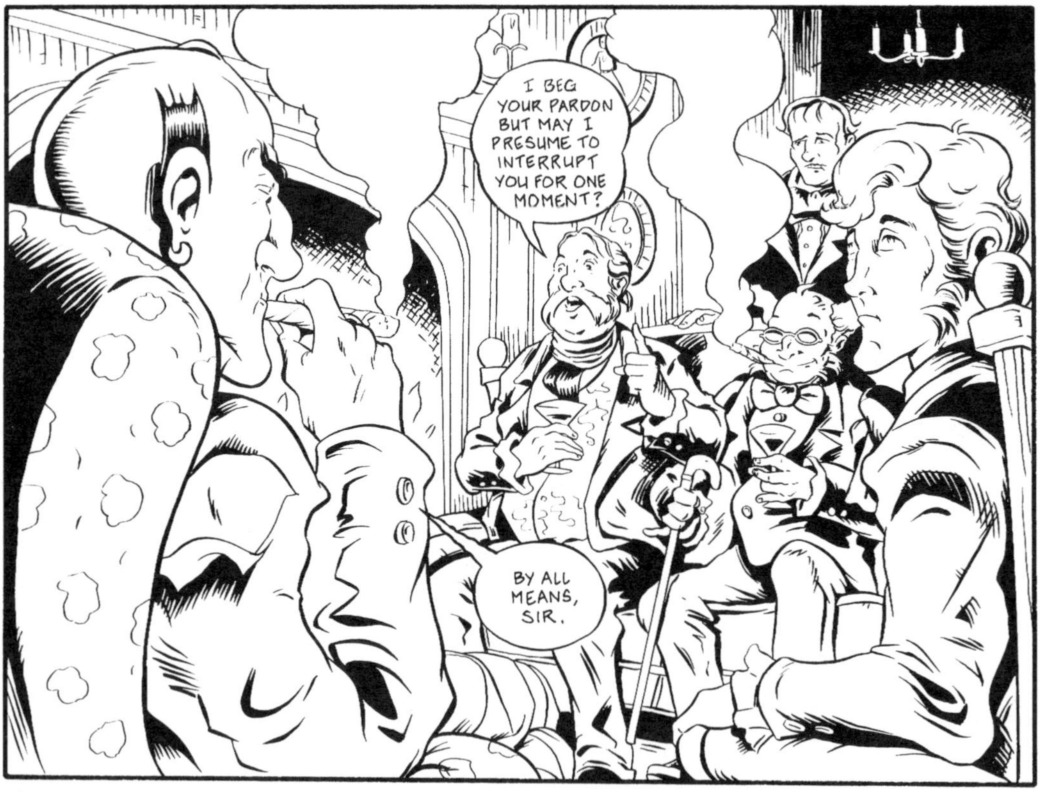
I BEG YOUR PARDON BUT MAY I PRESUME TO INTERRUPT YOU FOR ONE MOMENT?
BY ALL MEANS, SIR.

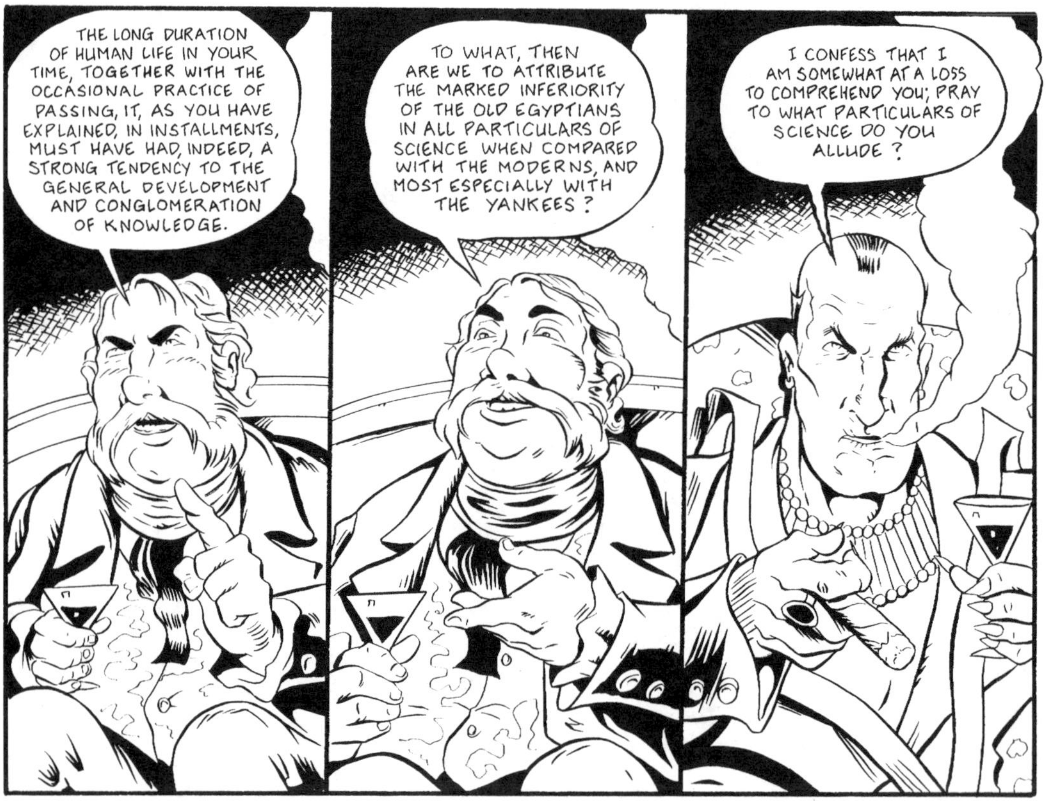
THE LONG DURATION OF HUMAN LIFE IN YOUR TIME, TOGETHER WITH THE OCCASIONAL PRACTICE OF PASSING IT, AS YOU HAVE EXPLAINED, IN INSTALLMENTS, MUST HAVE HAD, INDEED, A STRONG TENDENCY TO THE GENERAL DEVELOPMENT AND CONGLOMERATION OF KNOWLEDGE.
TO WHAT, THEN ARE WE TO ATTRIBUTE THE MARKED INFERIORITY OF THE OLD EGYPTIANS IN ALL PARTICULARS OF SCIENCE WHEN COMPARED WITH THE MODERNS, AND MOST ESPECIALLY WITH THE YANKEES?
I CONFESS THAT I AM SOMEWHAT AT A LOSS TO COMPREHEND YOU; PRAY TO WHAT PARTICULARS OF SCIENCE DO YOU ALLUDE?

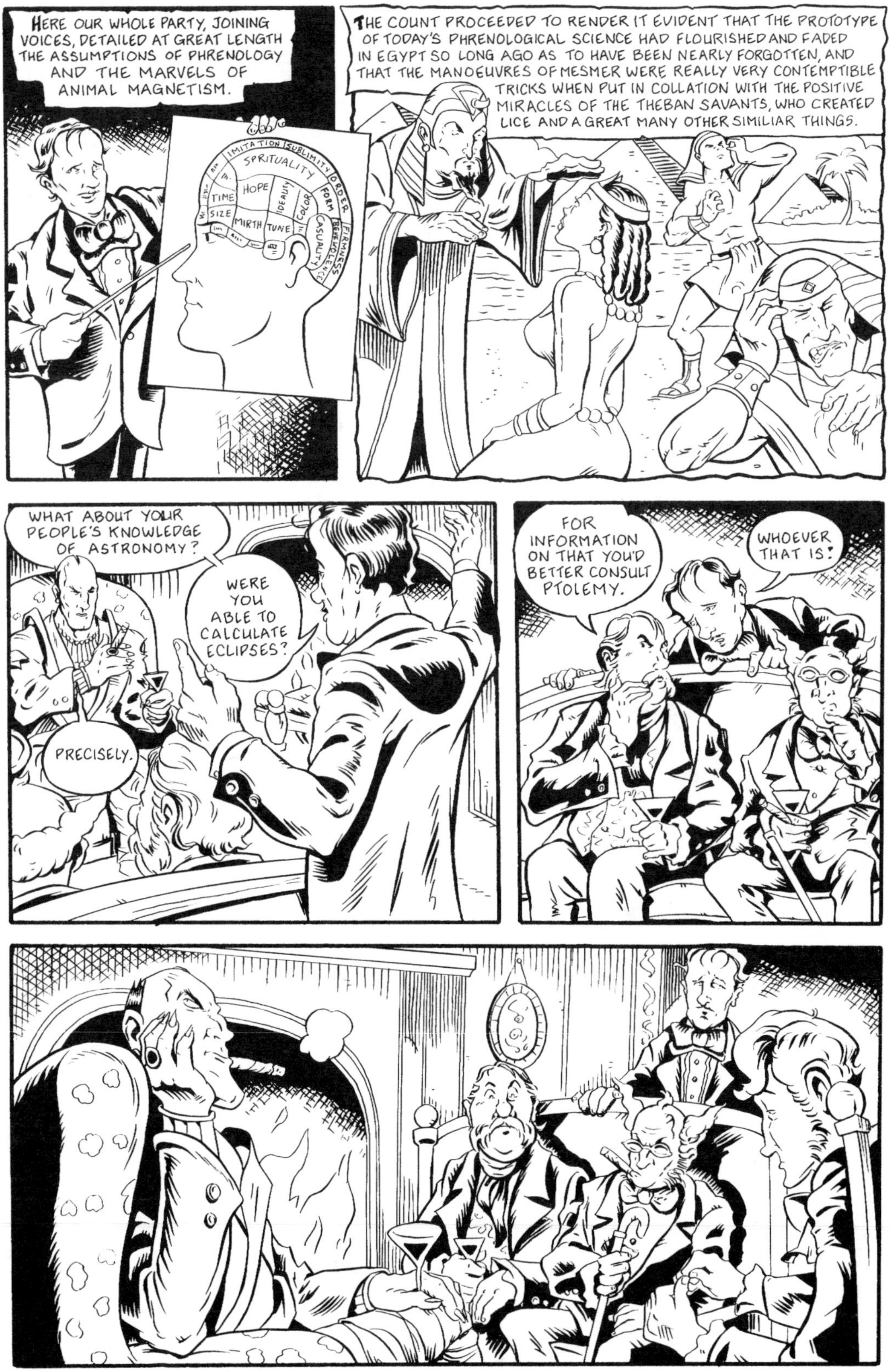
HERE OUR WHOLE PARTY, JOINING VOICES, DETAILED AT GREAT LENGTH THE ASSUMPTIONS OF PHRENOLOGY AND THE MARVELS OF ANIMAL MAGNETISM.
IMITATION
SUBLIMITY
SPRITUALITY
ORDER
HOPE
TIME
SIZE
MIRTH
TUNE
FORM
COLOR
CASUALITY
FIRMNESS
THE COUNT PROCEEDED TO RENDER IT EVIDENT THAT THE PROTOTYPE OF TODAY'S PHRENOLOGICAL SCIENCE HAD FLOURISHED AND FADED IN EGYPT SO LONG AGO AS TO HAVE BEEN NEARLY FORGOTTEN, AND THAT THE MANOEUVRES OF MESMER WERE REALLY VERY CONTEMPTIBLE TRICKS WHEN PUT IN COLLATION WITH THE POSITIVE MIRACLES OF THE THEBAN SAVANTS, WHO CREATED LICE AND A GREAT MANY OTHER SIMILIAR THINGS.
WHAT ABOUT YOUR PEOPLE'S KNOWLEDGE OF ASTRONOMY?
WERE YOU ABLE TO CALCULATE ECLIPSES?
PRECISELY.
FOR INFORMATION ON THAT YOU'D BETTER CONSULT PTOLEMY.
WHOEVER THAT IS!

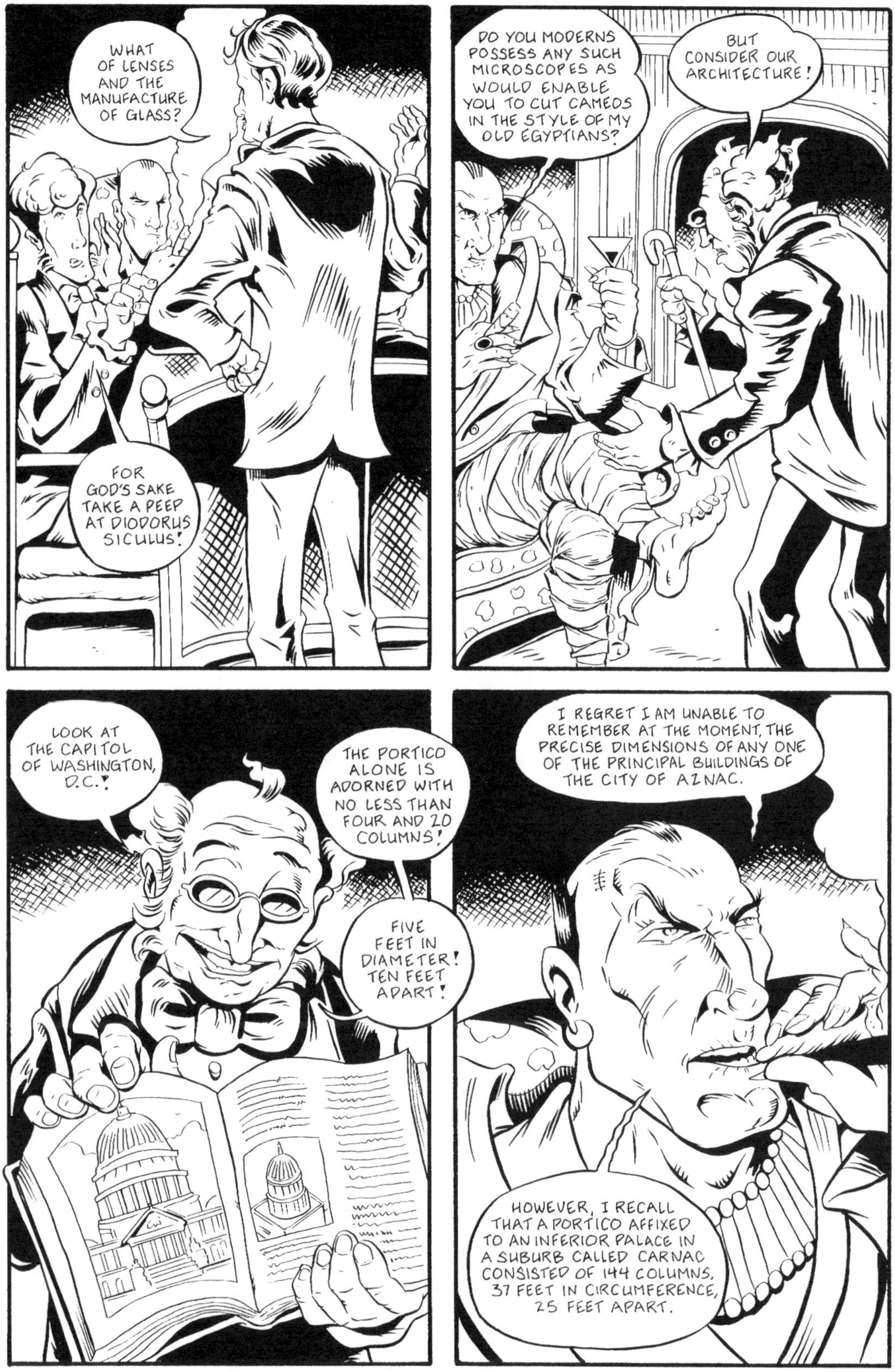
WHAT OF LENSES AND THE MANUFACTURE OF GLASS?
FOR GOD'S SAKE TAKE A PEEP AT DIODORUS SICULUS!
DO YOU MODERNS POSSESS ANY SUCH MICROSCOPES AS WOULD ENABLE YOU TO CUT CAMEOS IN THE STYLE OF MY OLD EGYPTIANS?
BUT CONSIDER OUR ARCHITECTURE!
LOOK AT THE CAPITOL OF WASHINGTON, D.C.!
THE PORTICO ALONE IS ADORNED WITH NO LESS THAN FOUR AND 20 COLUMNS!
FIVE FEET IN DIAMETER! TEN FEET APART!
I REGRET I AM UNABLE TO REMEMBER AT THE MOMENT, THE PRECISE DIMENSIONS OF ANY ONE OF THE PRINCIPAL BUILDINGS OF THE CITY OF AZNAC.
HOWEVER, I RECALL THAT A PORTICO AFFIXED TO AN INFERIOR PALACE IN A SUBURB CALLED CARNAC CONSISTED OF 144 COLUMNS, 37 FEET IN CIRCUMFERENCE, 25 FEET APART.

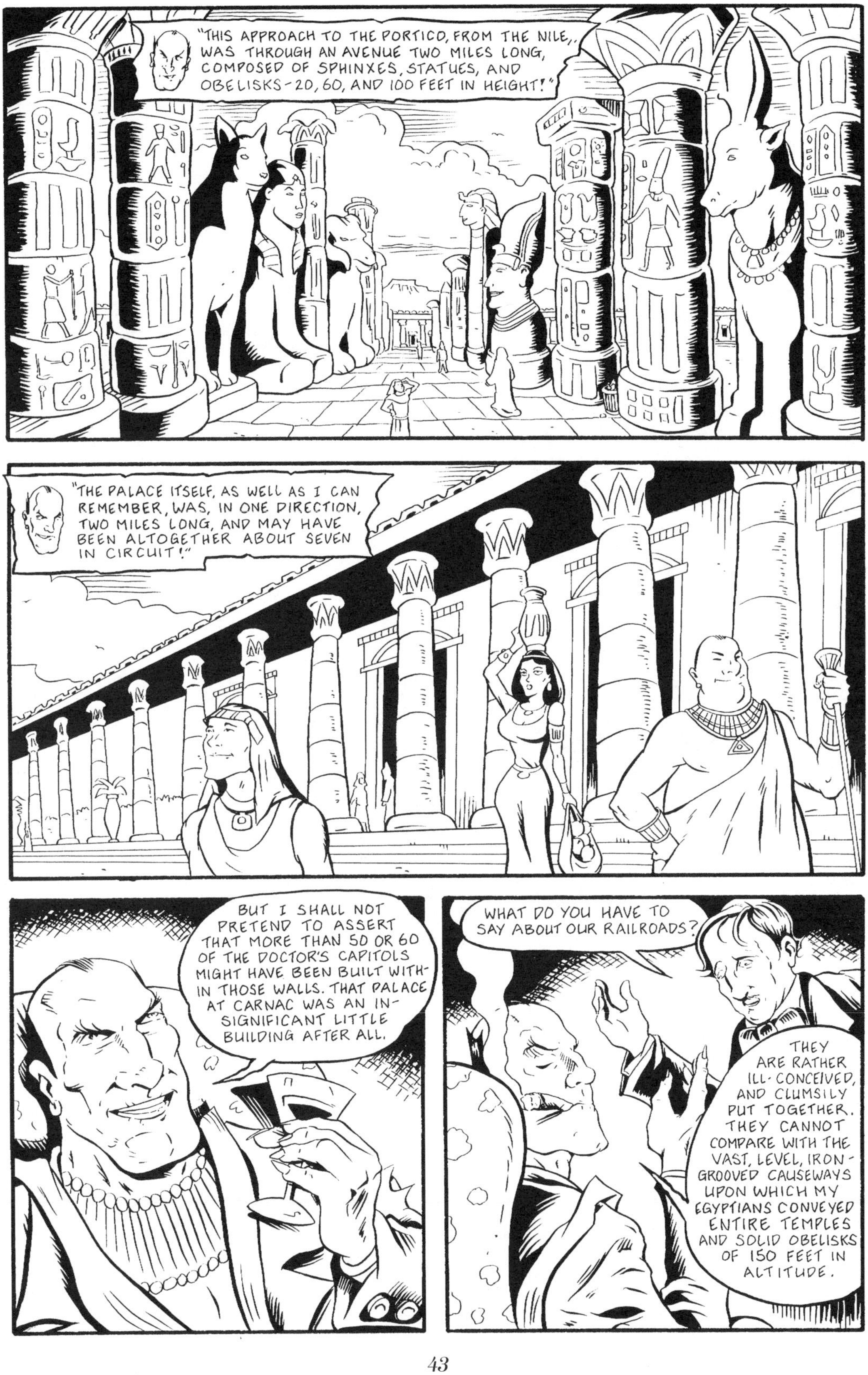
"THIS APPROACH TO THE PORTICO, FROM THE NILE, WAS THROUGH AN AVENUE TWO MILES LONG, COMPOSED OF SPHINXES, STATUES, AND OBELISKS - 20, 60, AND 100 FEET IN HEIGHT!"
"THE PALACE ITSELF, AS WELL AS I CAN REMEMBER, WAS, IN ONE DIRECTION, TWO MILES LONG, AND MAY HAVE BEEN ALTOGETHER ABOUT SEVEN IN CIRCUIT!"
BUT I SHALL NOT PRETEND TO ASSERT THAT MORE THAN 50 OR 60 OF THE DOCTOR'S CAPITOLS MIGHT HAVE BEEN BUILT WITHIN THOSE WALLS. THAT PALACE AT CARNAC WAS AN INSIGNIFICANT LITTLE BUILDING AFTER ALL.
WHAT DO YOU HAVE TO SAY ABOUT OUR RAILROADS?
THEY ARE RATHER ILL-CONCEIVED, AND CLUMSILY PUT TOGETHER. THEY CANNOT COMPARE WITH THE VAST, LEVEL, IRON-GROOVED CAUSEWAYS UPON WHICH MY EGYPTIANS CONVEYED ENTIRE TEMPLES AND SOLID OBELISKS OF 150 FEET IN ALTITUDE.

BUT WHAT OF OUR GIGANTIC MECHANICAL FORCES?

I AGREE THAT YOU KNOW SOMETHING IN THAT WAY, BUT HOW SHOULD YOU HAVE GONE TO WORK IN GETTING UP THE IMPOSTS ON THE LINTELS OF EVEN THE LITTLE PALACE AT CARNAC?

THIS DISCONCERTED US SO GREATLY THAT WE THOUGHT IT ADVISABLE TO VARY THE ATTACK.

WE SPOKE OF THE GREAT BEAUTY AND IMPORTANCE OF DEMOCRACY, AND WERE AT MUCH TROUBLE IN IMPRESSING THE COUNT WITH A DUE SENSE OF THE ADVANTAGES WE ENJOYED IN LIVING WHERE THERE WAS SUFFRAGE AD LIBITUM AND NO KING.

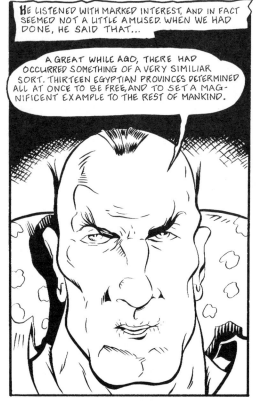

HE LISTENED WITH MARKED INTEREST, AND IN FACT SEEMED NOT A LITTLE AMUSED. WHEN WE HAD DONE, HE SAID THAT...

A GREAT WHILE AGO, THERE HAD OCCURRED SOMETHING OF A VERY SIMILIAR SORT. THIRTEEN EGYPTIAN PROVINCES DETERMINED ALL AT ONCE TO BE FREE, AND TO SET A MAGNIFICENT EXAMPLE TO THE REST OF MANKIND.

THEY ASSEMBLED THEIR WISE MEN, AND CONCOCTED THE MOST INGENIOUS CONSTITUTION IT IS POSSIBLE TO CONCEIVE. FOR A WHILE THEY MANAGED REMARKABLY WELL; ONLY THEIR HABIT OF BRAGGING WAS PRODIGIOUS.

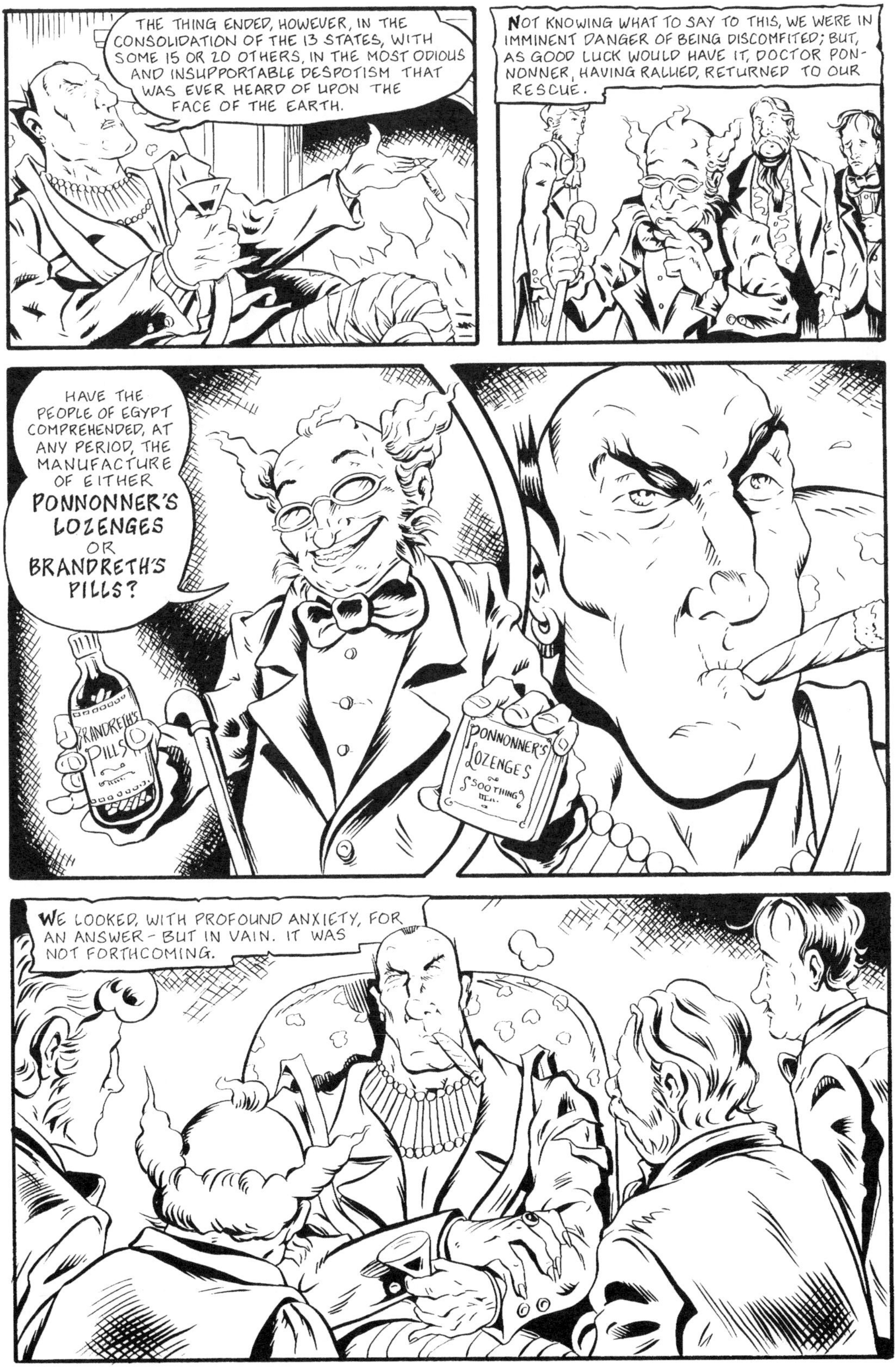
THE THING ENDED, HOWEVER, IN THE CONSOLIDATION OF THE 13 STATES, WITH SOME 15 OR 20 OTHERS, IN THE MOST ODIOUS AND INSUPPORTABLE DESPOTISM THAT WAS EVER HEARD OF UPON THE FACE OF THE EARTH.
NOT KNOWING WHAT TO SAY TO THIS, WE WERE IN IMMINENT DANGER OF BEING DISCOMFITED; BUT, AS GOOD LUCK WOULD HAVE IT, DOCTOR PONNONNER, HAVING RALLIED, RETURNED TO OUR RESCUE.
HAVE THE PEOPLE OF EGYPT COMPREHENDED, AT ANY PERIOD, THE MANUFACTURE OF EITHER PONNONNER'S LOZENGES OR BRANDRETH'S PILLS?
BRANDRETH'S PILLS
PONNONNER'S LOZENGES SOOTHING
WE LOOKED, WITH PROFOUND ANXIETY, FOR AN ANSWER - BUT IN VAIN. IT WAS NOT FORTHCOMING.

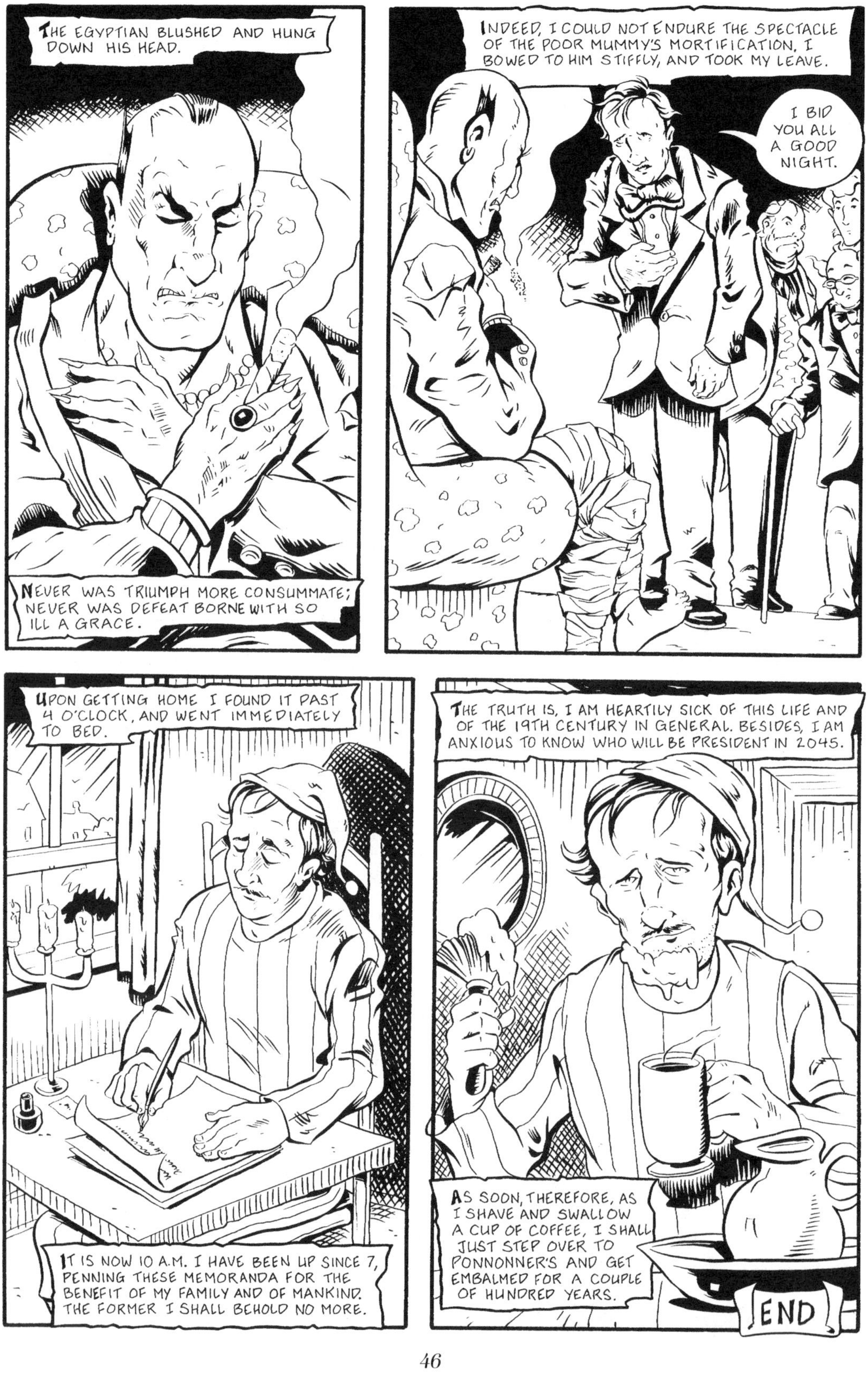
THE EGYPTIAN BLUSHED AND HUNG DOWN HIS HEAD.
NEVER WAS TRIUMPH MORE CONSUMMATE; NEVER WAS DEFEAT BORNE WITH SO ILL A GRACE.
INDEED, I COULD NOT ENDURE THE SPECTACLE OF THE POOR MUMMY'S MORTIFICATION. I BOWED TO HIM STIFFLY, AND TOOK MY LEAVE.
I BID YOU ALL A GOOD NIGHT.
UPON GETTING HOME I FOUND IT PAST 4 O'CLOCK, AND WENT IMMEDIATELY TO BED.
IT IS NOW 10 A.M. I HAVE BEEN UP SINCE 7, PENNING THESE MEMORANDA FOR THE BENEFIT OF MY FAMILY AND OF MANKIND. THE FORMER I SHALL BEHOLD NO MORE.
THE TRUTH IS, I AM HEARTILY SICK OF THIS LIFE AND OF THE 19TH CENTURY IN GENERAL. BESIDES, I AM ANXIOUS TO KNOW WHO WILL BE PRESIDENT IN 2045.
AS SOON, THEREFORE, AS I SHAVE AND SWALLOW A CUP OF COFFEE, I SHALL JUST STEP OVER TO PONNONNER'S AND GET EMBALMED FOR A COUPLE OF HUNDRED YEARS.
END

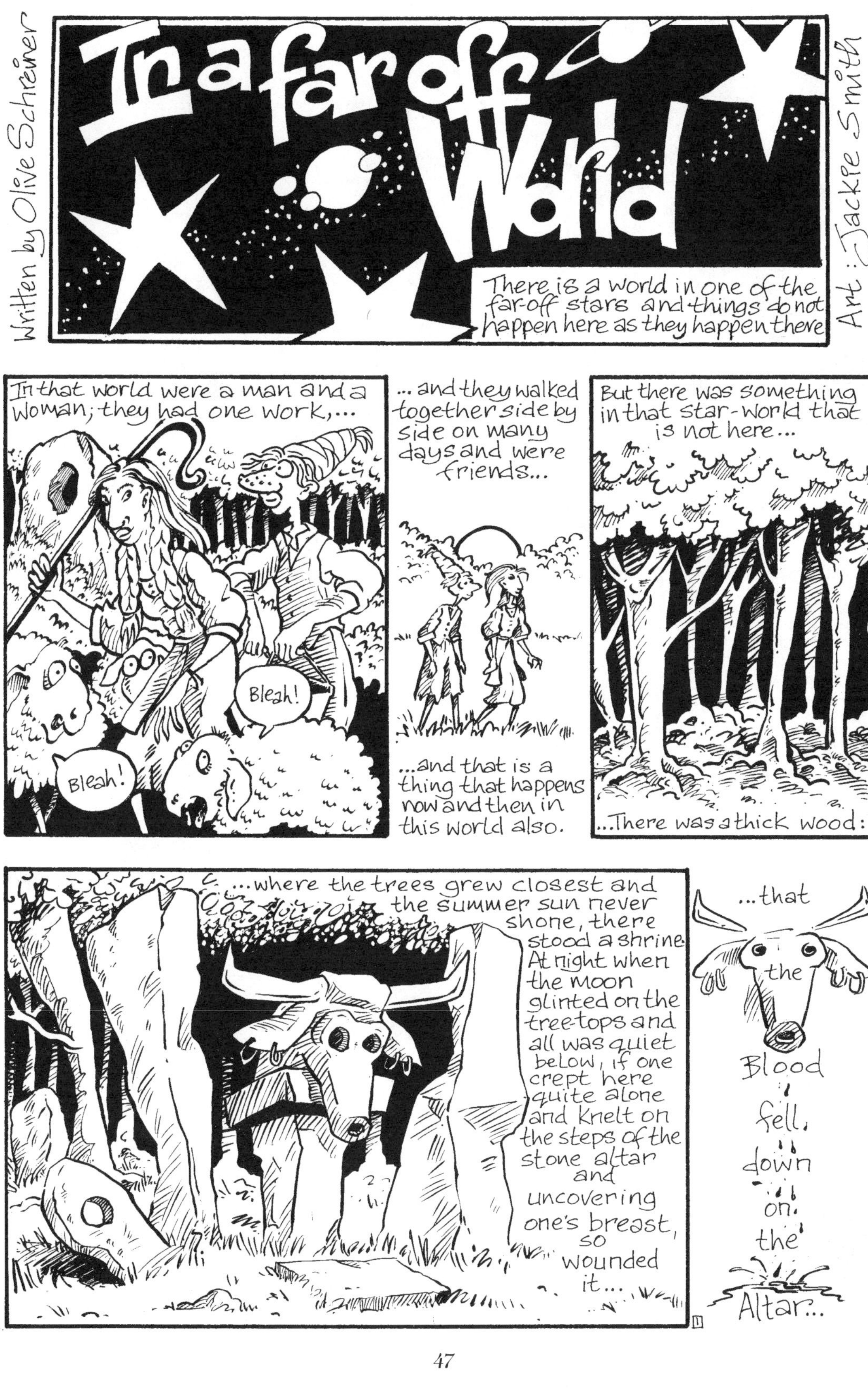
Written by Olive Schreiner
In a far off World
Art: Jackie Smith
There is a world in one of the far-off stars and things do not happen here as they happen there
In that world were a man and a woman; they had one work,...
Bleah!
Bleah!
...and they walked together side by side on many days and were friends...
...and that is a thing that happens now and then in this world also.
But there was something in that star-world that is not here...
...There was a thick wood:
...where the trees grew closest and the summer sun never shone, there stood a shrine. At night when the moon glinted on the tree-tops and all was quiet below, if one crept here quite alone and knelt on the steps of the stone altar and uncovering one's breast, so wounded it...
1
...that the Blood fell down on the Altar...

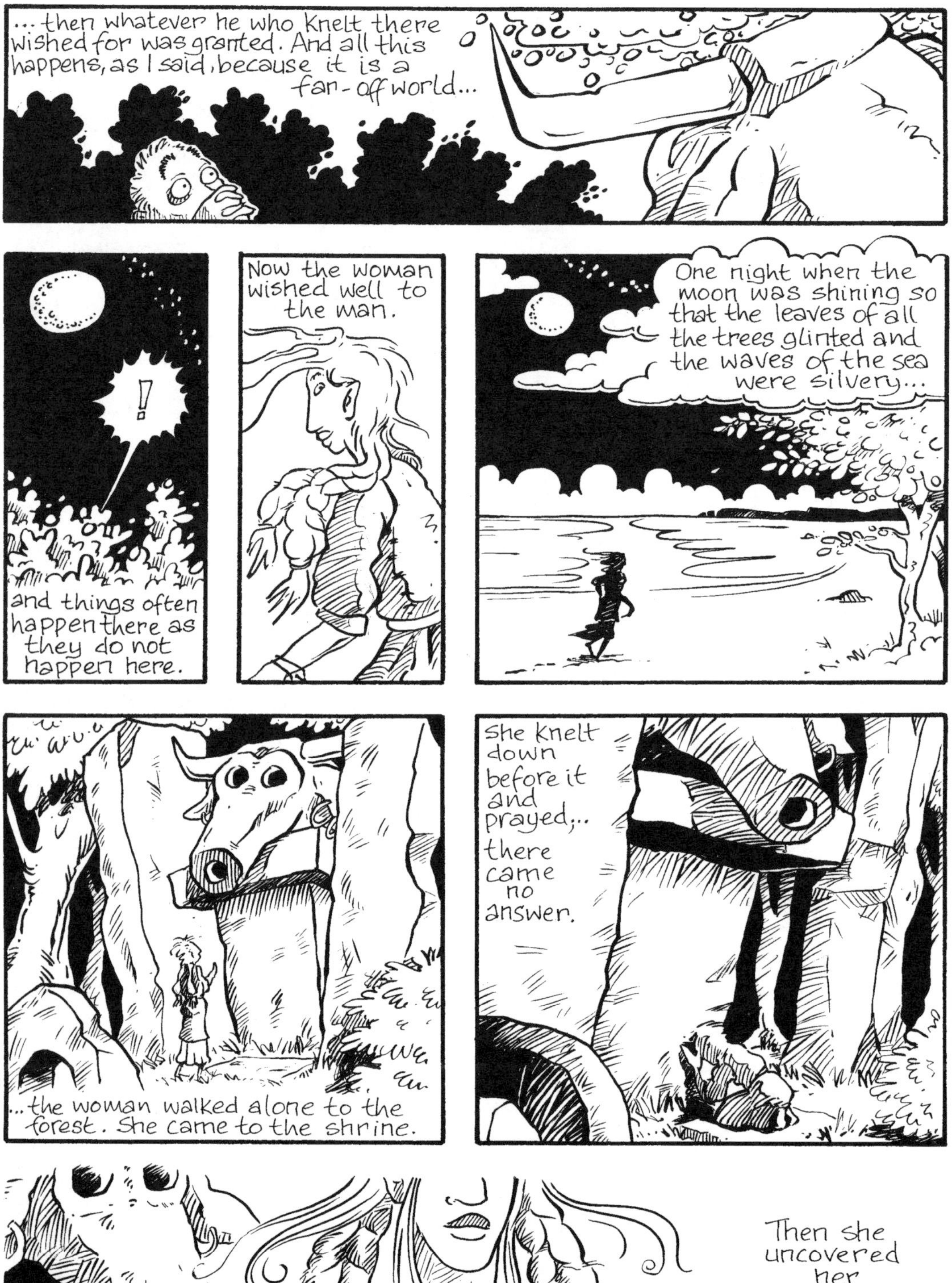
...then whatever he who knelt there wished for was granted. And all this happens, as I said, because it is a far-off world...
!
and things often happen there as they do not happen here.
Now the woman wished well to the man.
One night when the moon was shining so that the leaves of all the trees glinted and the waves of the sea were silvery...
...the woman walked alone to the forest. She came to the shrine.
She knelt down before it and prayed,... there came no answer.
Then she uncovered her breast...
2

With a sharp stone that lay there she wounded it.

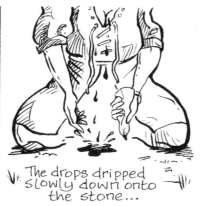

The drops dripped slowly down onto the stone...

..AND A VOICE CRIED..

WHAT DO YOU SEEK ?....

TH..TH.. THERE IS A MAN..

I KNOW NOT...BUT THAT WHICH IS MOST GOOD FOR HIM I WISH HIM TO HAVE!

..I HOLD HIM NEARER THAN ANYTHING, I WOULD GIVE HIM THE BEST OF ALL BLESSINGS.

WHAT IS IT!

YOUR PRAYER IS ANSWERED.

HE SHALL HAVE IT.

3

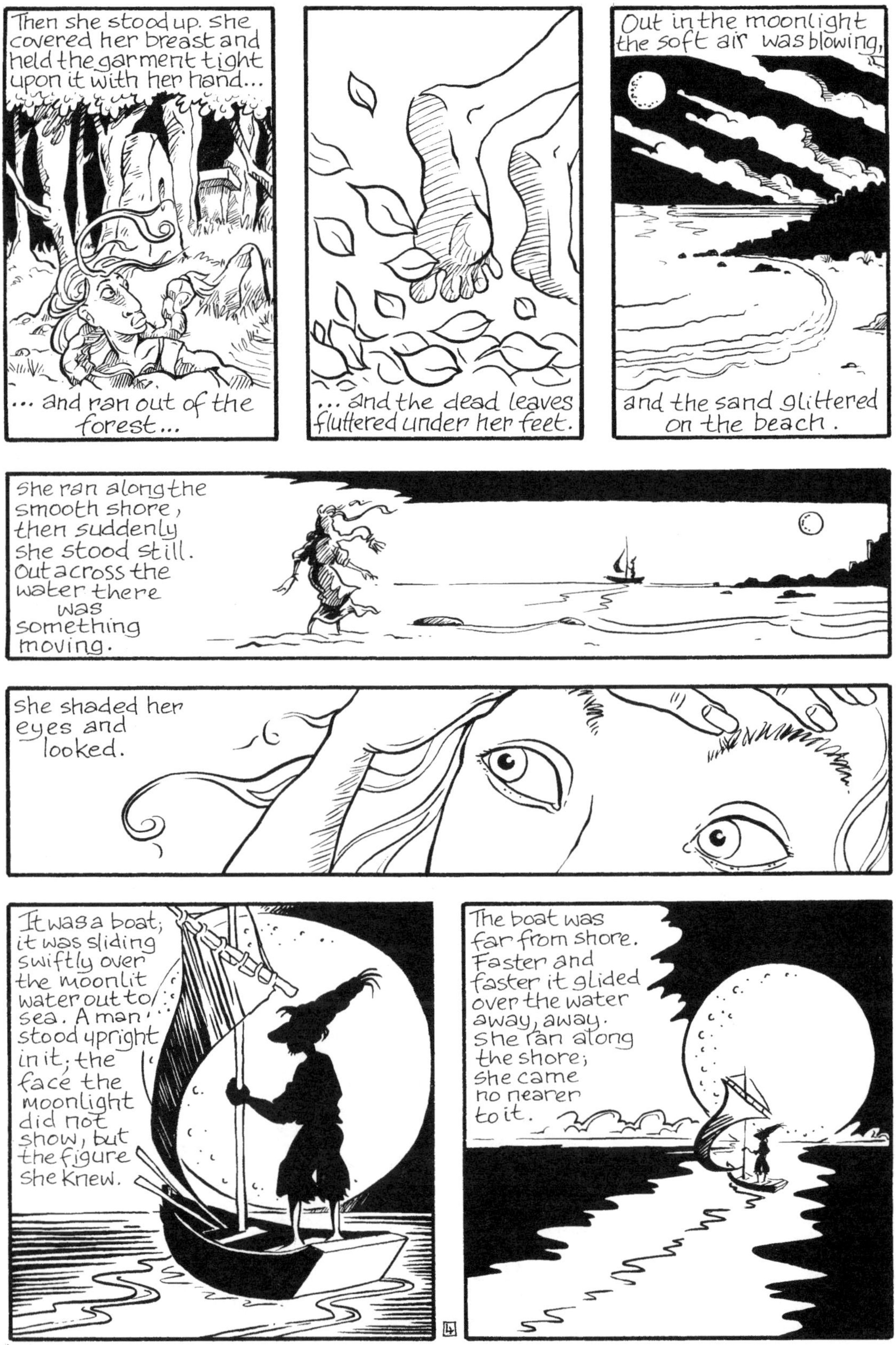
Then she stood up. She covered her breast and held the garment tight upon it with her hand...
... and ran out of the forest...
... and the dead leaves fluttered under her feet.
Out in the moonlight the soft air was blowing,
and the sand glittered on the beach.
She ran along the smooth shore, then suddenly she stood still. Out across the water there was something moving.
She shaded her eyes and looked.
It was a boat; it was sliding swiftly over the moonlit water out to sea. A man stood upright in it; the face the moonlight did not show, but the figure she knew.
The boat was far from shore. Faster and faster it glided over the water away, away. She ran along the shore; she came no nearer to it.

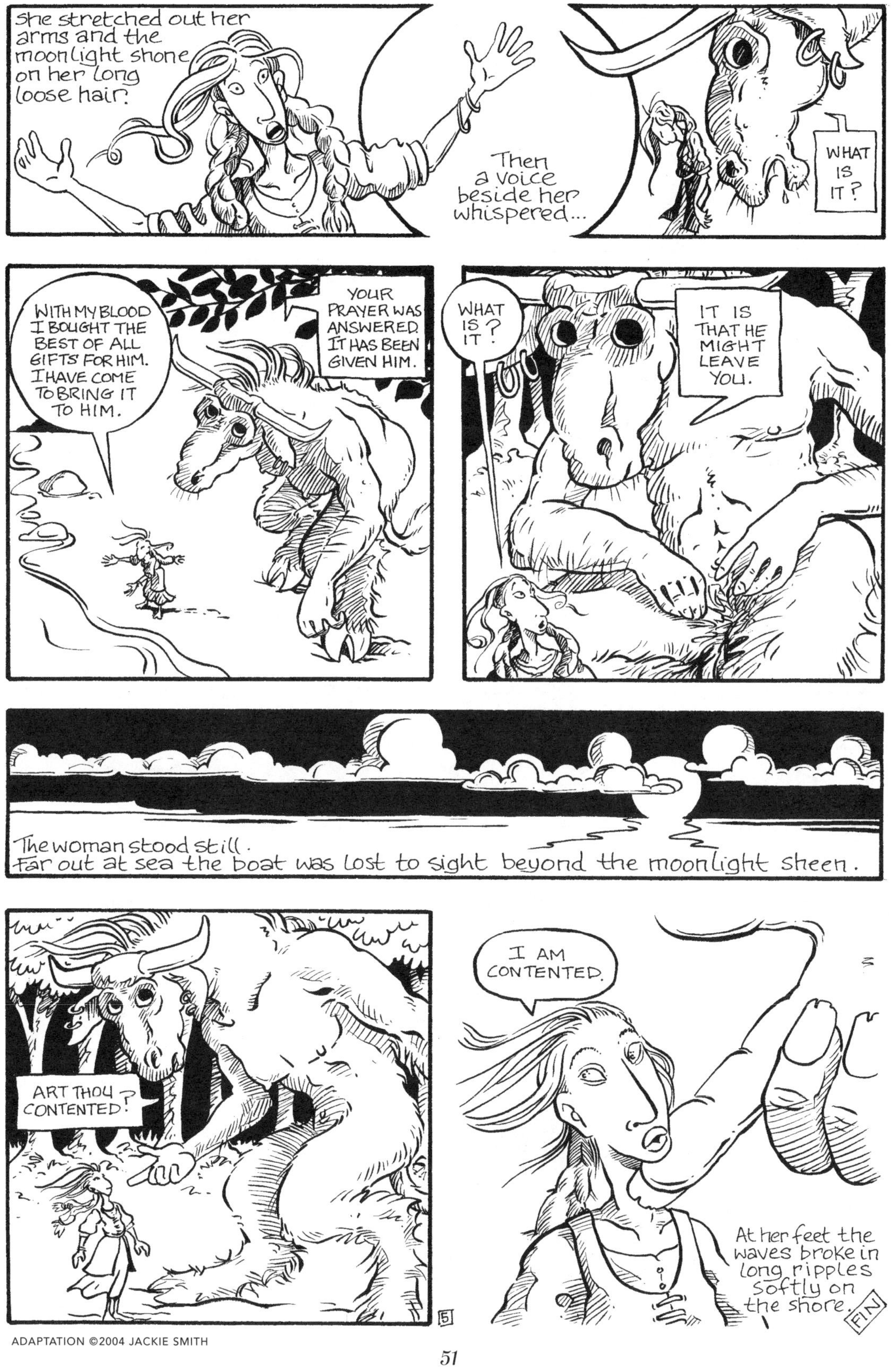
She stretched out her arms and the moonlight shone on her long loose hair.
Then a voice beside her whispered...
WHAT IS IT?
WITH MY BLOOD I BOUGHT THE BEST OF ALL GIFTS FOR HIM. I HAVE COME TO BRING IT TO HIM.
YOUR PRAYER WAS ANSWERED. IT HAS BEEN GIVEN HIM.
WHAT IS IT?
IT IS THAT HE MIGHT LEAVE YOU.
The woman stood still.
Far out at sea the boat was lost to sight beyond the moonlight sheen.
ART THOU CONTENTED?
5
I AM CONTENTED.
At her feet the waves broke in long ripples softly on the shore.
FIN

THE THING AT GHENT

STORY BY HONORÉ De BALZAC   PICTURES BY MARK DANCEY

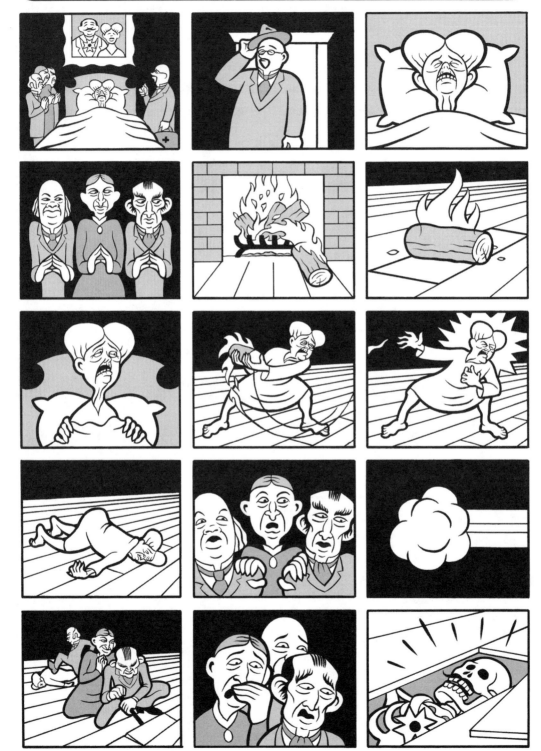

ADAPTATION ©2004 MARK DANCEY

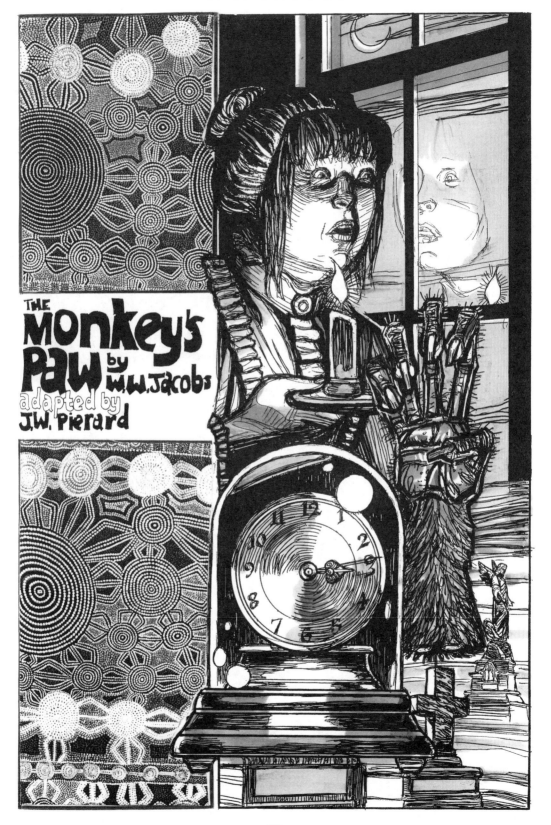

THE MONKEY'S PAW by W.W.Jacobs
adapted by J.W. Pierard

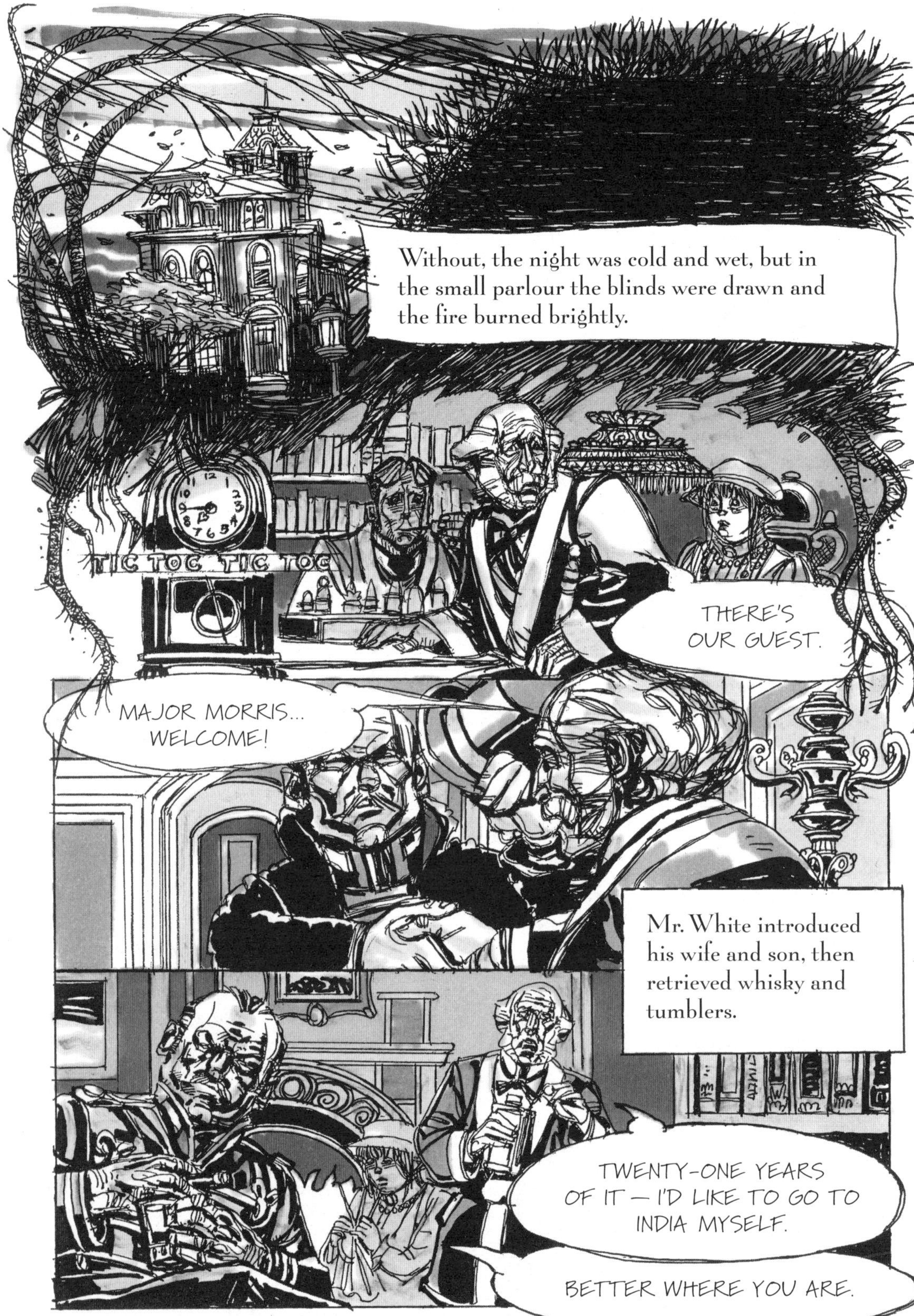
Without, the night was cold and wet, but in the small parlour the blinds were drawn and the fire burned brightly.
TIC TOC TIC TOC
THERE'S OUR GUEST.
MAJOR MORRIS... WELCOME!
Mr. White introduced his wife and son, then retrieved whisky and tumblers.
TWENTY-ONE YEARS OF IT — I'D LIKE TO GO TO INDIA MYSELF.
BETTER WHERE YOU ARE.

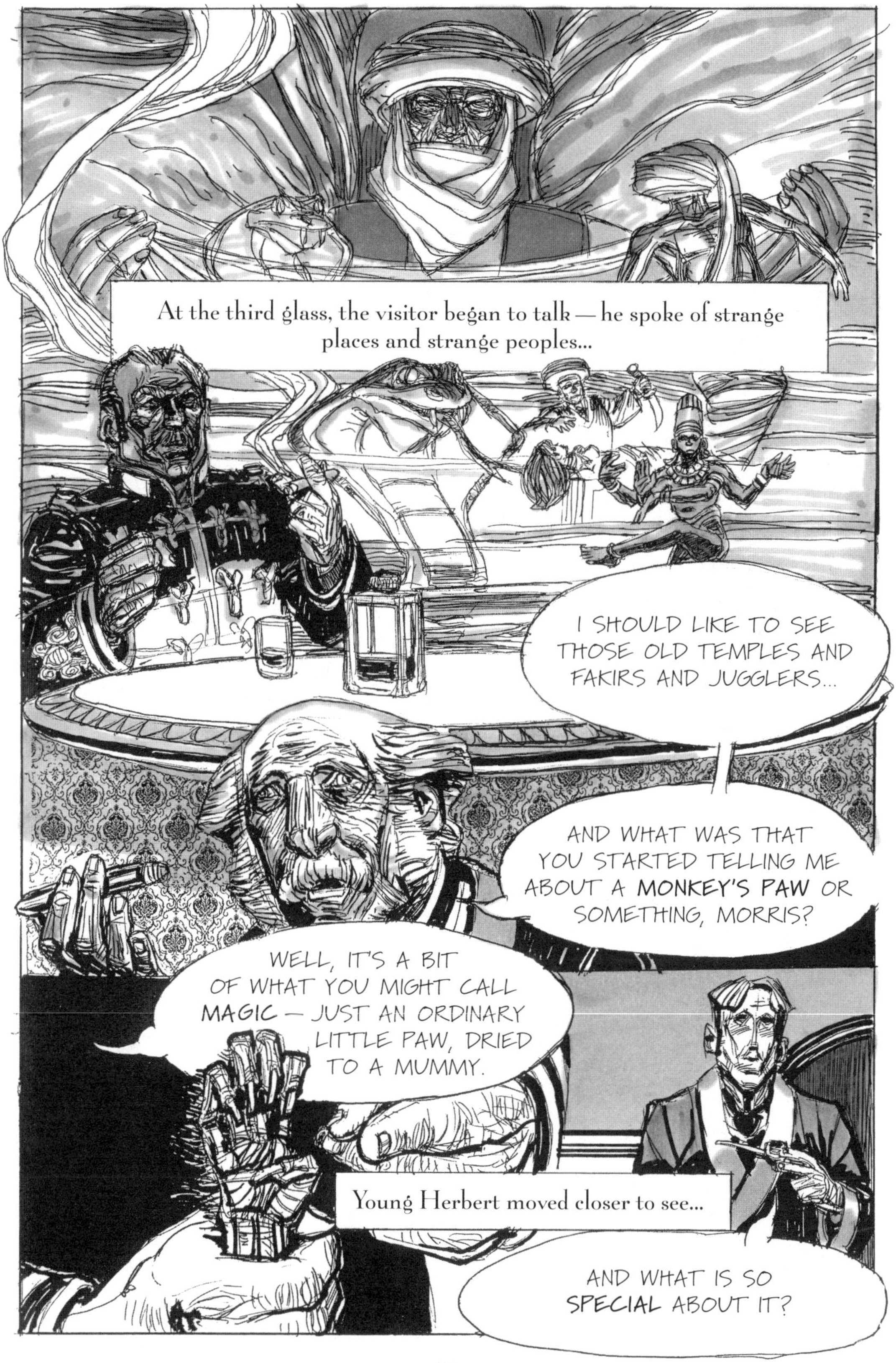
At the third glass, the visitor began to talk — he spoke of strange places and strange peoples...
I SHOULD LIKE TO SEE THOSE OLD TEMPLES AND FAKIRS AND JUGGLERS...
AND WHAT WAS THAT YOU STARTED TELLING ME ABOUT A MONKEY'S PAW OR SOMETHING, MORRIS?
WELL, IT'S A BIT OF WHAT YOU MIGHT CALL MAGIC — JUST AN ORDINARY LITTLE PAW, DRIED TO A MUMMY.
Young Herbert moved closer to see...
AND WHAT IS SO SPECIAL ABOUT IT?

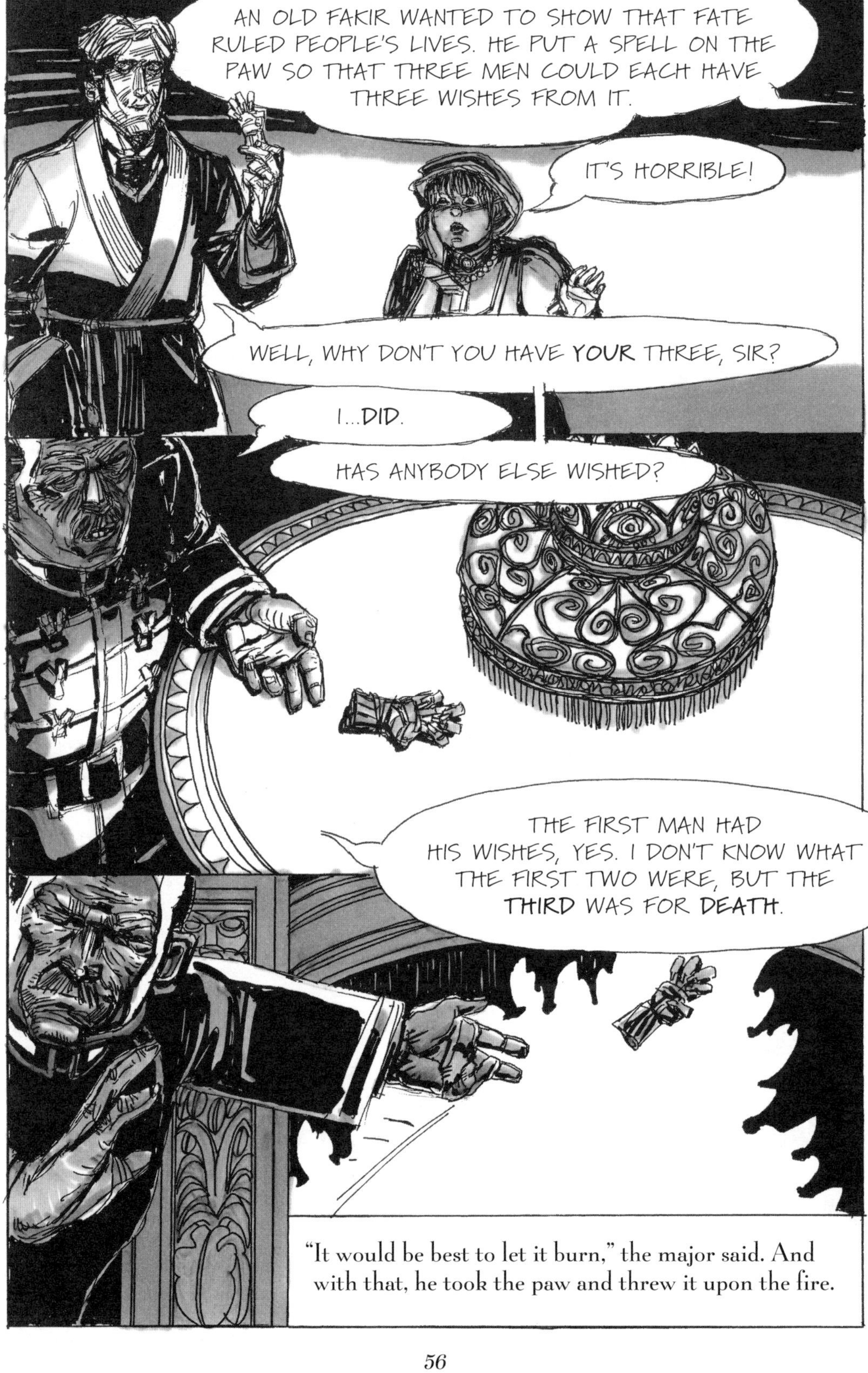
AN OLD FAKIR WANTED TO SHOW THAT FATE RULED PEOPLE'S LIVES. HE PUT A SPELL ON THE PAW SO THAT THREE MEN COULD EACH HAVE THREE WISHES FROM IT.
IT'S HORRIBLE!
WELL, WHY DON'T YOU HAVE **YOUR** THREE, SIR?
I...**DID**.
HAS ANYBODY ELSE WISHED?
THE FIRST MAN HAD HIS WISHES, YES. I DON'T KNOW WHAT THE FIRST TWO WERE, BUT THE **THIRD** WAS FOR **DEATH**.

"It would be best to let it burn," the major said. And with that, he took the paw and threw it upon the fire.

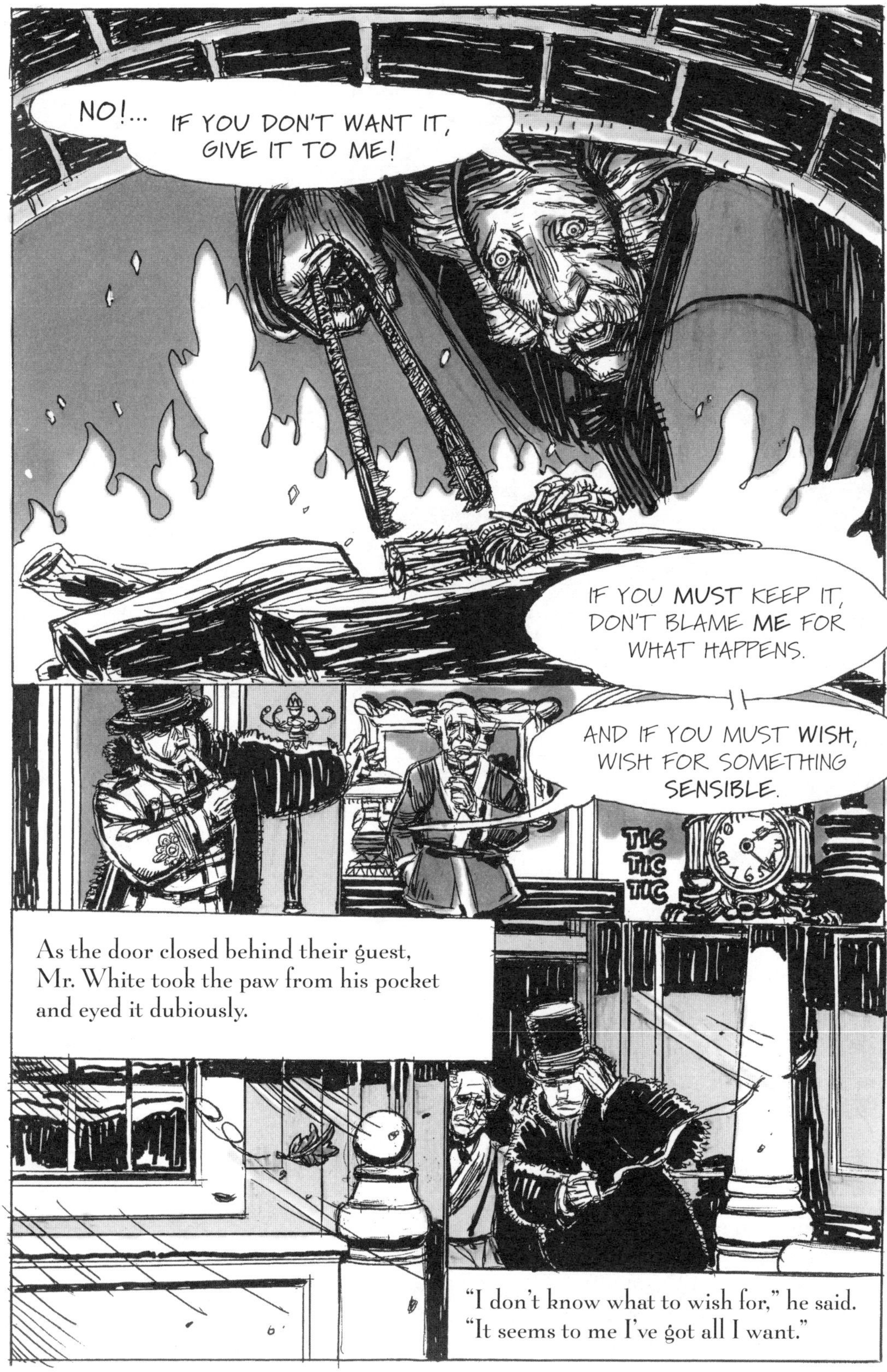
NO!... IF YOU DON'T WANT IT, GIVE IT TO ME!
IF YOU MUST KEEP IT, DON'T BLAME ME FOR WHAT HAPPENS.
AND IF YOU MUST WISH, WISH FOR SOMETHING SENSIBLE.
TIC TIC TIC
As the door closed behind their guest, Mr. White took the paw from his pocket and eyed it dubiously.
"I don't know what to wish for," he said. "It seems to me I've got all I want."

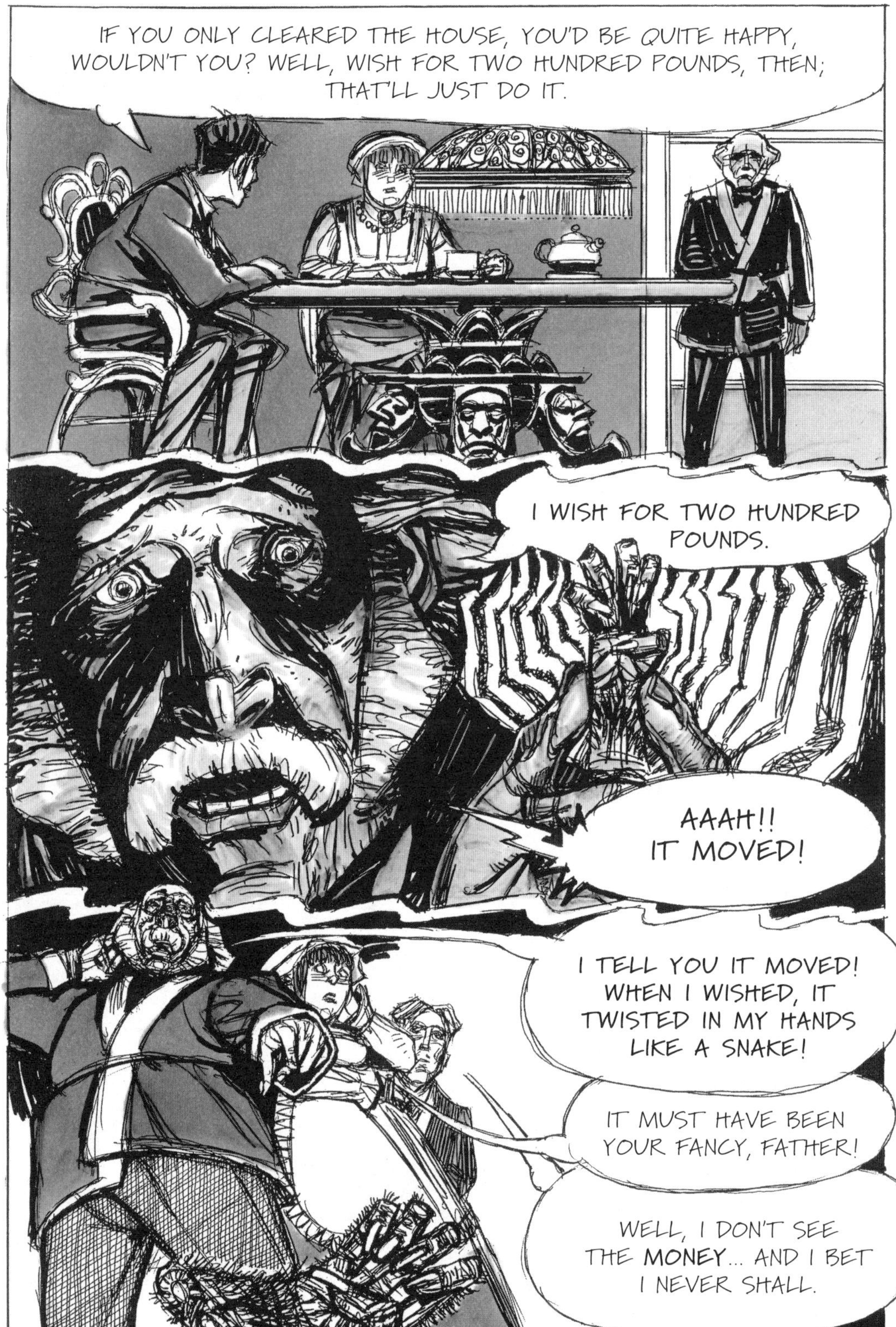
IF YOU ONLY CLEARED THE HOUSE, YOU'D BE QUITE HAPPY, WOULDN'T YOU? WELL, WISH FOR TWO HUNDRED POUNDS, THEN; THAT'LL JUST DO IT.
I WISH FOR TWO HUNDRED POUNDS.
AAAH!! IT MOVED!
I TELL YOU IT MOVED! WHEN I WISHED, IT TWISTED IN MY HANDS LIKE A SNAKE!
IT MUST HAVE BEEN YOUR FANCY, FATHER!
WELL, I DON'T SEE THE MONEY... AND I BET I NEVER SHALL.

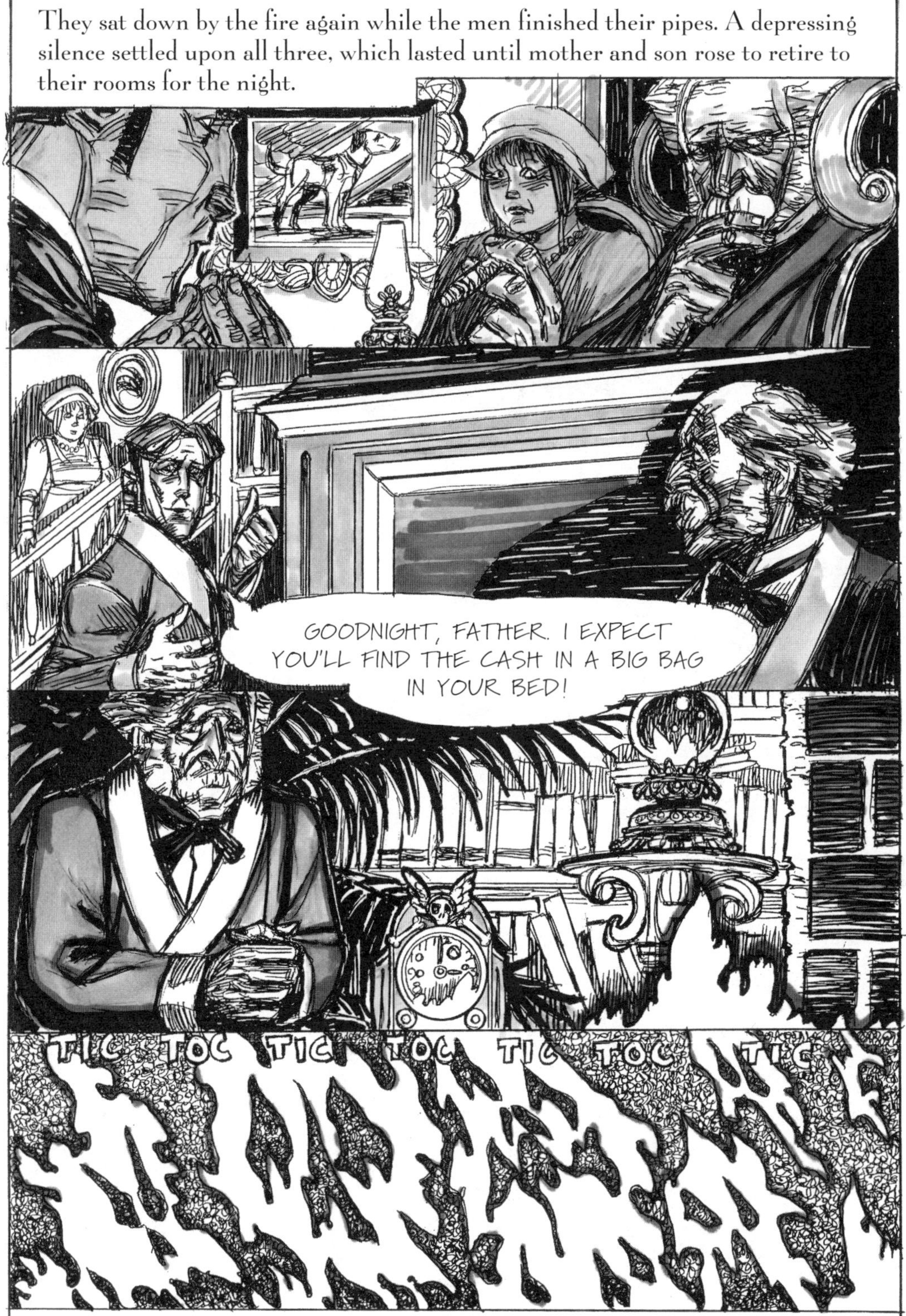
They sat down by the fire again while the men finished their pipes. A depressing silence settled upon all three, which lasted until mother and son rose to retire to their rooms for the night.
GOODNIGHT, FATHER. I EXPECT YOU'LL FIND THE CASH IN A BIG BAG IN YOUR BED!
TIC TOC TIC TOC TIC TOC TIC
He sat alone, seeing faces in the dying fire. Then, with a shiver, he went up to bed.

In the brightness of the sun the next morning, the old man forgot his fears.

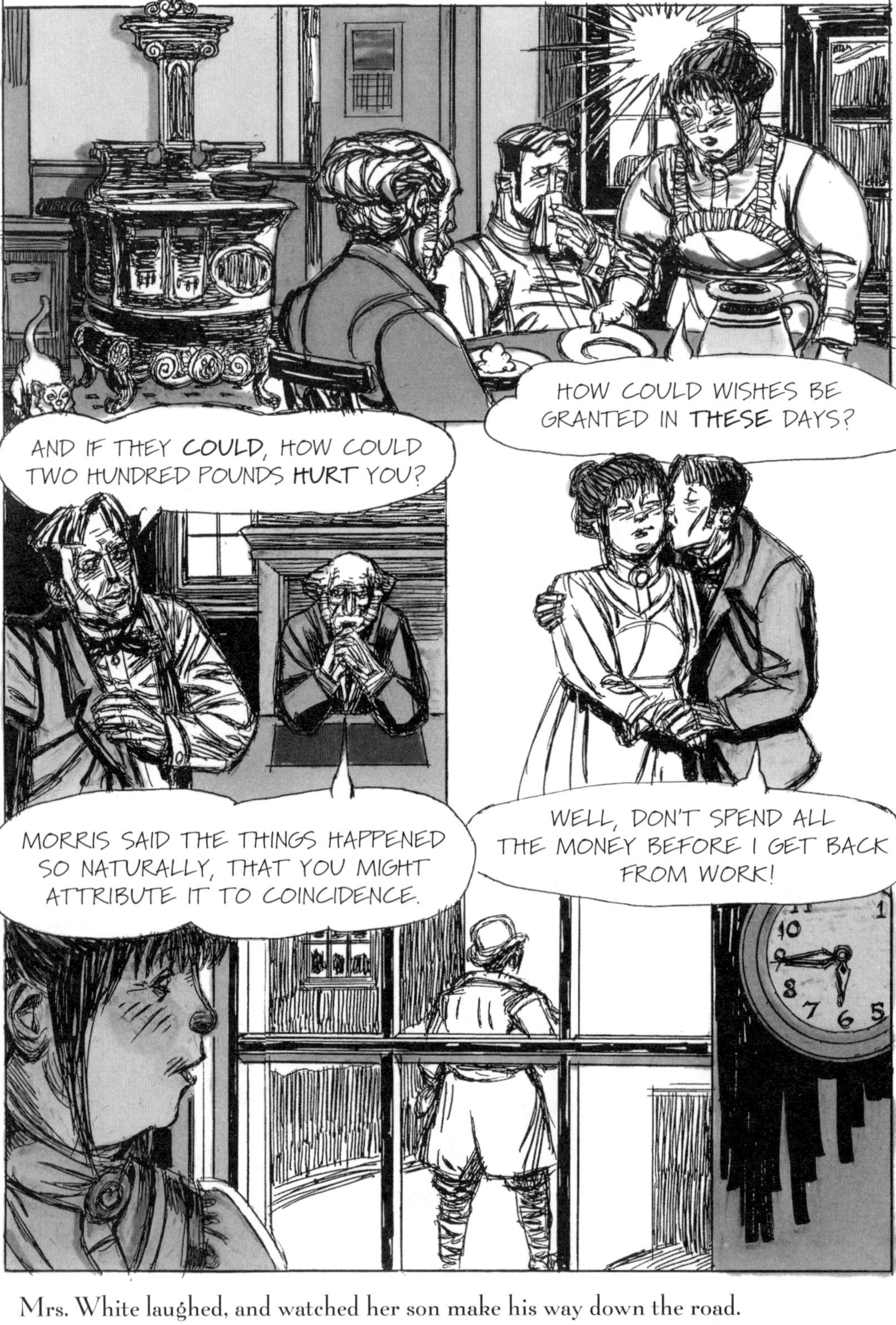
HOW COULD WISHES BE GRANTED IN THESE DAYS?
AND IF THEY COULD, HOW COULD TWO HUNDRED POUNDS HURT YOU?
MORRIS SAID THE THINGS HAPPENED SO NATURALLY, THAT YOU MIGHT ATTRIBUTE IT TO COINCIDENCE.
WELL, DON'T SPEND ALL THE MONEY BEFORE I GET BACK FROM WORK!

Mrs. White laughed, and watched her son make his way down the road.

The day passed pleasantly until late afternoon, when Mrs. White noticed a man outside, who appeared to be trying to make up his mind whether to enter the house.

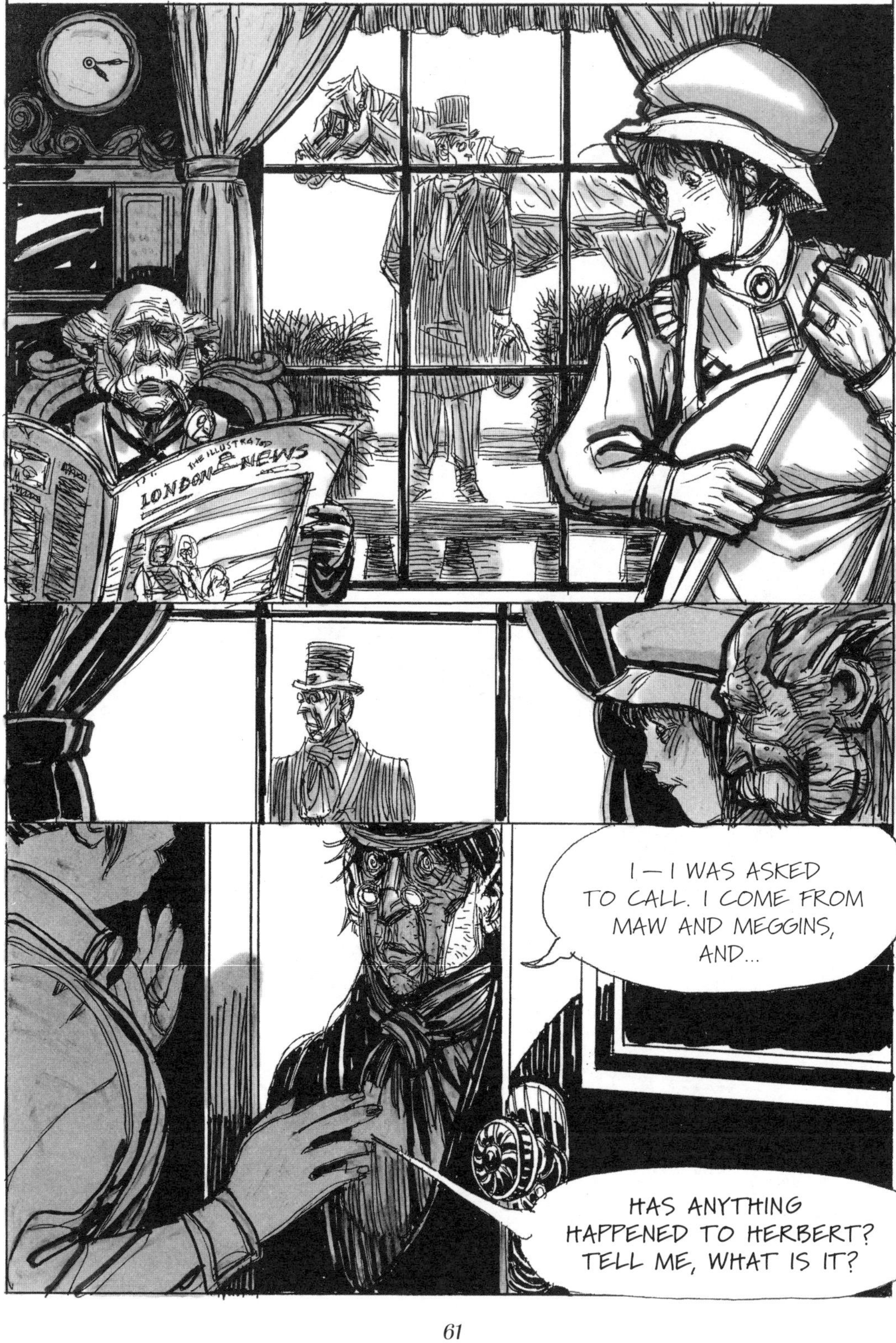
THE ILLUSTRATED LONDON NEWS
I—I WAS ASKED TO CALL. I COME FROM MAW AND MEGGINS, AND...
HAS ANYTHING HAPPENED TO HERBERT? TELL ME, WHAT IS IT?

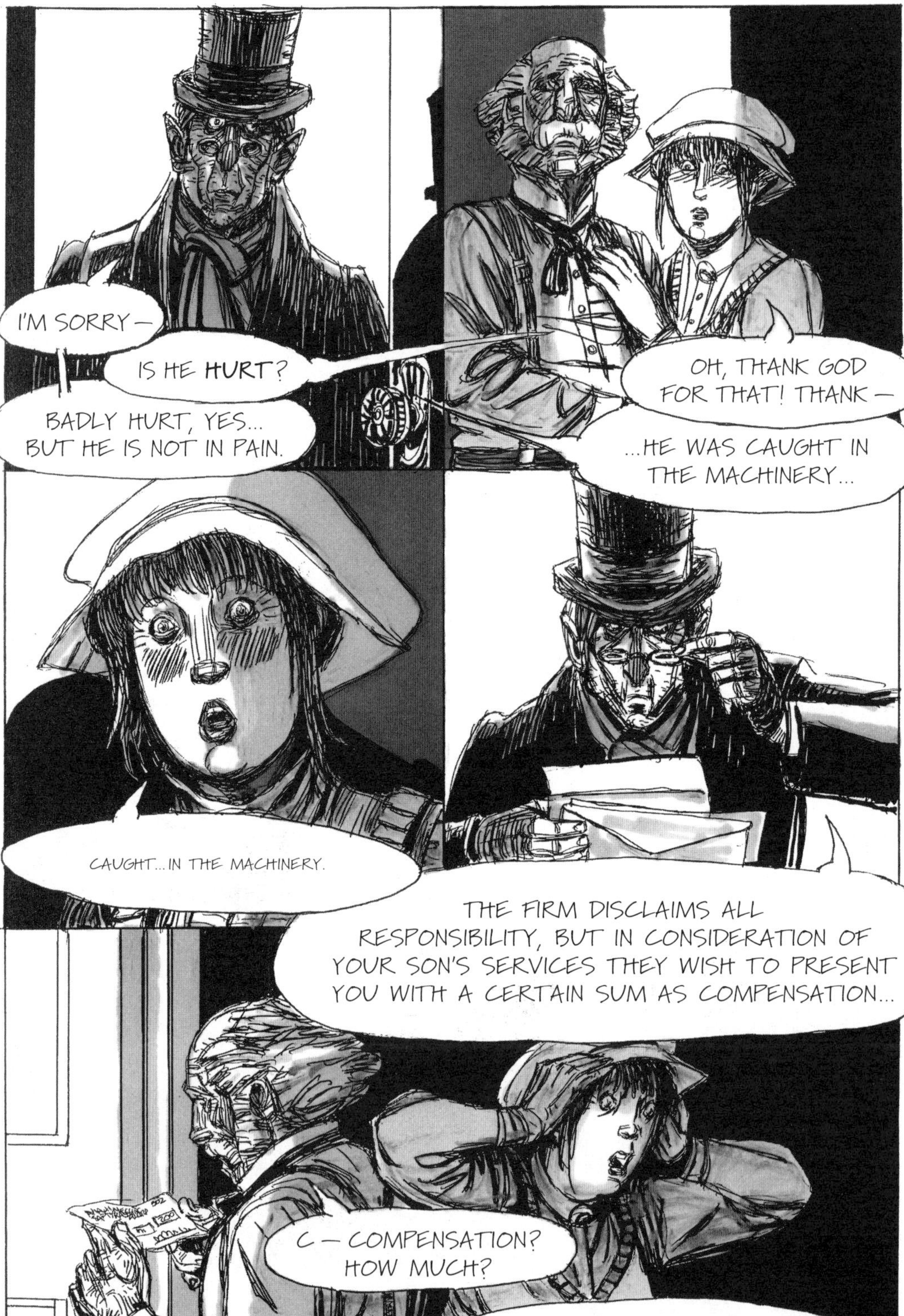
I'M SORRY—
IS HE HURT?
BADLY HURT, YES... BUT HE IS NOT IN PAIN.
OH, THANK GOD FOR THAT! THANK—
...HE WAS CAUGHT IN THE MACHINERY...
CAUGHT...IN THE MACHINERY.
THE FIRM DISCLAIMS ALL RESPONSIBILITY, BUT IN CONSIDERATION OF YOUR SON'S SERVICES THEY WISH TO PRESENT YOU WITH A CERTAIN SUM AS COMPENSATION...
C—COMPENSATION? HOW MUCH?
TWO HUNDRED POUNDS.

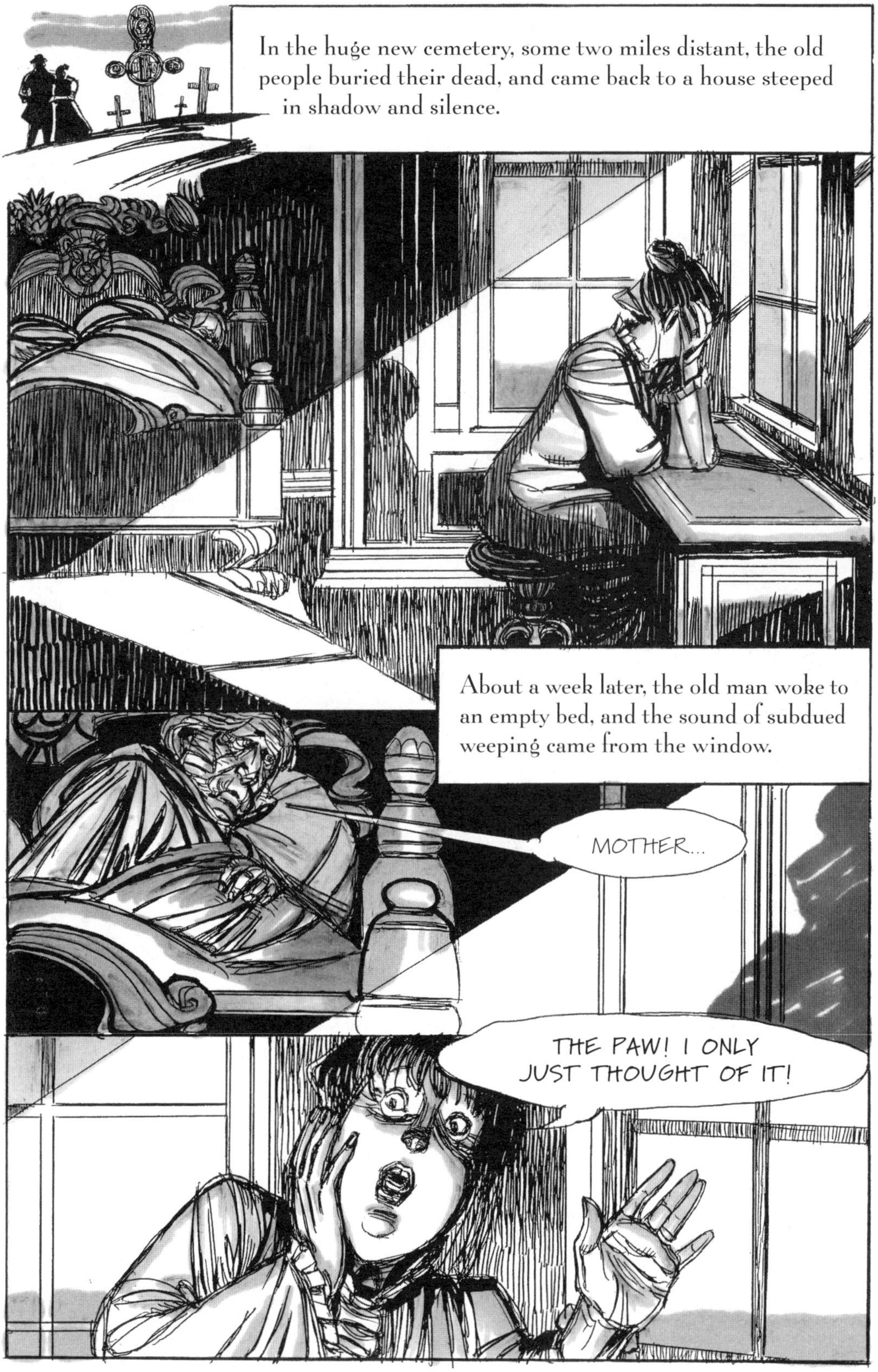
In the huge new cemetery, some two miles distant, the old people buried their dead, and came back to a house steeped in shadow and silence.
About a week later, the old man woke to an empty bed, and the sound of subdued weeping came from the window.
MOTHER...
THE PAW! I ONLY JUST THOUGHT OF IT!

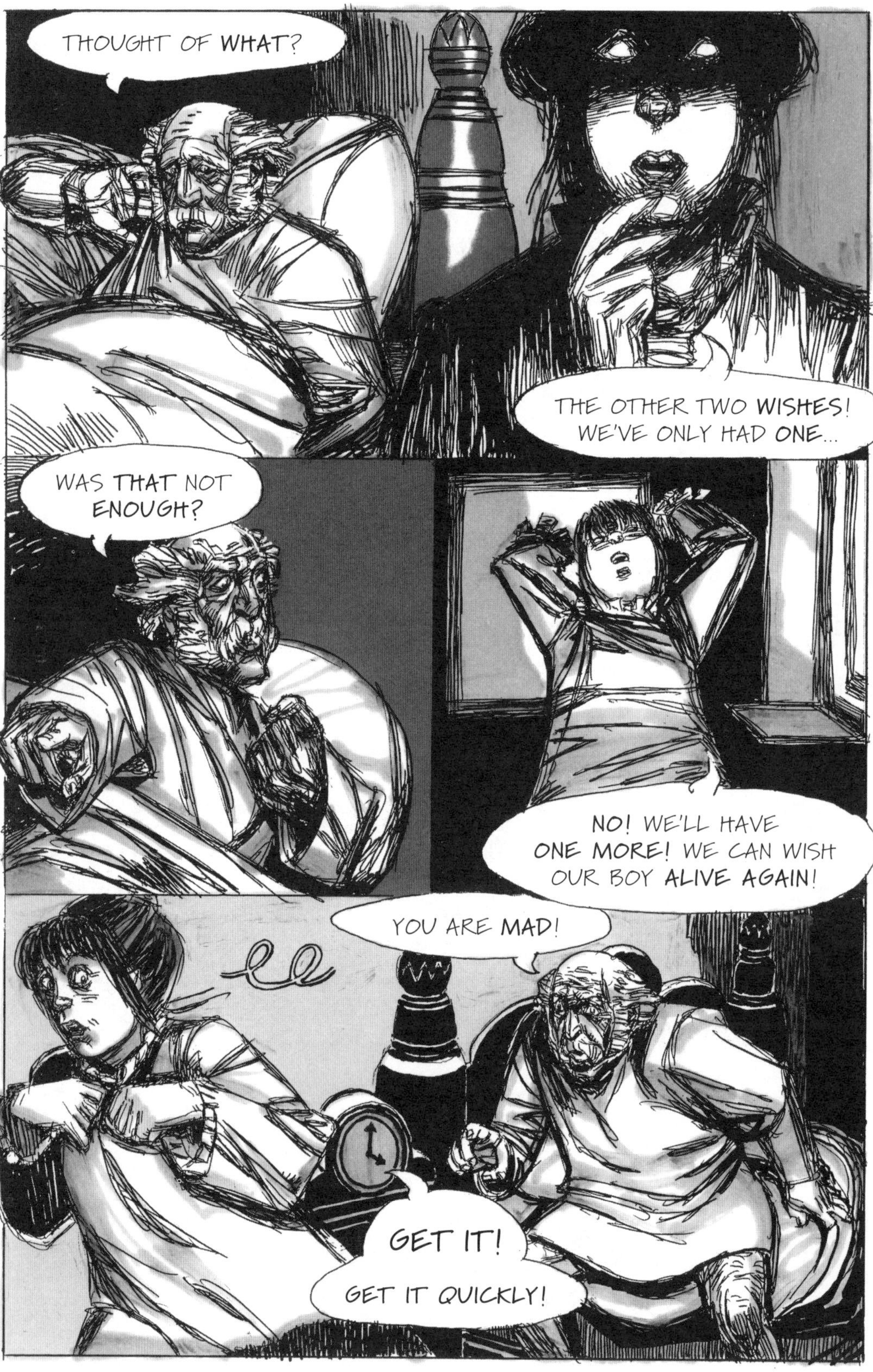
THOUGHT OF WHAT?
THE OTHER TWO WISHES! WE'VE ONLY HAD ONE...
WAS THAT NOT ENOUGH?
NO! WE'LL HAVE ONE MORE! WE CAN WISH OUR BOY ALIVE AGAIN!
YOU ARE MAD!
GET IT!
GET IT QUICKLY!

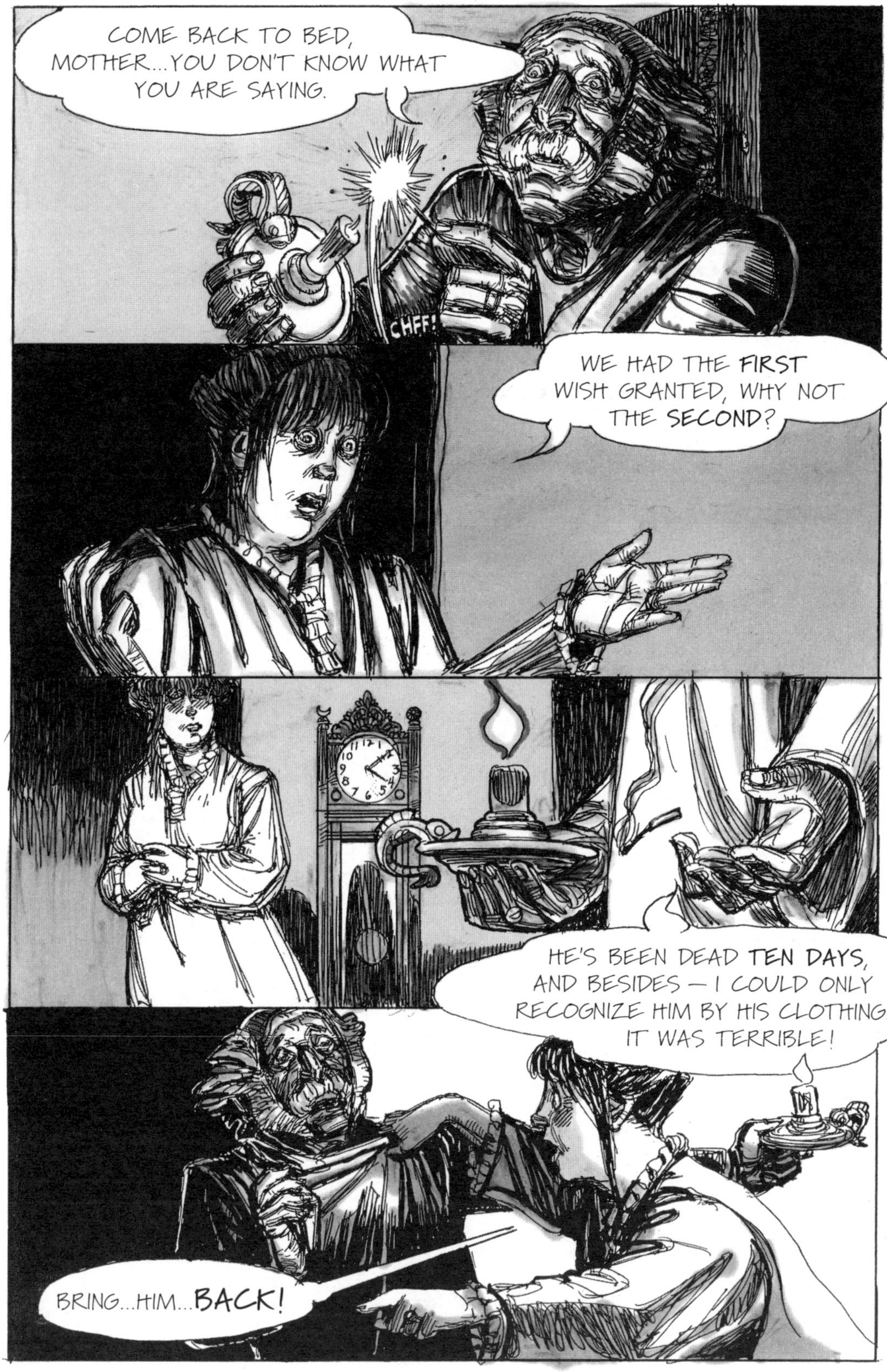
COME BACK TO BED, MOTHER...YOU DON'T KNOW WHAT YOU ARE SAYING.
CHFF!
WE HAD THE FIRST WISH GRANTED, WHY NOT THE SECOND?
HE'S BEEN DEAD TEN DAYS, AND BESIDES — I COULD ONLY RECOGNIZE HIM BY HIS CLOTHING. IT WAS TERRIBLE!
BRING...HIM...BACK!

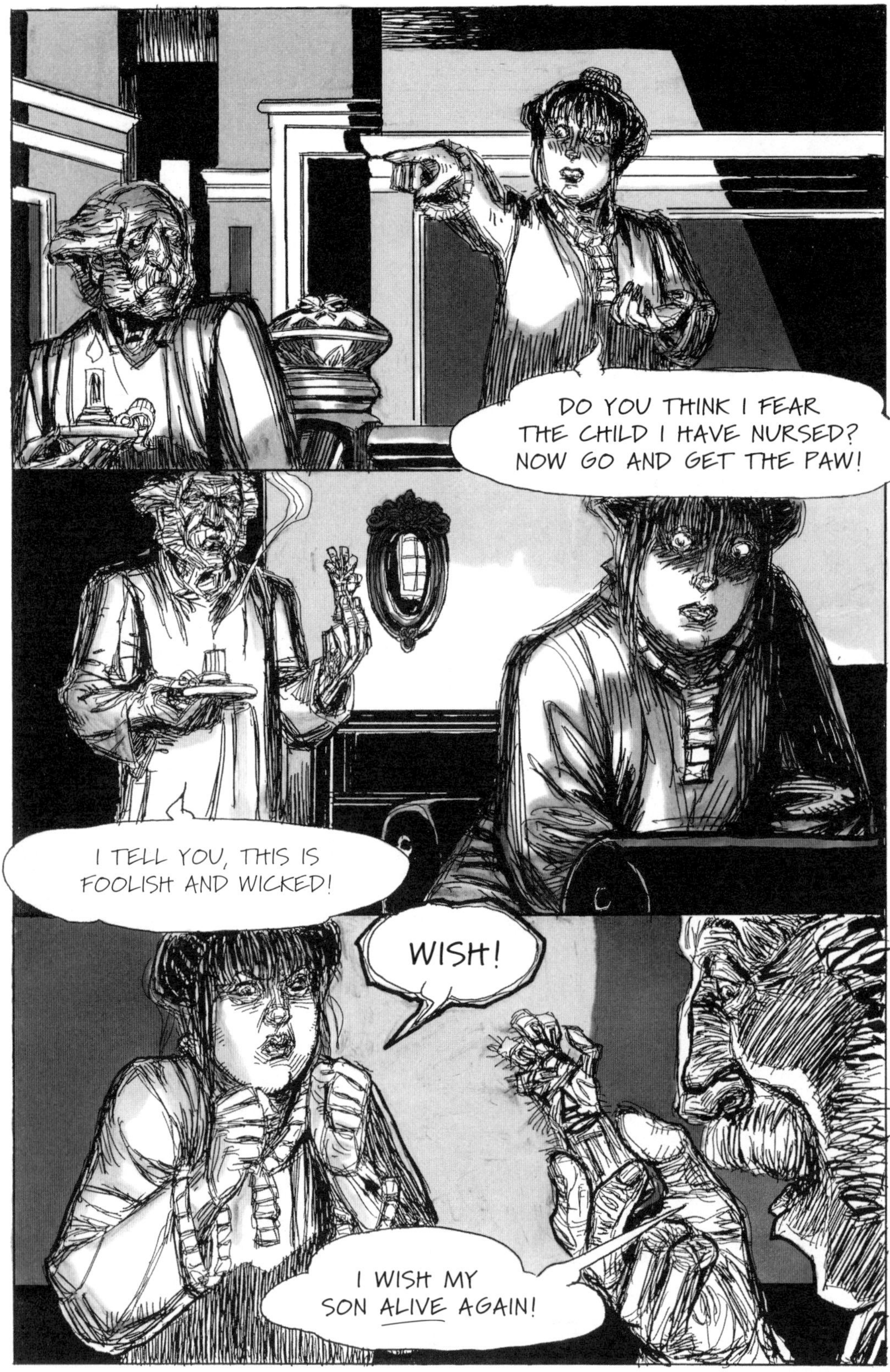
DO YOU THINK I FEAR THE CHILD I HAVE NURSED? NOW GO AND GET THE PAW!
I TELL YOU, THIS IS FOOLISH AND WICKED!
WISH!
I WISH MY SON ALIVE AGAIN!

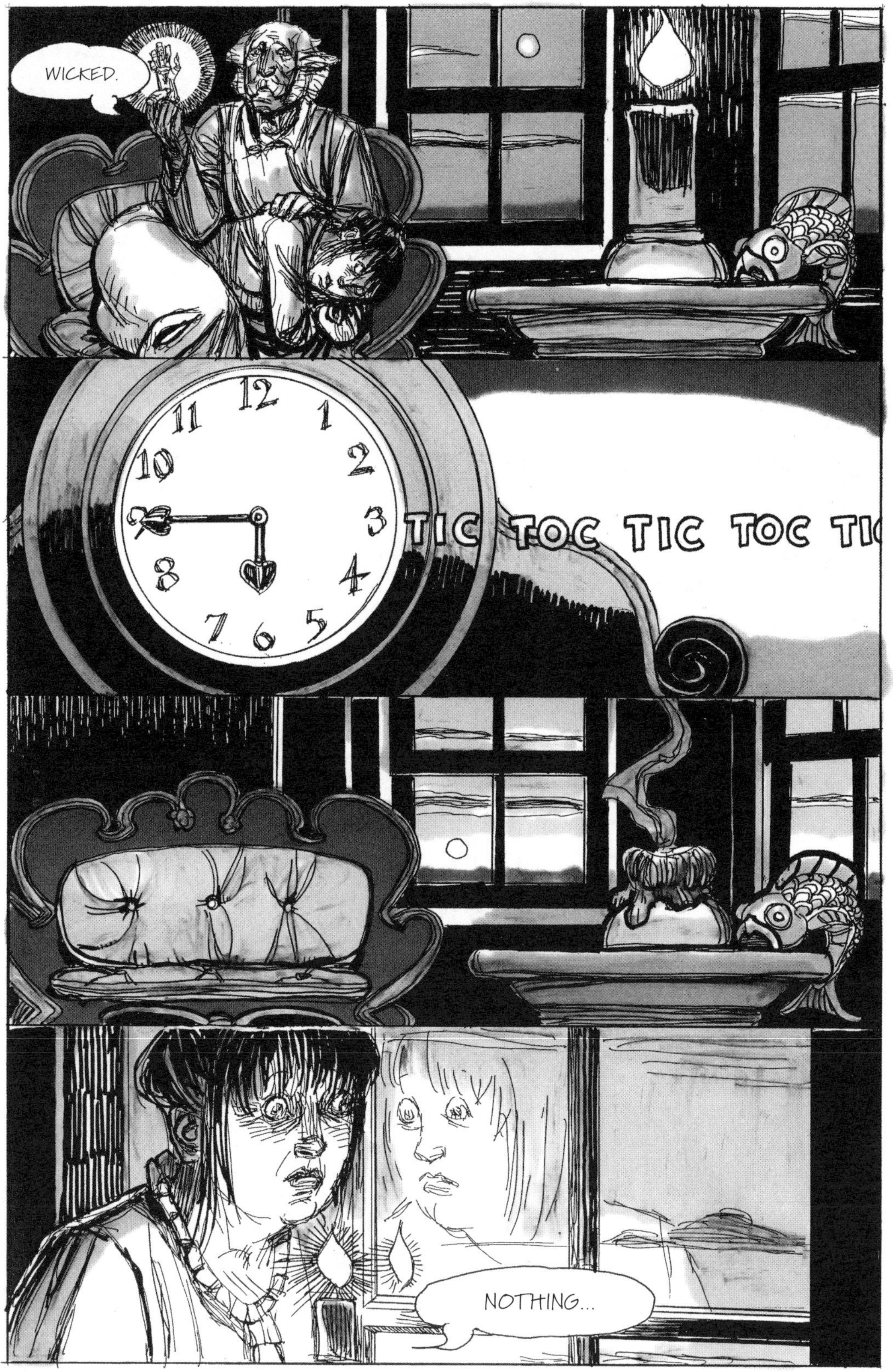
WICKED.
TIC TOC TIC TOC TI
NOTHING...

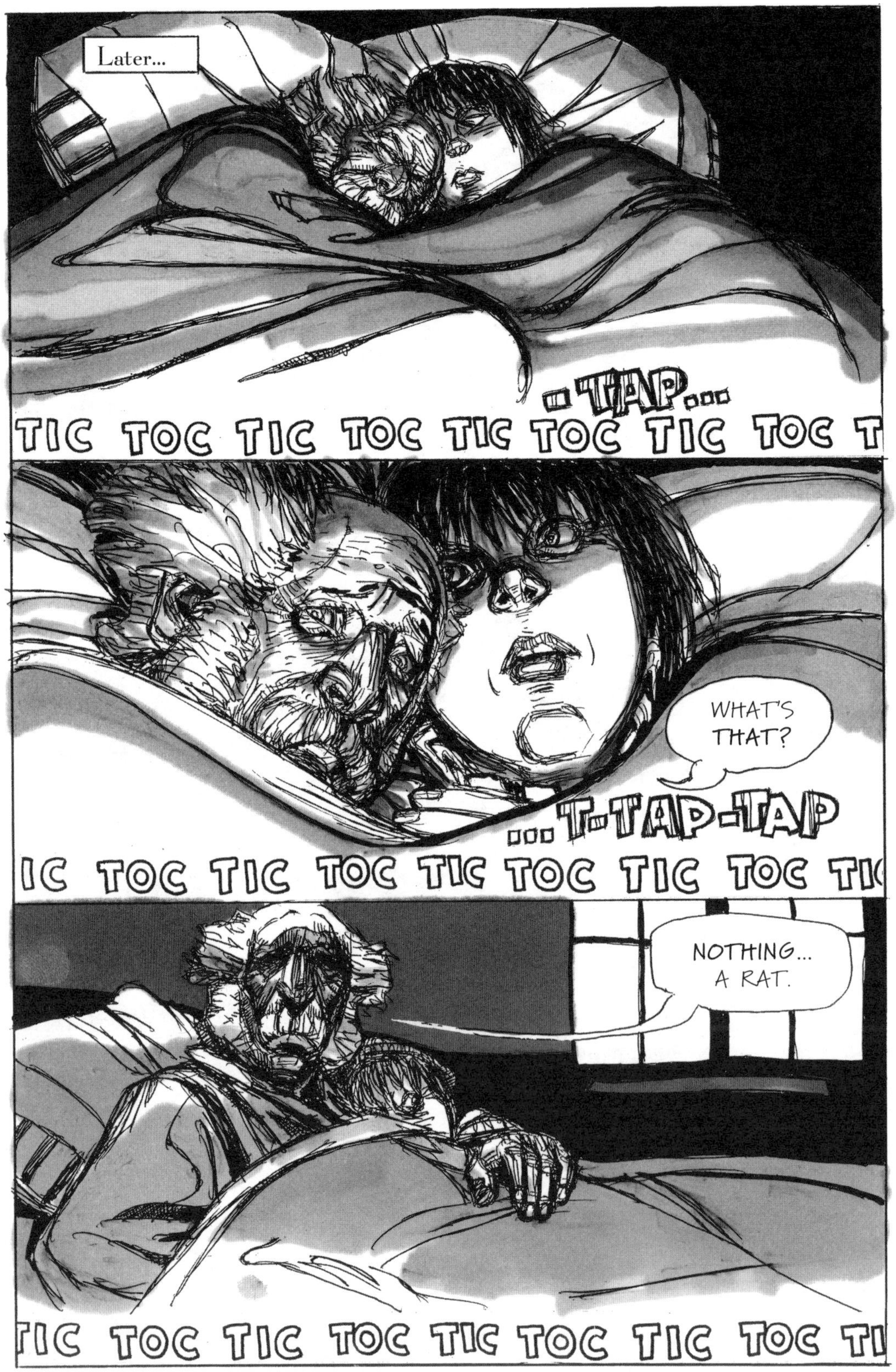
Later...
...TAP...
TIC TOC TIC TOC TIC TOC TIC TOC T
WHAT'S THAT?
...T-TAP-TAP
IC TOC TIC TOC TIC TOC TIC TOC TI
NOTHING... A RAT.
TIC TOC TIC TOC TIC TOC TIC TOC TI

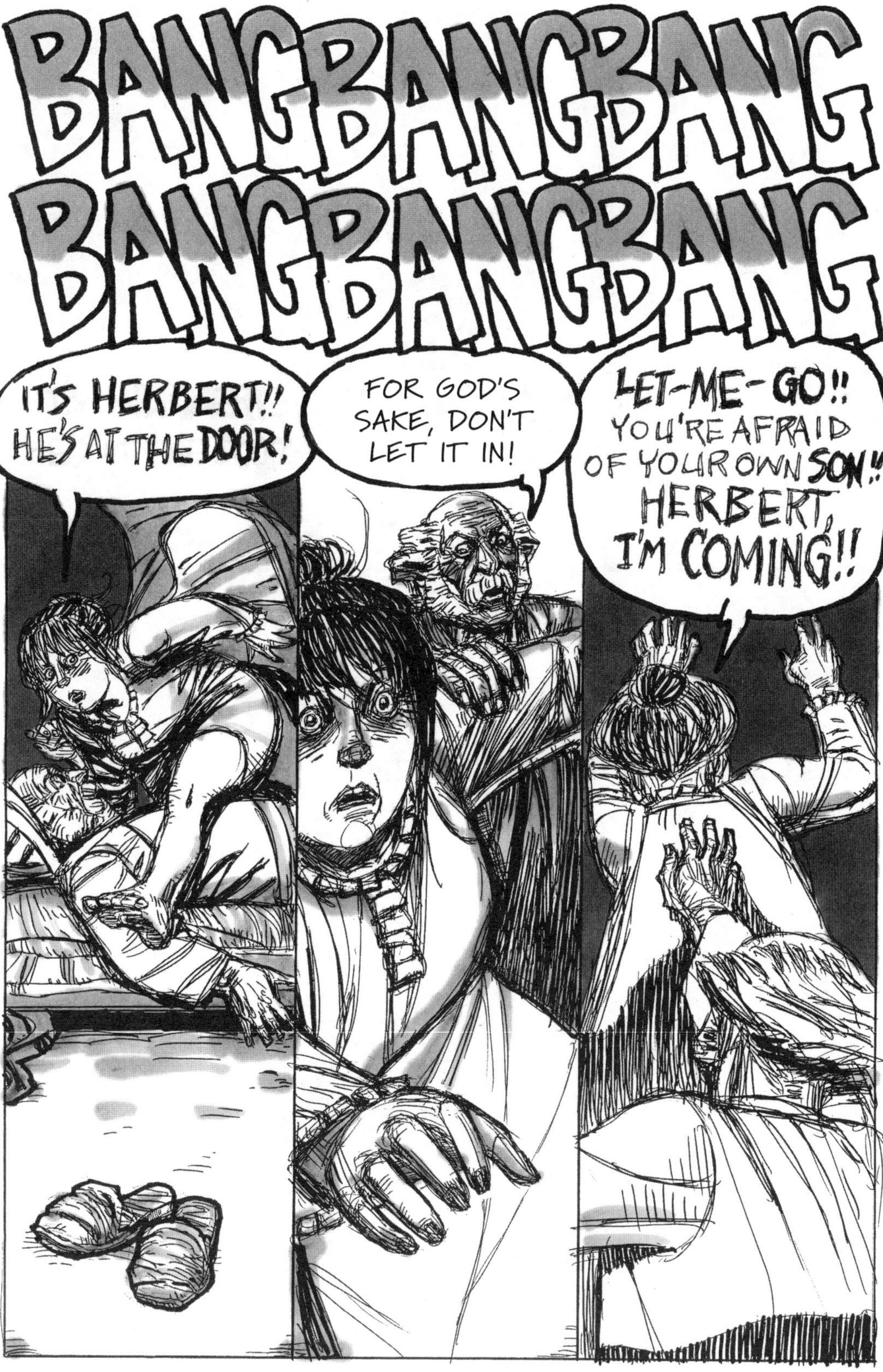
BANGBANGBANG
BANGBANGBANG
IT'S HERBERT!! HE'S AT THE DOOR!
FOR GOD'S SAKE, DON'T LET IT IN!
LET-ME-GO!! YOU'RE AFRAID OF YOUR OWN SON!! HERBERT, I'M COMING!!

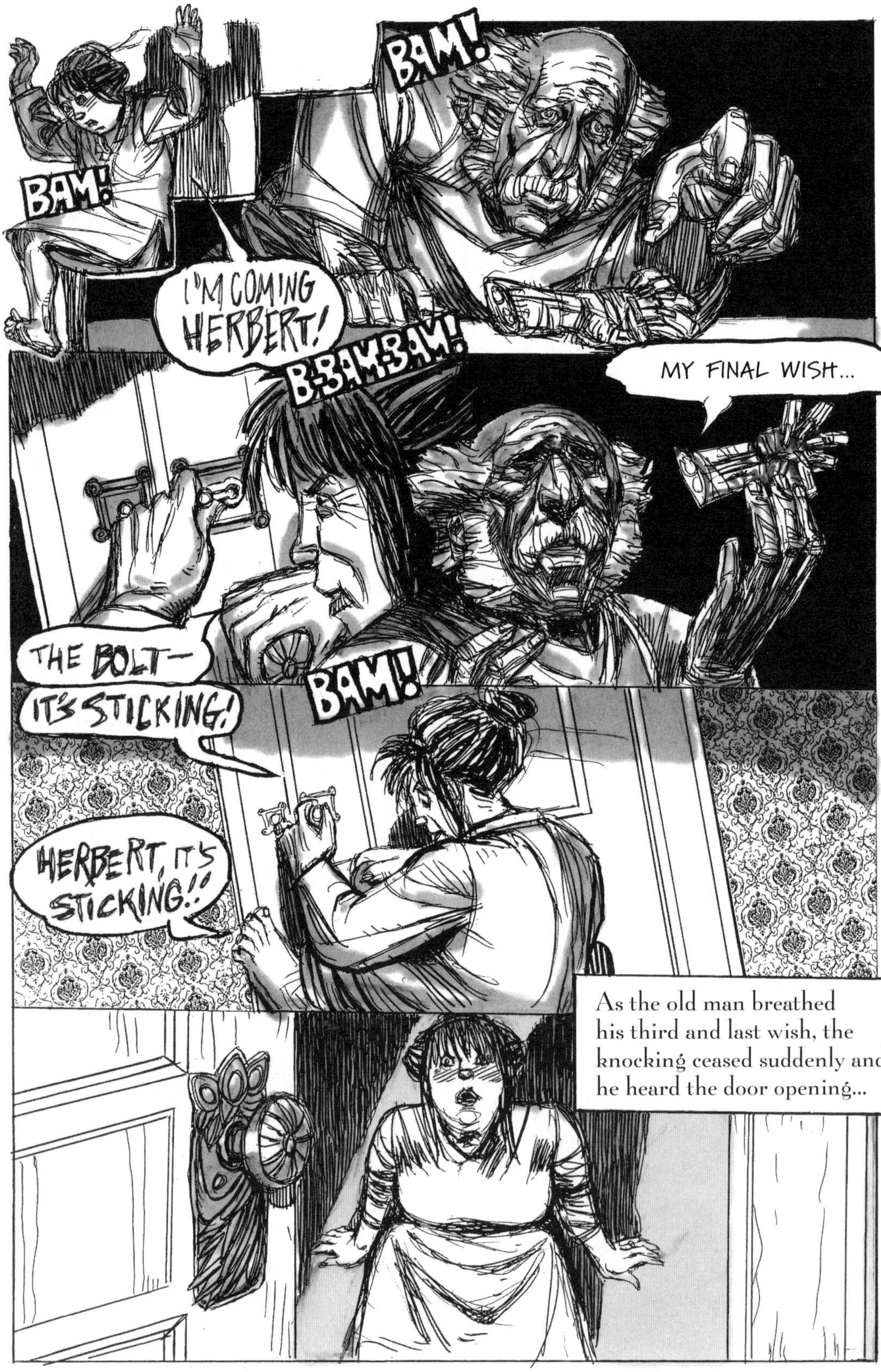
BAM!
BAM!
I'M COMING HERBERT!
B-BAM-BAM!
MY FINAL WISH...
THE BOLT— IT'S STICKING!
BAM!
HERBERT, IT'S STICKING!!
As the old man breathed his third and last wish, the knocking ceased suddenly and he heard the door opening...

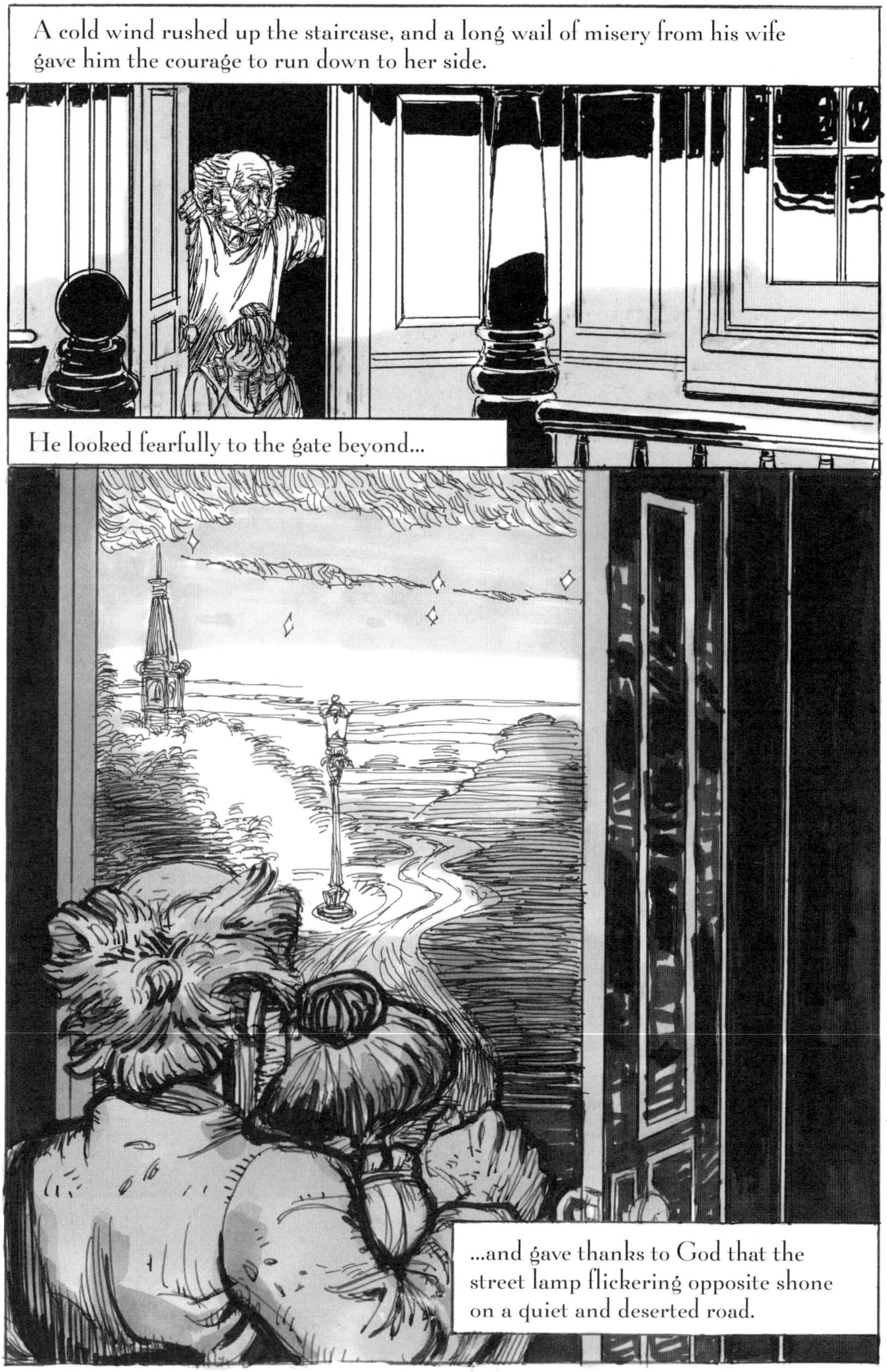
A cold wind rushed up the staircase, and a long wail of misery from his wife gave him the courage to run down to her side.
He looked fearfully to the gate beyond...
...and gave thanks to God that the street lamp flickering opposite shone on a quiet and deserted road.

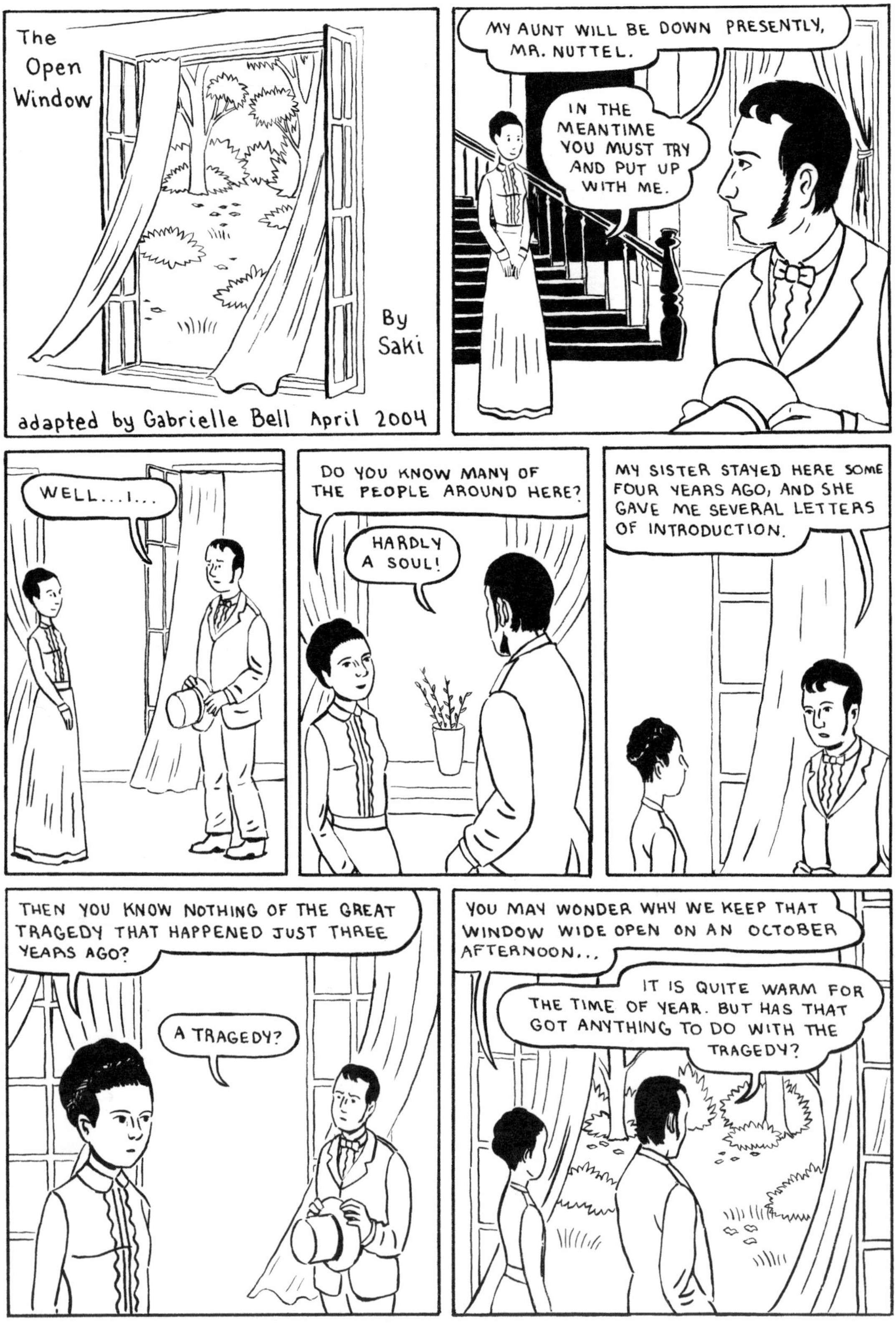
The Open Window
By Saki
adapted by Gabrielle Bell April 2004
MY AUNT WILL BE DOWN PRESENTLY, MR. NUTTEL.
IN THE MEANTIME YOU MUST TRY AND PUT UP WITH ME.
WELL...I...
DO YOU KNOW MANY OF THE PEOPLE AROUND HERE?
HARDLY A SOUL!
MY SISTER STAYED HERE SOME FOUR YEARS AGO, AND SHE GAVE ME SEVERAL LETTERS OF INTRODUCTION.
THEN YOU KNOW NOTHING OF THE GREAT TRAGEDY THAT HAPPENED JUST THREE YEARS AGO?
A TRAGEDY?
YOU MAY WONDER WHY WE KEEP THAT WINDOW WIDE OPEN ON AN OCTOBER AFTERNOON...
IT IS QUITE WARM FOR THE TIME OF YEAR. BUT HAS THAT GOT ANYTHING TO DO WITH THE TRAGEDY?

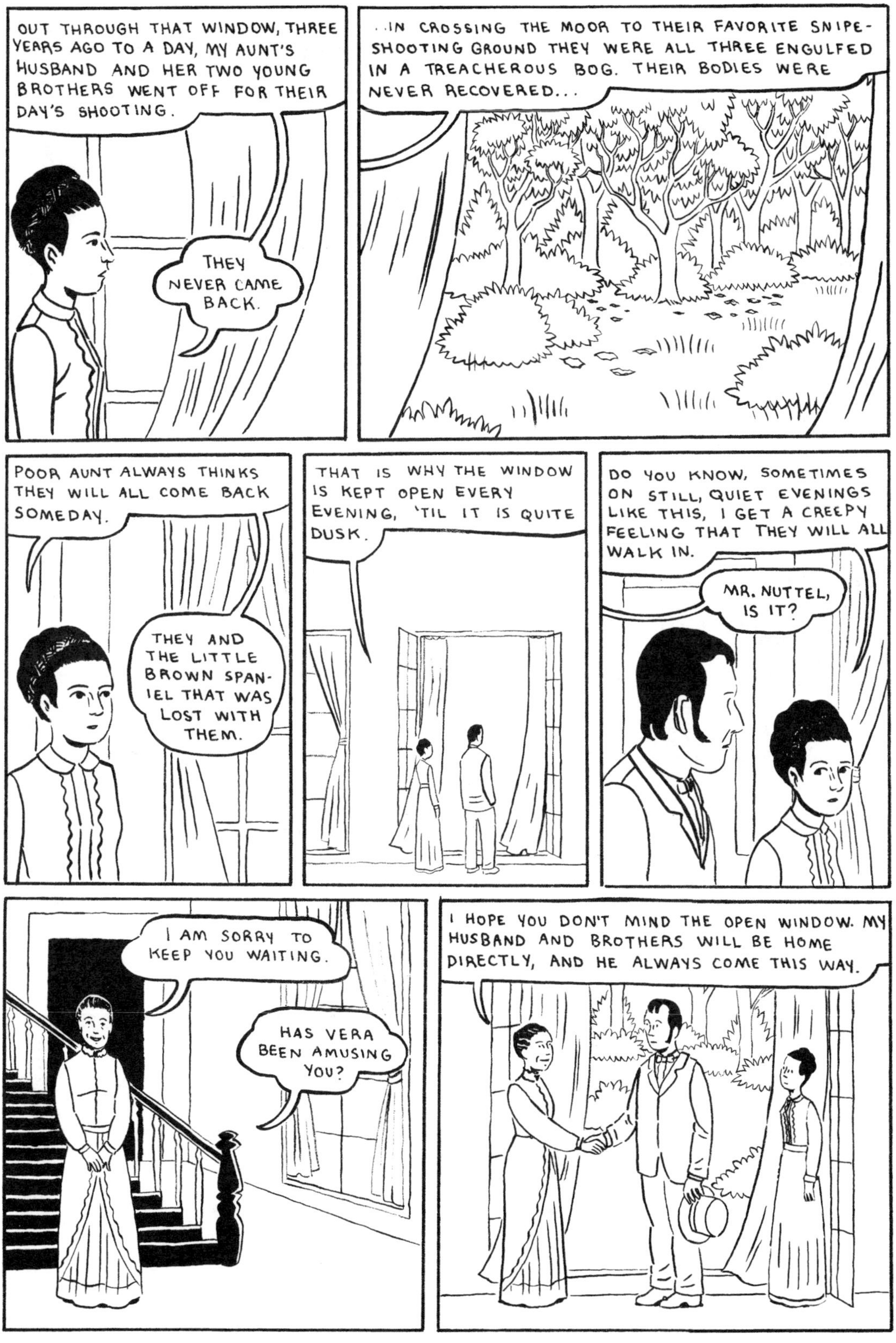
OUT THROUGH THAT WINDOW, THREE YEARS AGO TO A DAY, MY AUNT'S HUSBAND AND HER TWO YOUNG BROTHERS WENT OFF FOR THEIR DAY'S SHOOTING.
THEY NEVER CAME BACK.
..IN CROSSING THE MOOR TO THEIR FAVORITE SNIPE-SHOOTING GROUND THEY WERE ALL THREE ENGULFED IN A TREACHEROUS BOG. THEIR BODIES WERE NEVER RECOVERED...
POOR AUNT ALWAYS THINKS THEY WILL ALL COME BACK SOMEDAY.
THEY AND THE LITTLE BROWN SPANIEL THAT WAS LOST WITH THEM.
THAT IS WHY THE WINDOW IS KEPT OPEN EVERY EVENING, 'TIL IT IS QUITE DUSK.
DO YOU KNOW, SOMETIMES ON STILL, QUIET EVENINGS LIKE THIS, I GET A CREEPY FEELING THAT THEY WILL ALL WALK IN.
MR. NUTTEL, IS IT?
I AM SORRY TO KEEP YOU WAITING.
HAS VERA BEEN AMUSING YOU?
I HOPE YOU DON'T MIND THE OPEN WINDOW. MY HUSBAND AND BROTHERS WILL BE HOME DIRECTLY, AND HE ALWAYS COME THIS WAY.

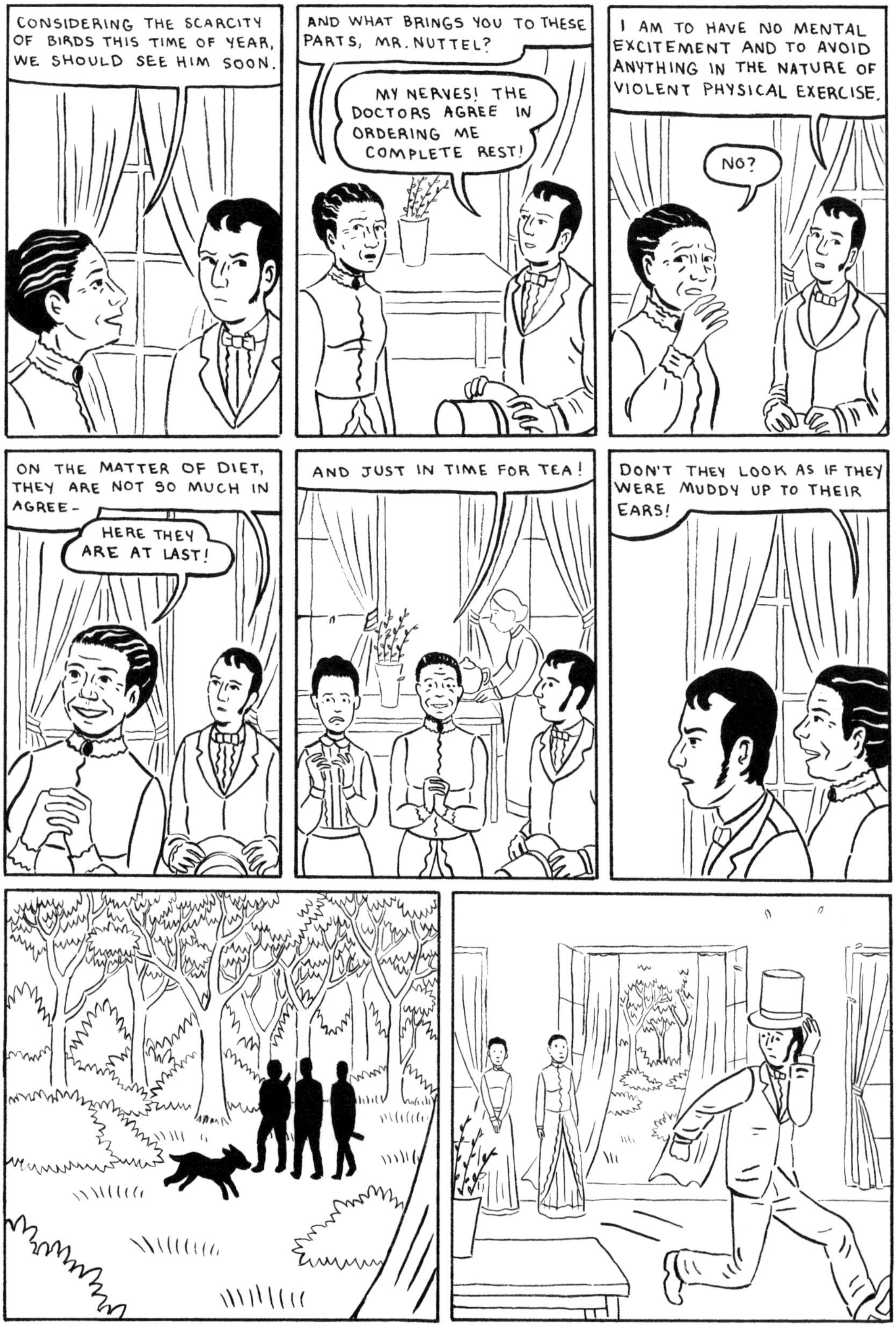
CONSIDERING THE SCARCITY OF BIRDS THIS TIME OF YEAR, WE SHOULD SEE HIM SOON.
AND WHAT BRINGS YOU TO THESE PARTS, MR. NUTTEL?
MY NERVES! THE DOCTORS AGREE IN ORDERING ME COMPLETE REST!
I AM TO HAVE NO MENTAL EXCITEMENT AND TO AVOID ANYTHING IN THE NATURE OF VIOLENT PHYSICAL EXERCISE.
NO?
ON THE MATTER OF DIET, THEY ARE NOT SO MUCH IN AGREE-
HERE THEY ARE AT LAST!
AND JUST IN TIME FOR TEA!
DON'T THEY LOOK AS IF THEY WERE MUDDY UP TO THEIR EARS!

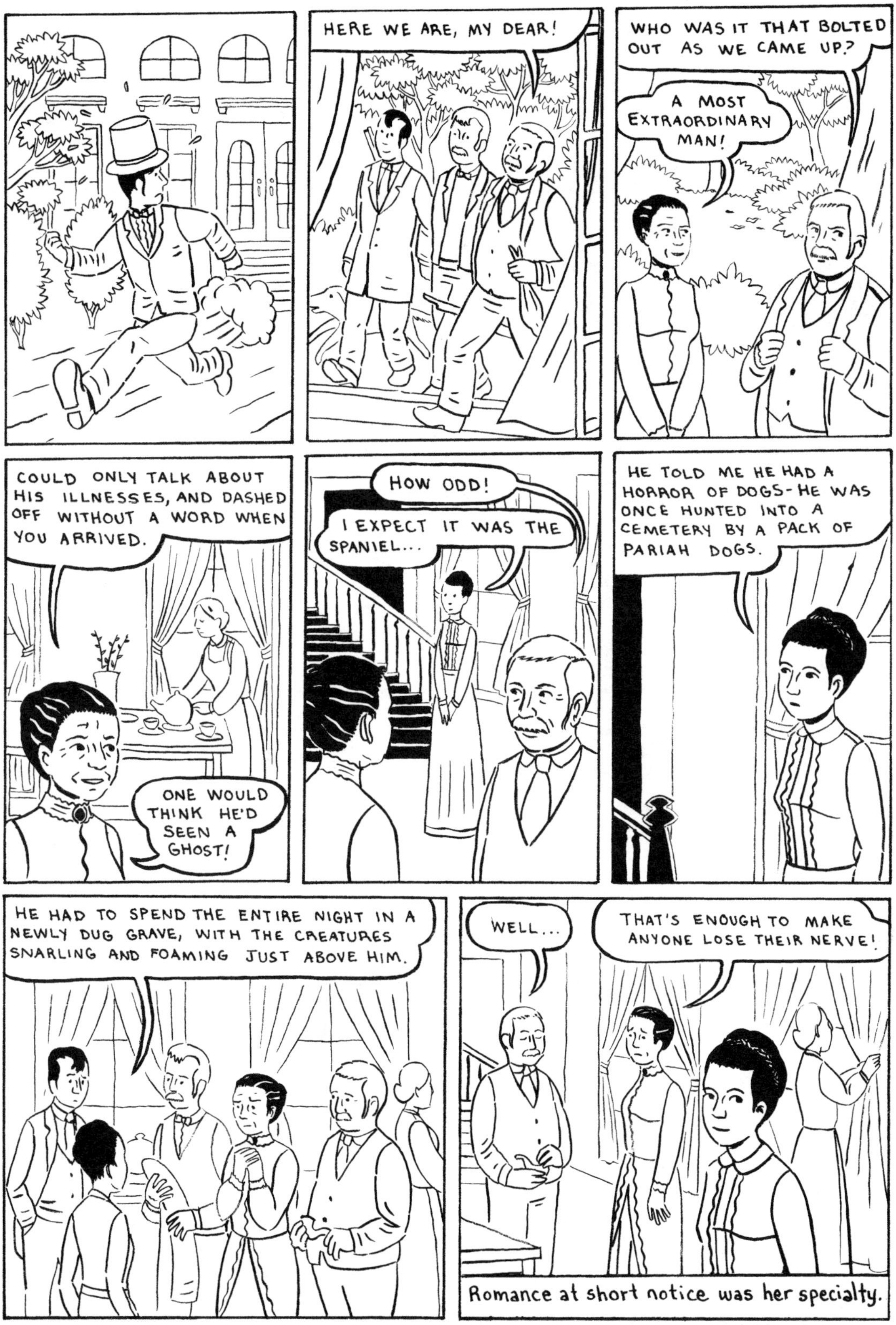
HERE WE ARE, MY DEAR!
WHO WAS IT THAT BOLTED OUT AS WE CAME UP?
A MOST EXTRAORDINARY MAN!
COULD ONLY TALK ABOUT HIS ILLNESSES, AND DASHED OFF WITHOUT A WORD WHEN YOU ARRIVED.
ONE WOULD THINK HE'D SEEN A GHOST!
HOW ODD!
I EXPECT IT WAS THE SPANIEL...
HE TOLD ME HE HAD A HORROR OF DOGS- HE WAS ONCE HUNTED INTO A CEMETERY BY A PACK OF PARIAH DOGS.
HE HAD TO SPEND THE ENTIRE NIGHT IN A NEWLY DUG GRAVE, WITH THE CREATURES SNARLING AND FOAMING JUST ABOVE HIM.
WELL...
THAT'S ENOUGH TO MAKE ANYONE LOSE THEIR NERVE!
Romance at short notice was her specialty.

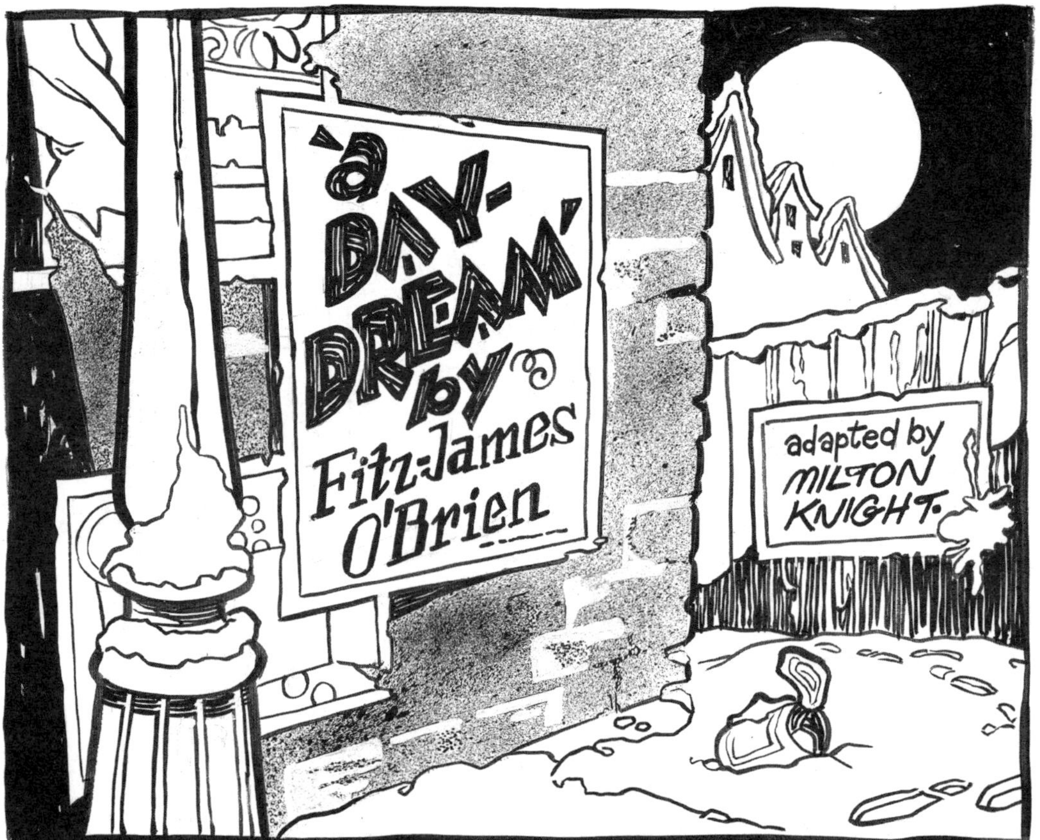
'a DAY-DREAM' by Fitz-James O'Brien
adapted by MILTON KNIGHT.

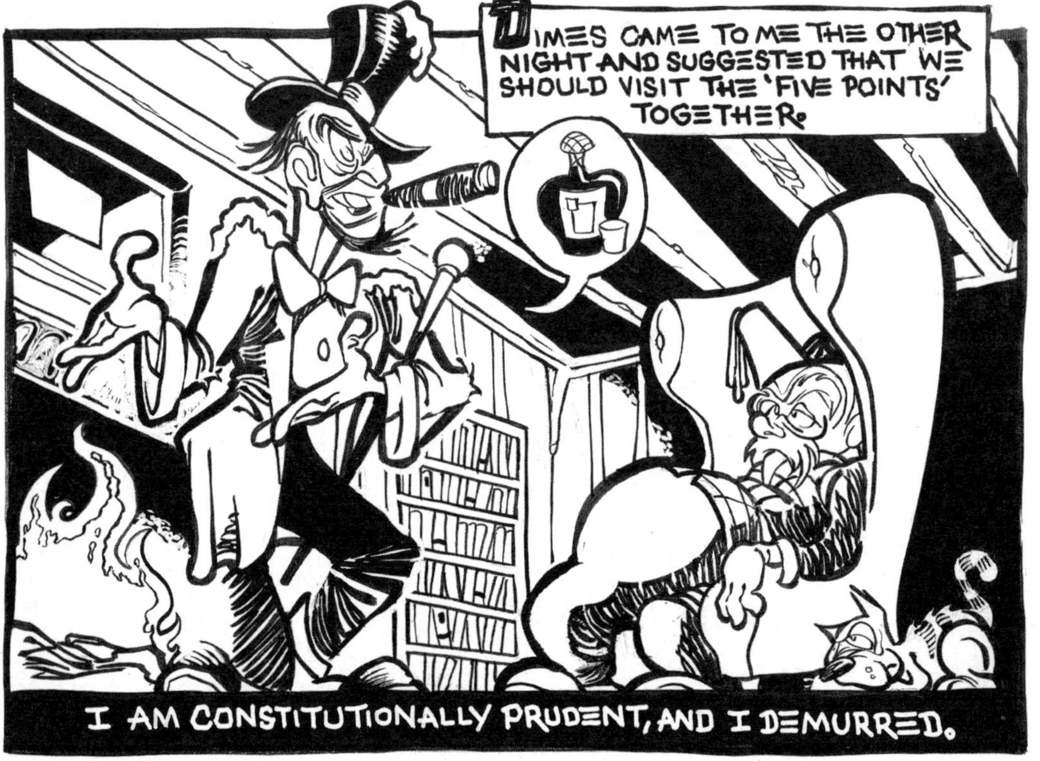
DIMES CAME TO ME THE OTHER NIGHT AND SUGGESTED THAT WE SHOULD VISIT THE 'FIVE POINTS' TOGETHER.
I AM CONSTITUTIONALLY PRUDENT, AND I DEMURRED.

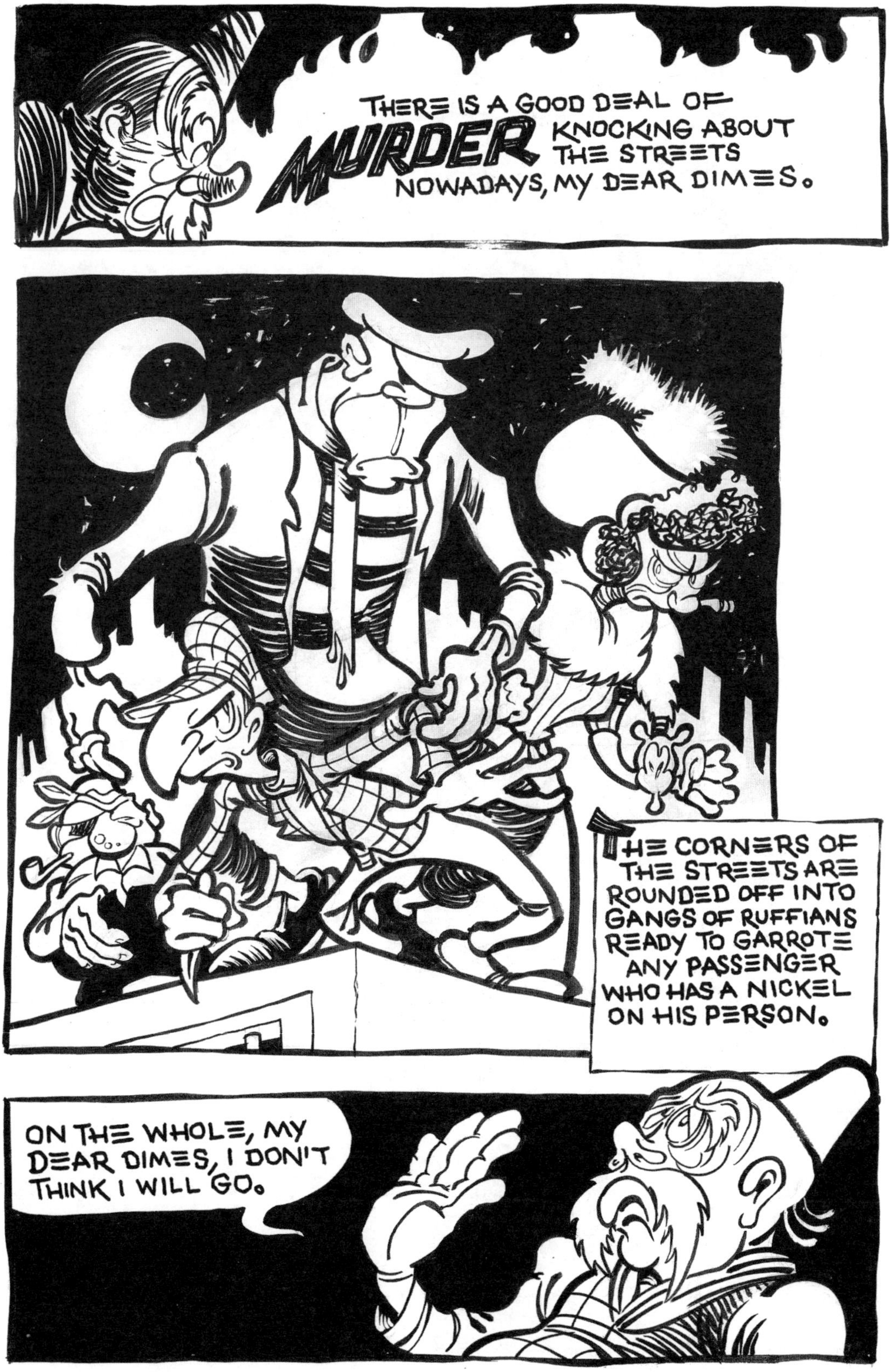
THERE IS A GOOD DEAL OF MURDER KNOCKING ABOUT THE STREETS NOWADAYS, MY DEAR DIMES.
THE CORNERS OF THE STREETS ARE ROUNDED OFF INTO GANGS OF RUFFIANS READY TO GARROTE ANY PASSENGER WHO HAS A NICKEL ON HIS PERSON.
ON THE WHOLE, MY DEAR DIMES, I DON'T THINK I WILL GO.

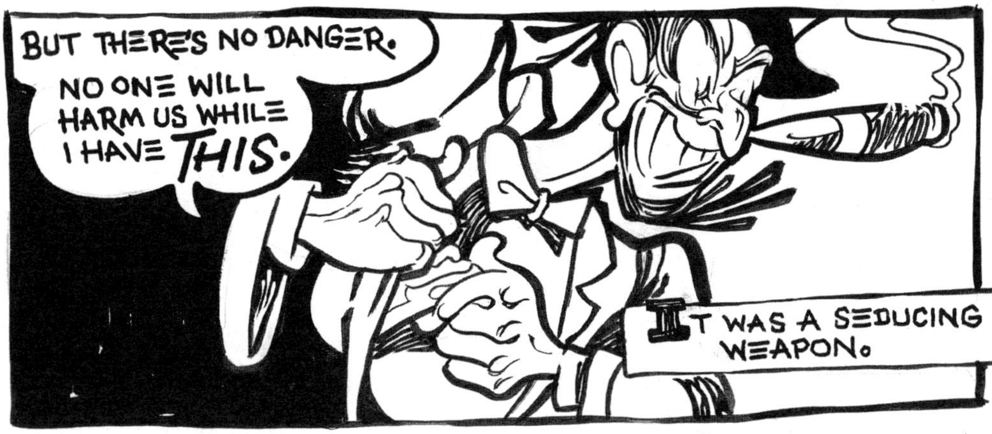
BUT THERE'S NO DANGER.
NO ONE WILL HARM US WHILE I HAVE THIS.
IT WAS A SEDUCING WEAPON.

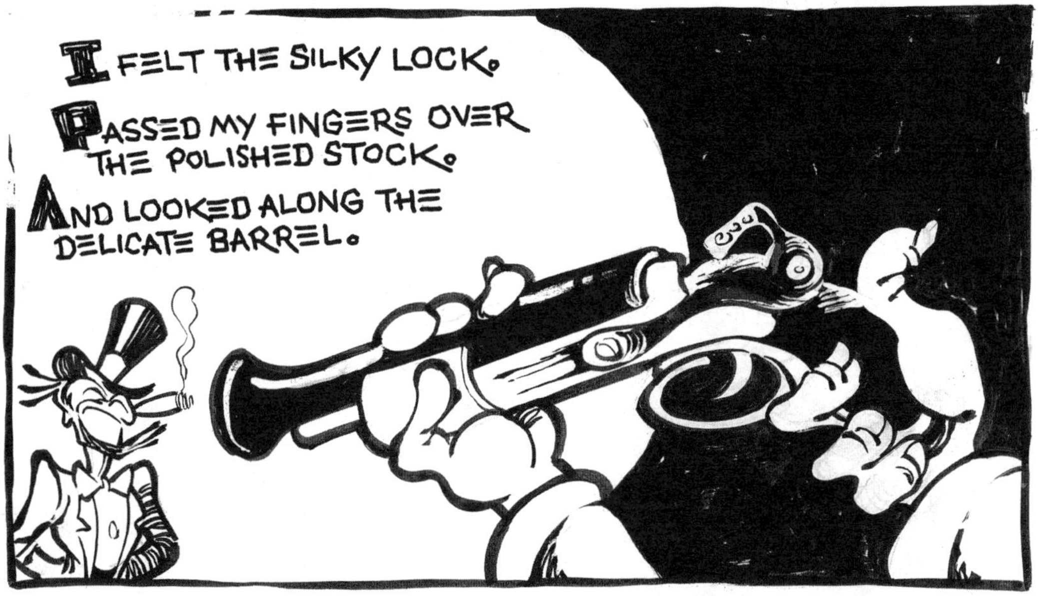
I FELT THE SILKY LOCK.
PASSED MY FINGERS OVER THE POLISHED STOCK.
AND LOOKED ALONG THE DELICATE BARREL.

I FOUND MYSELF SPECULATING ON WHAT WERE TO OCCUR IF I WERE TO *shoot* DIMES.

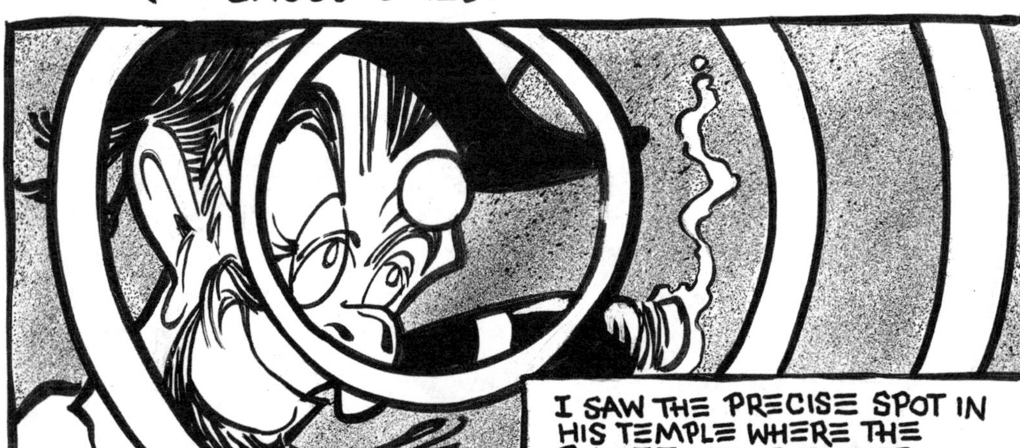
I SAW THE PRECISE SPOT IN HIS TEMPLE WHERE THE BULLET WOULD ENTER.

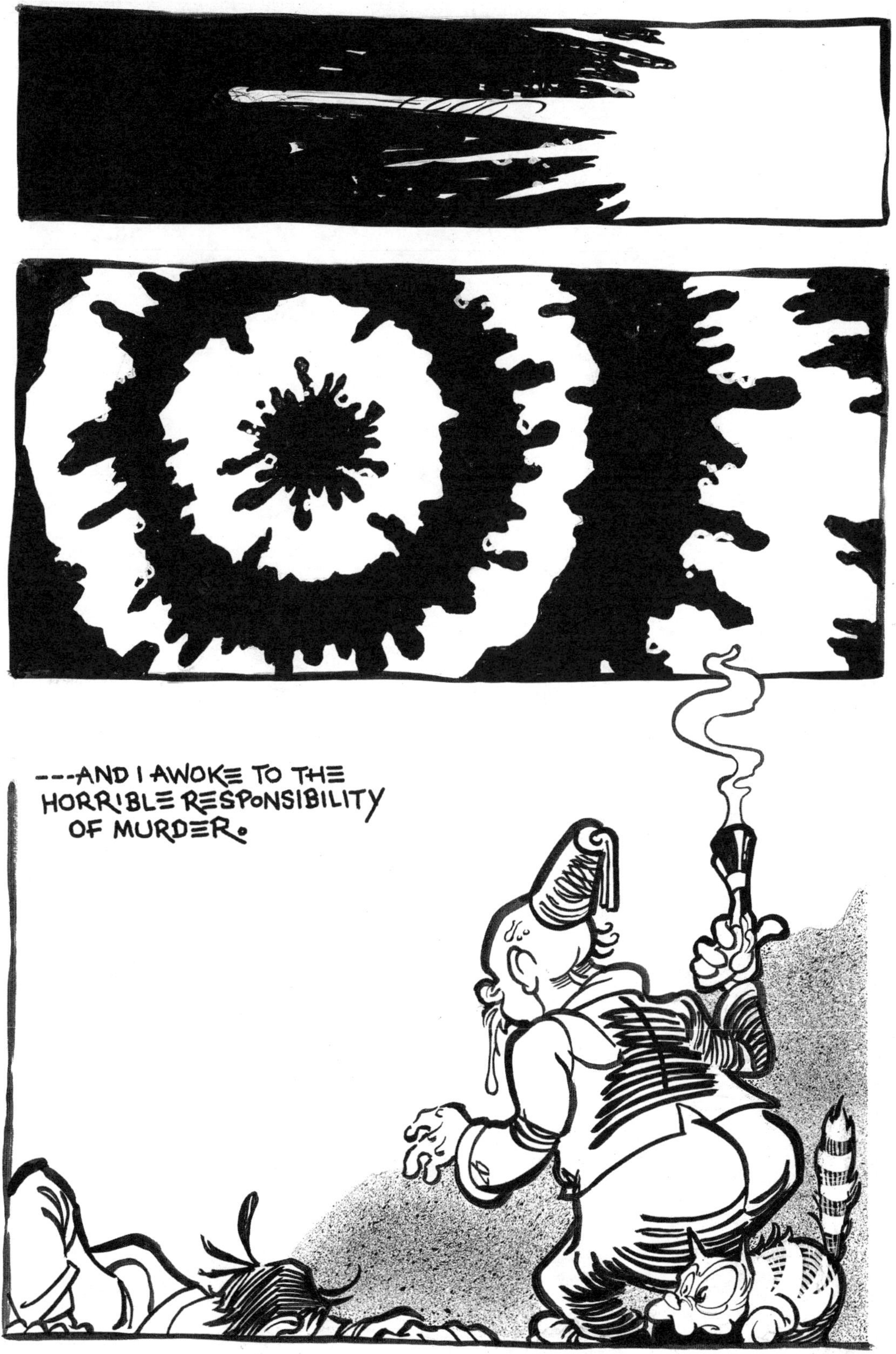
---AND I AWOKE TO THE HORRIBLE RESPONSIBILITY OF MURDER.

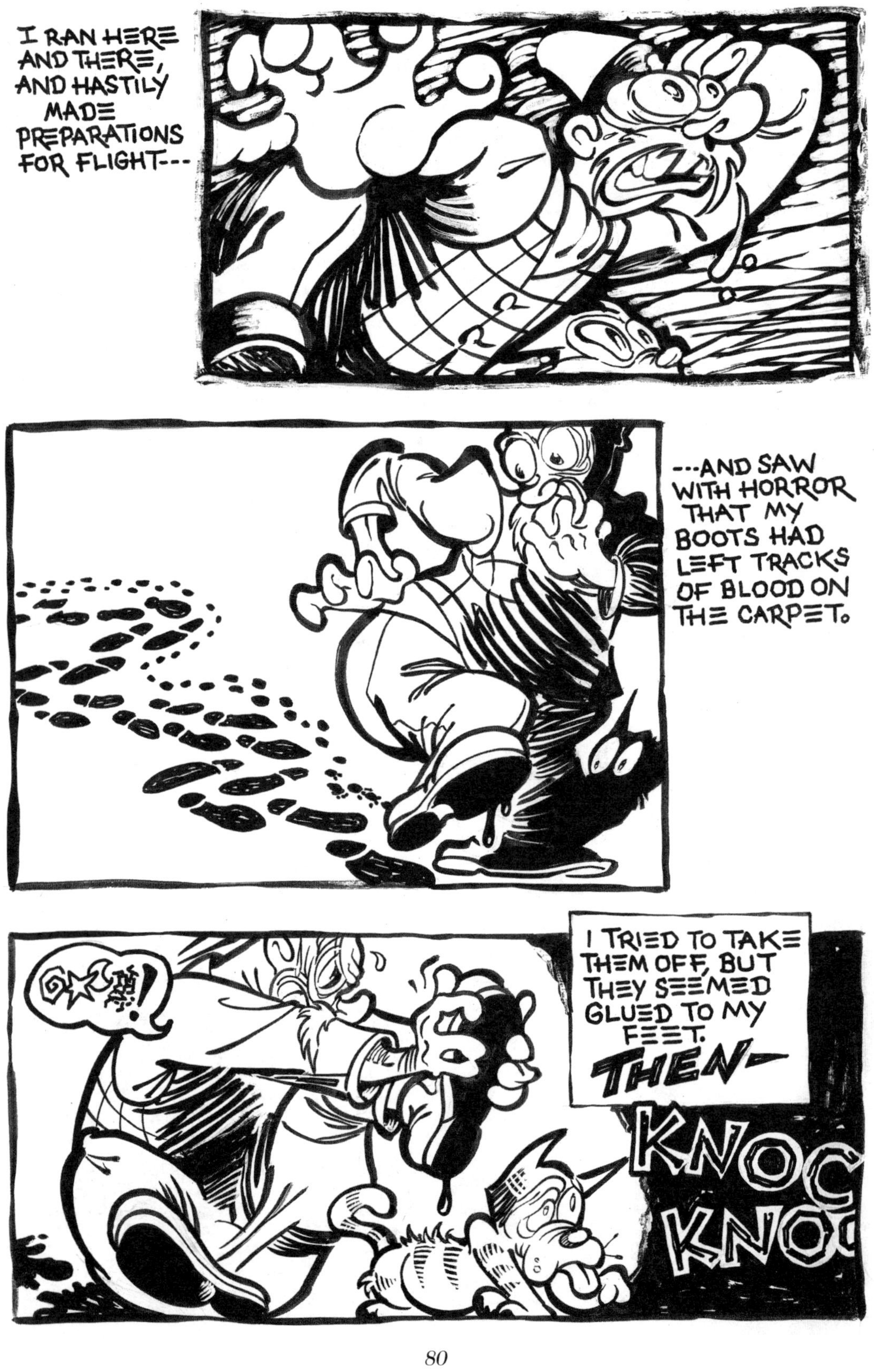
I RAN HERE AND THERE, AND HASTILY MADE PREPARATIONS FOR FLIGHT---
---AND SAW WITH HORROR THAT MY BOOTS HAD LEFT TRACKS OF BLOOD ON THE CARPET.
I TRIED TO TAKE THEM OFF, BUT THEY SEEMED GLUED TO MY FEET.
THEN-
KNOC
KNOC

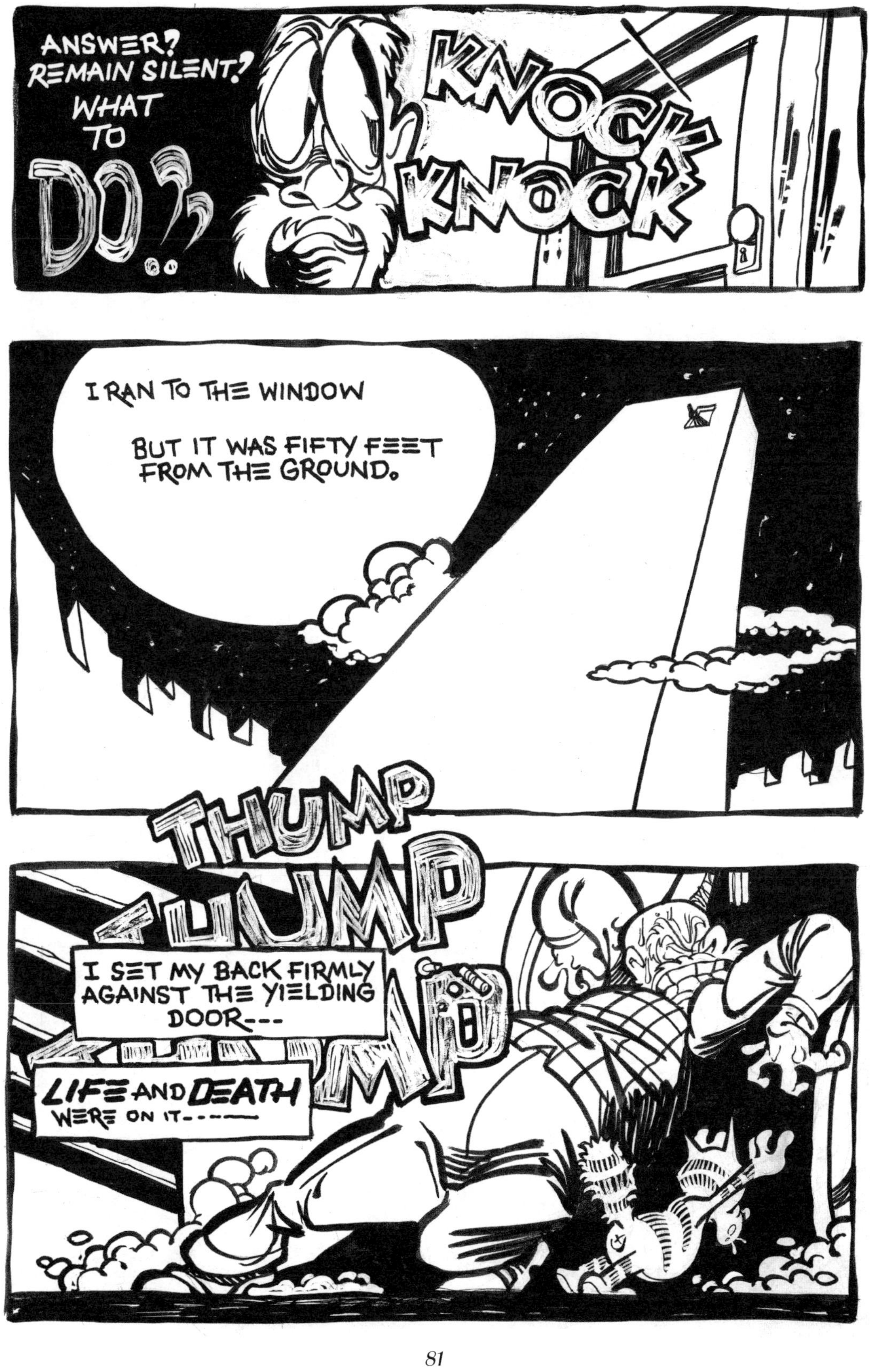
ANSWER? REMAIN SILENT? WHAT TO DO??
KNOCK KNOCK
I RAN TO THE WINDOW
BUT IT WAS FIFTY FEET FROM THE GROUND.
THUMP
THUMP
I SET MY BACK FIRMLY AGAINST THE YIELDING DOOR---
LIFE AND DEATH WERE ON IT-----

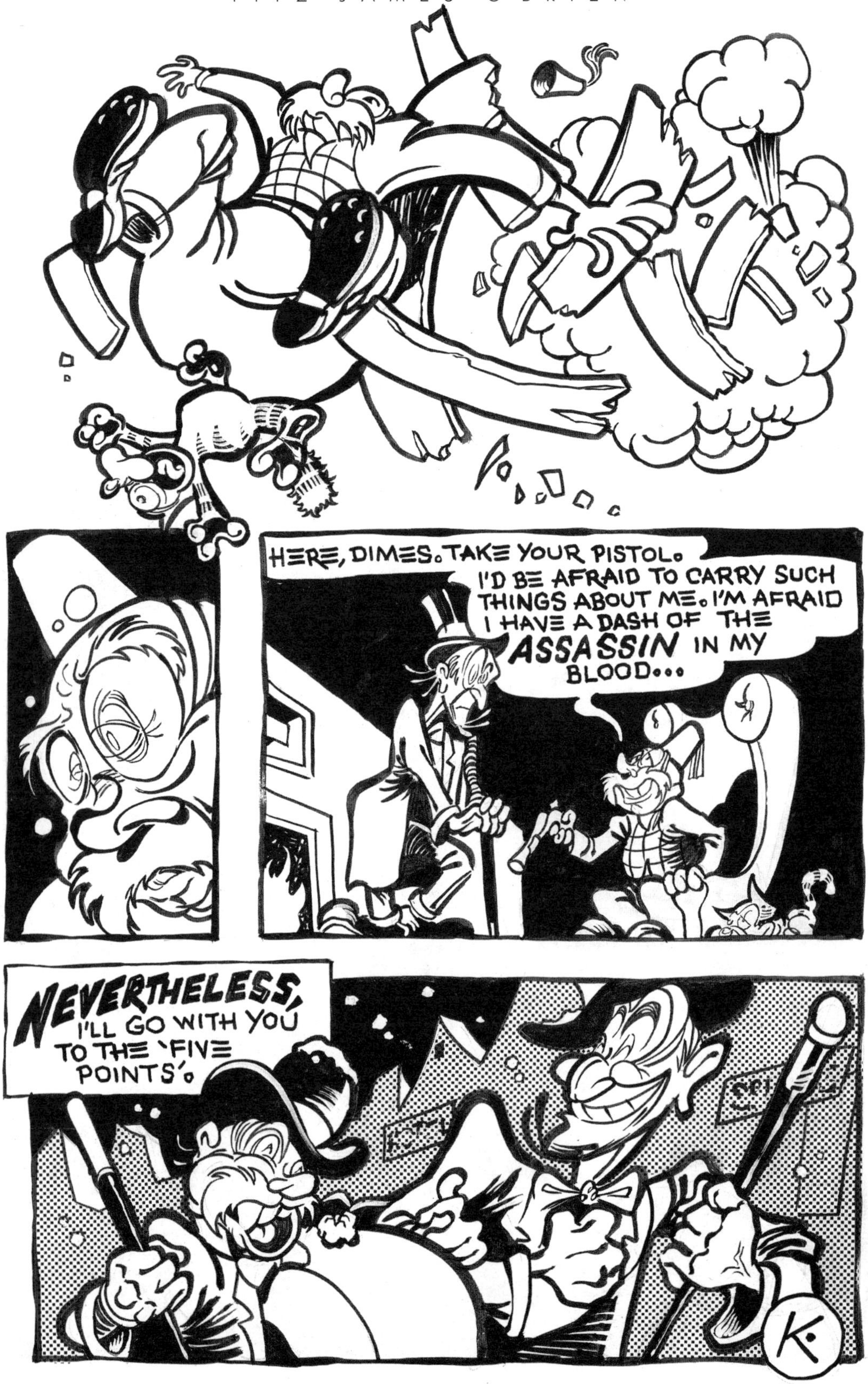
HERE, DIMES. TAKE YOUR PISTOL.
I'D BE AFRAID TO CARRY SUCH THINGS ABOUT ME. I'M AFRAID I HAVE A DASH OF THE ASSASSIN IN MY BLOOD...
NEVERTHELESS, I'LL GO WITH YOU TO THE 'FIVE POINTS'.

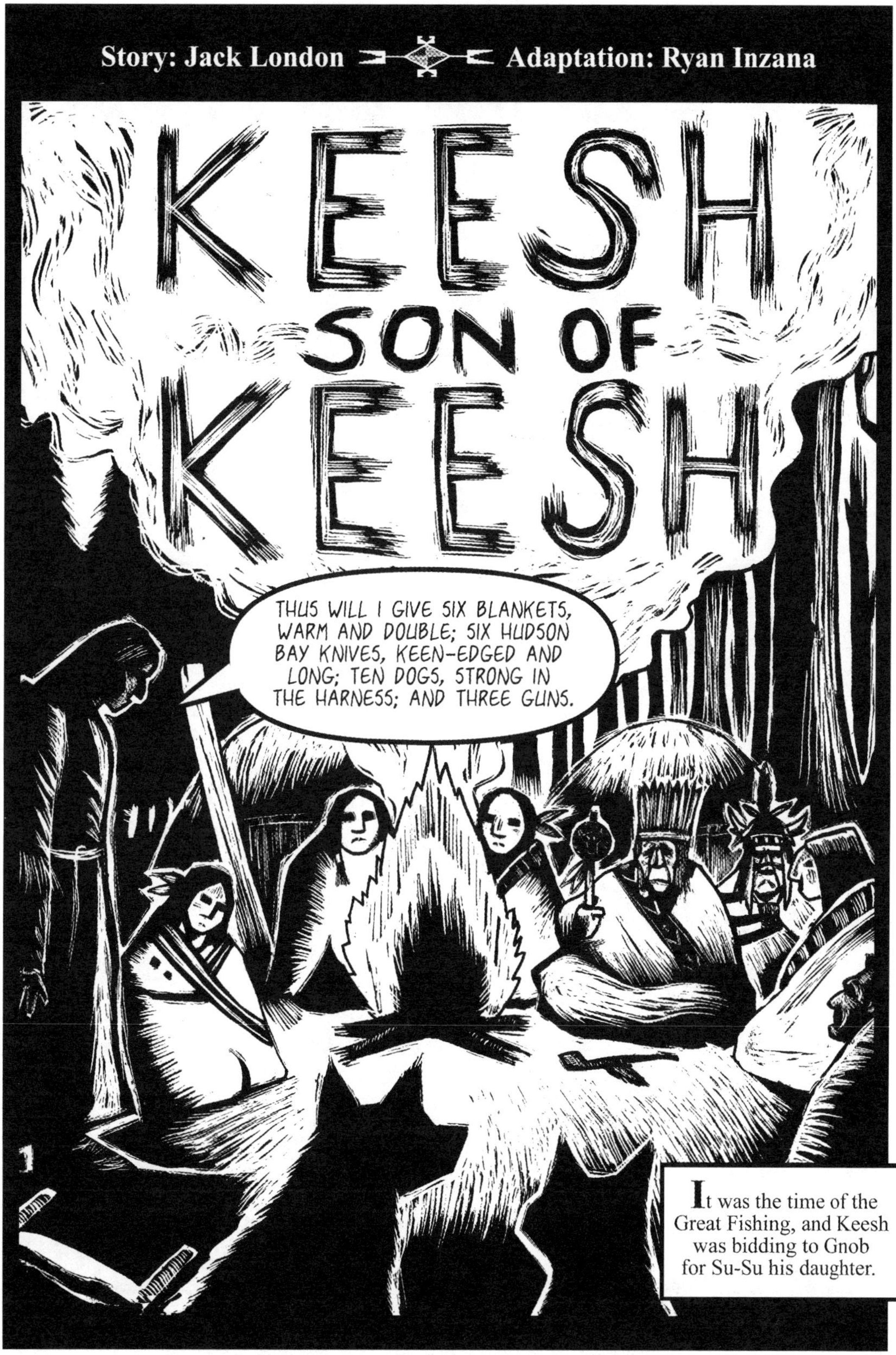
Story: Jack London
Adaptation: Ryan Inzana
KEESH SON OF KEESH
THUS WILL I GIVE SIX BLANKETS, WARM AND DOUBLE; SIX HUDSON BAY KNIVES, KEEN-EDGED AND LONG; TEN DOGS, STRONG IN THE HARNESS; AND THREE GUNS.
It was the time of the Great Fishing, and Keesh was bidding to Gnob for Su-Su his daughter.

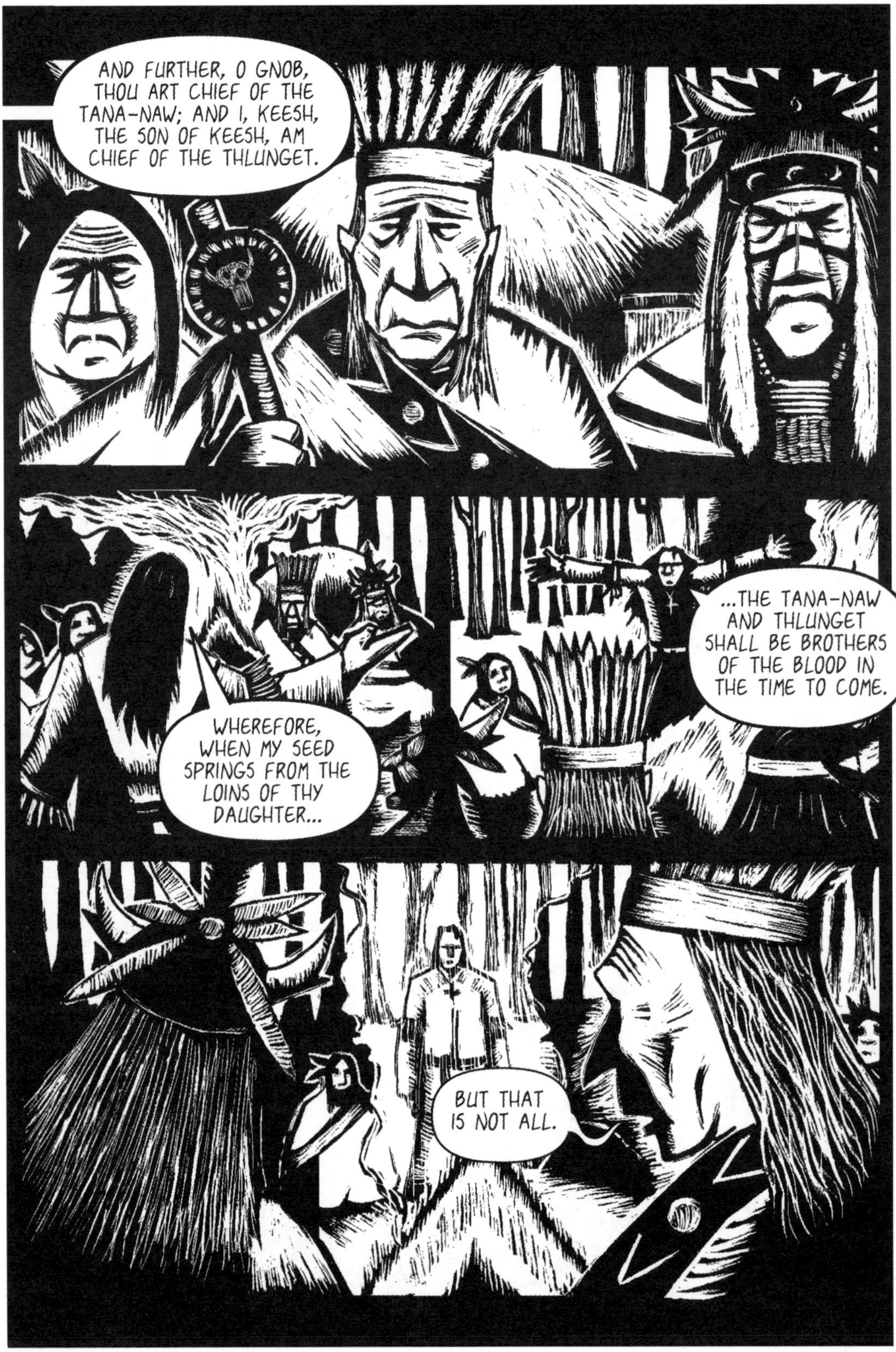
AND FURTHER, O GNOB, THOU ART CHIEF OF THE TANA-NAW; AND I, KEESH, THE SON OF KEESH, AM CHIEF OF THE THLUNGET.
WHEREFORE, WHEN MY SEED SPRINGS FROM THE LOINS OF THY DAUGHTER...
...THE TANA-NAW AND THLUNGET SHALL BE BROTHERS OF THE BLOOD IN THE TIME TO COME.
BUT THAT IS NOT ALL.

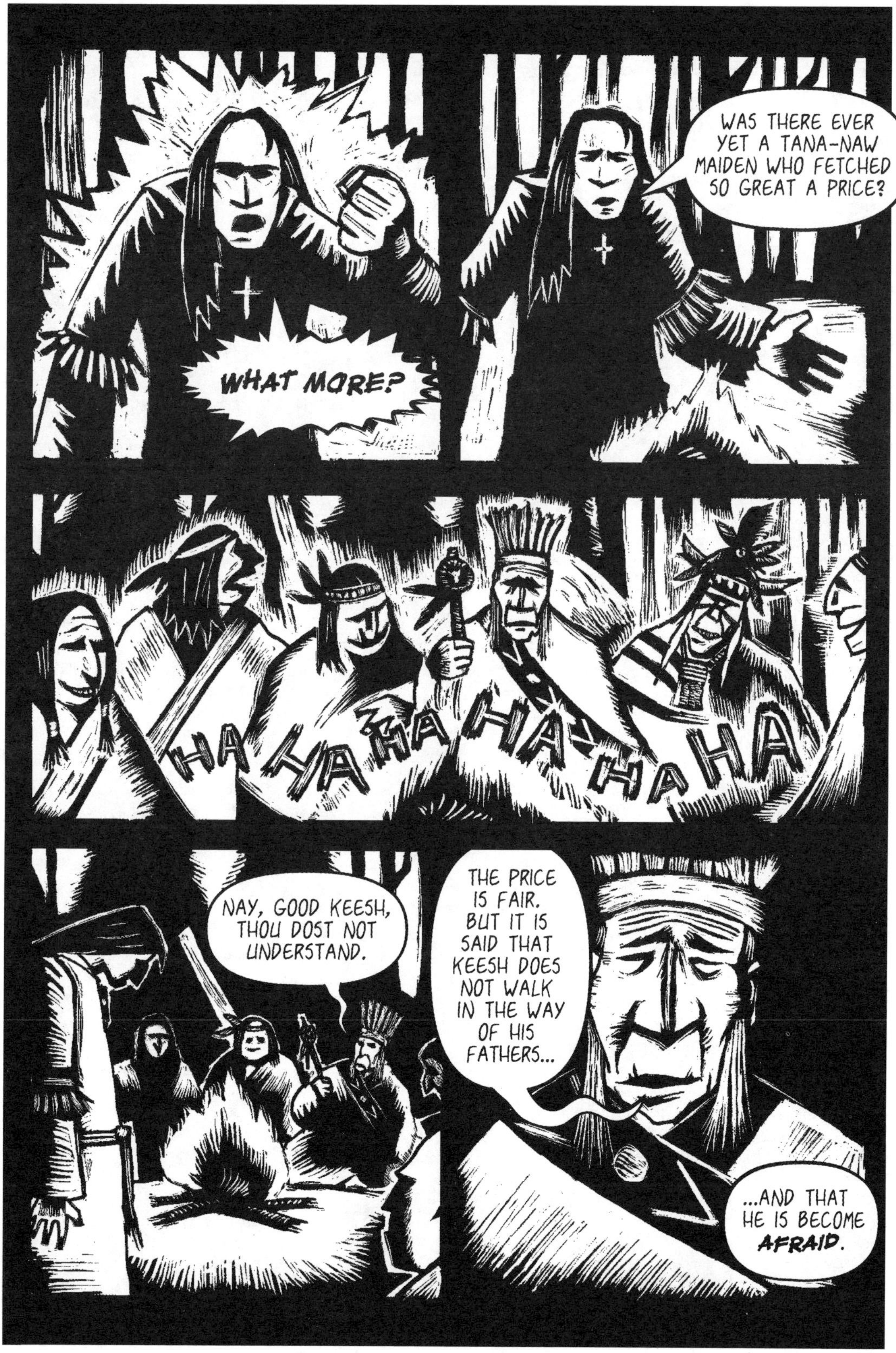
WHAT MORE?
WAS THERE EVER YET A TANA-NAW MAIDEN WHO FETCHED SO GREAT A PRICE?
HA HA HA HA HA HA HA
NAY, GOOD KEESH, THOU DOST NOT UNDERSTAND.
THE PRICE IS FAIR. BUT IT IS SAID THAT KEESH DOES NOT WALK IN THE WAY OF HIS FATHERS...
...AND THAT HE IS BECOME AFRAID.

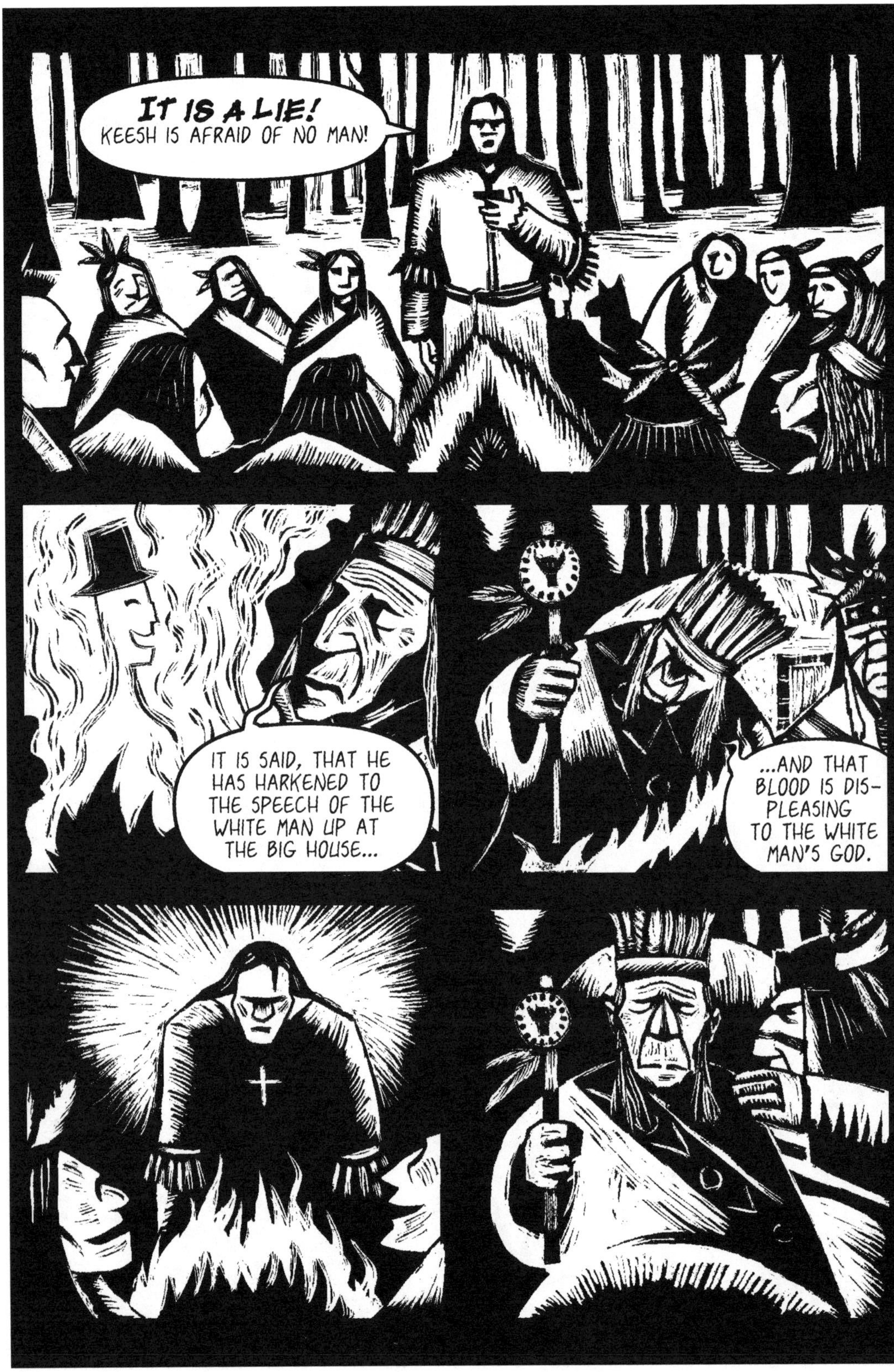
IT IS A LIE! KEESH IS AFRAID OF NO MAN!
IT IS SAID, THAT HE HAS HARKENED TO THE SPEECH OF THE WHITE MAN UP AT THE BIG HOUSE...
...AND THAT BLOOD IS DIS-PLEASING TO THE WHITE MAN'S GOD.

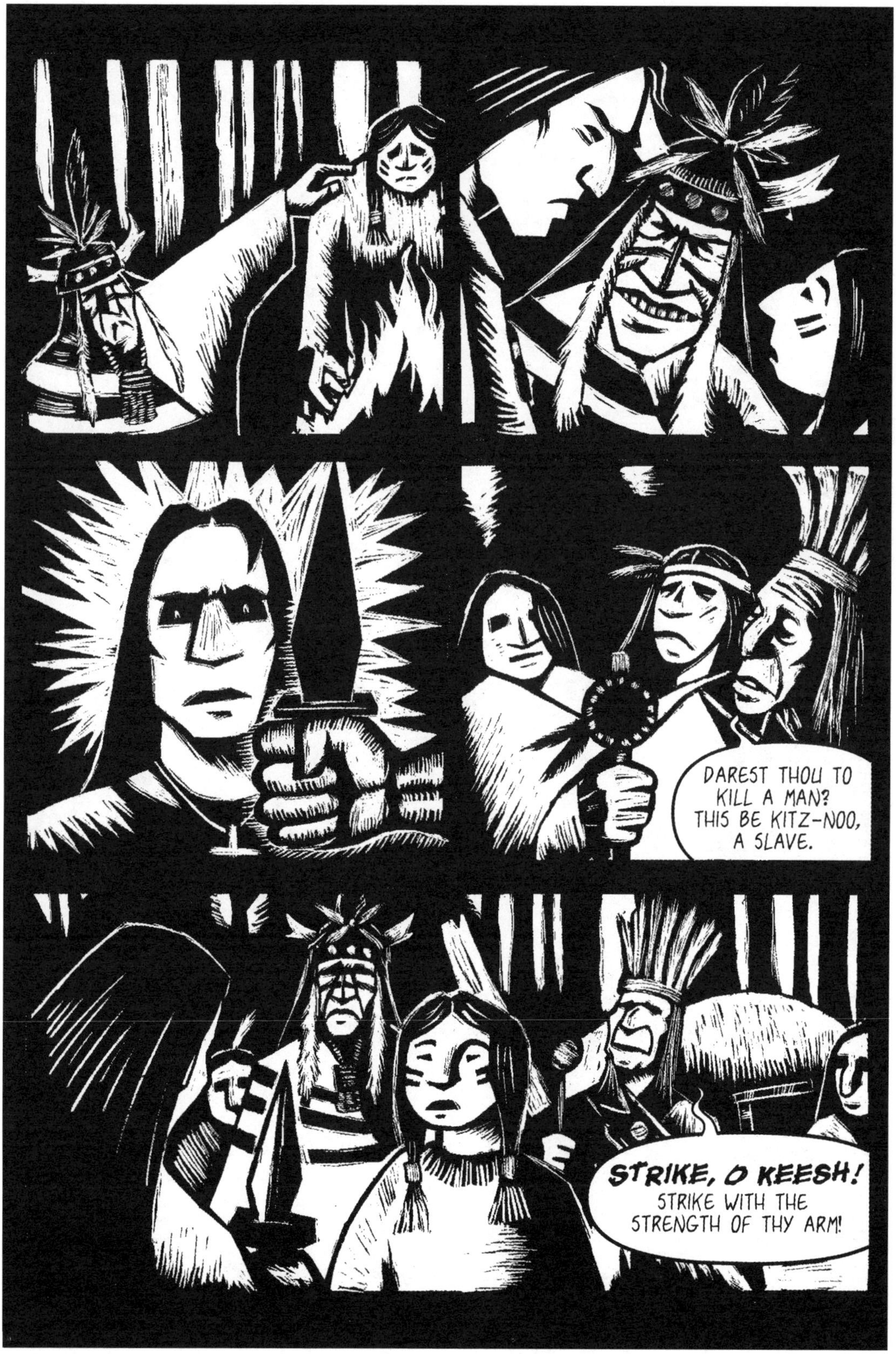
DAREST THOU TO KILL A MAN? THIS BE KITZ-NOO, A SLAVE.
STRIKE, O KEESH! STRIKE WITH THE STRENGTH OF THY ARM!

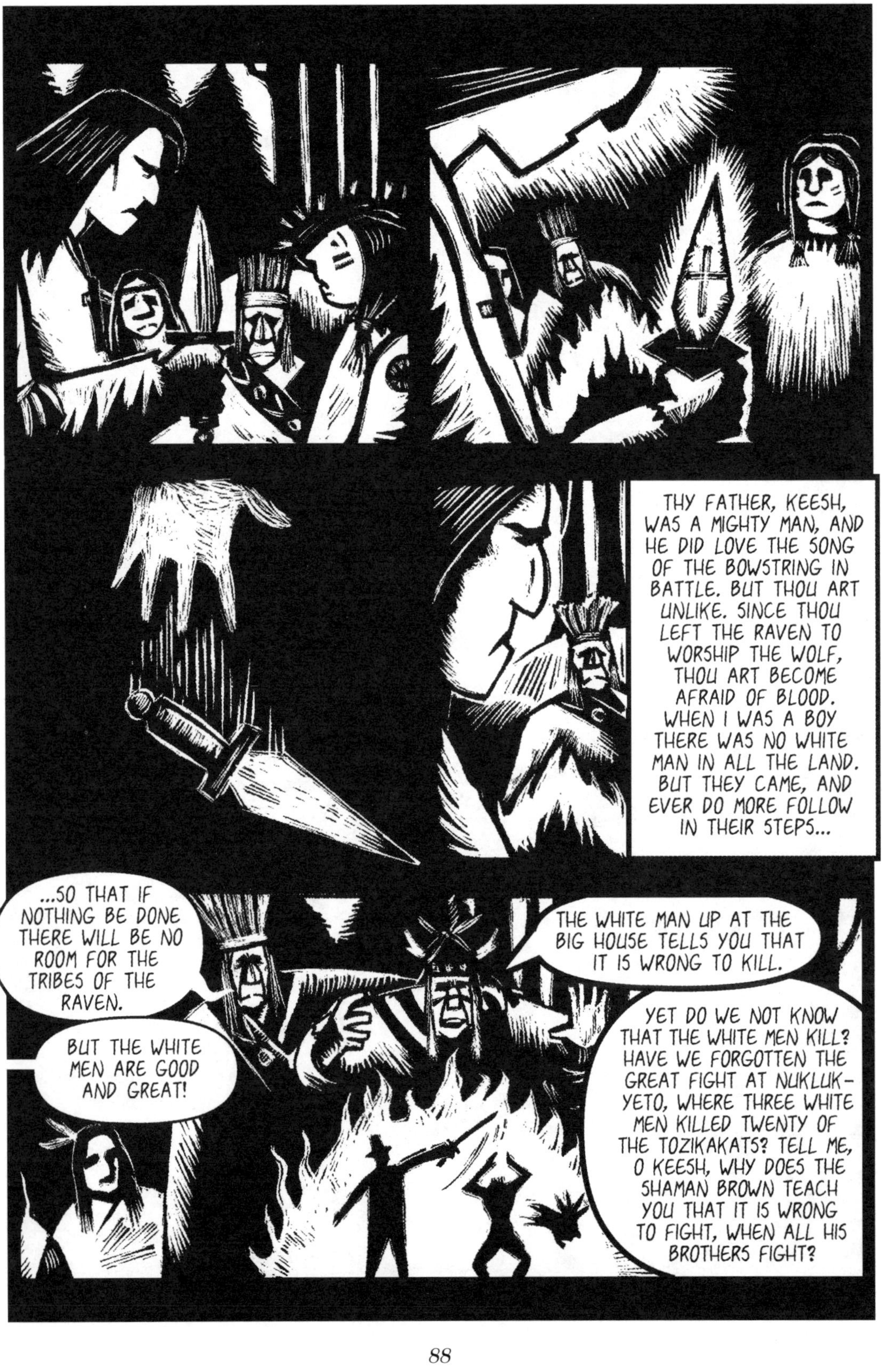
THY FATHER, KEESH, WAS A MIGHTY MAN, AND HE DID LOVE THE SONG OF THE BOWSTRING IN BATTLE. BUT THOU ART UNLIKE. SINCE THOU LEFT THE RAVEN TO WORSHIP THE WOLF, THOU ART BECOME AFRAID OF BLOOD. WHEN I WAS A BOY THERE WAS NO WHITE MAN IN ALL THE LAND. BUT THEY CAME, AND EVER DO MORE FOLLOW IN THEIR STEPS...
...SO THAT IF NOTHING BE DONE THERE WILL BE NO ROOM FOR THE TRIBES OF THE RAVEN.
BUT THE WHITE MEN ARE GOOD AND GREAT!
THE WHITE MAN UP AT THE BIG HOUSE TELLS YOU THAT IT IS WRONG TO KILL.
YET DO WE NOT KNOW THAT THE WHITE MEN KILL? HAVE WE FORGOTTEN THE GREAT FIGHT AT NUKLUK-YETO, WHERE THREE WHITE MEN KILLED TWENTY OF THE TOZIKAKATS? TELL ME, O KEESH, WHY DOES THE SHAMAN BROWN TEACH YOU THAT IT IS WRONG TO FIGHT, WHEN ALL HIS BROTHERS FIGHT?

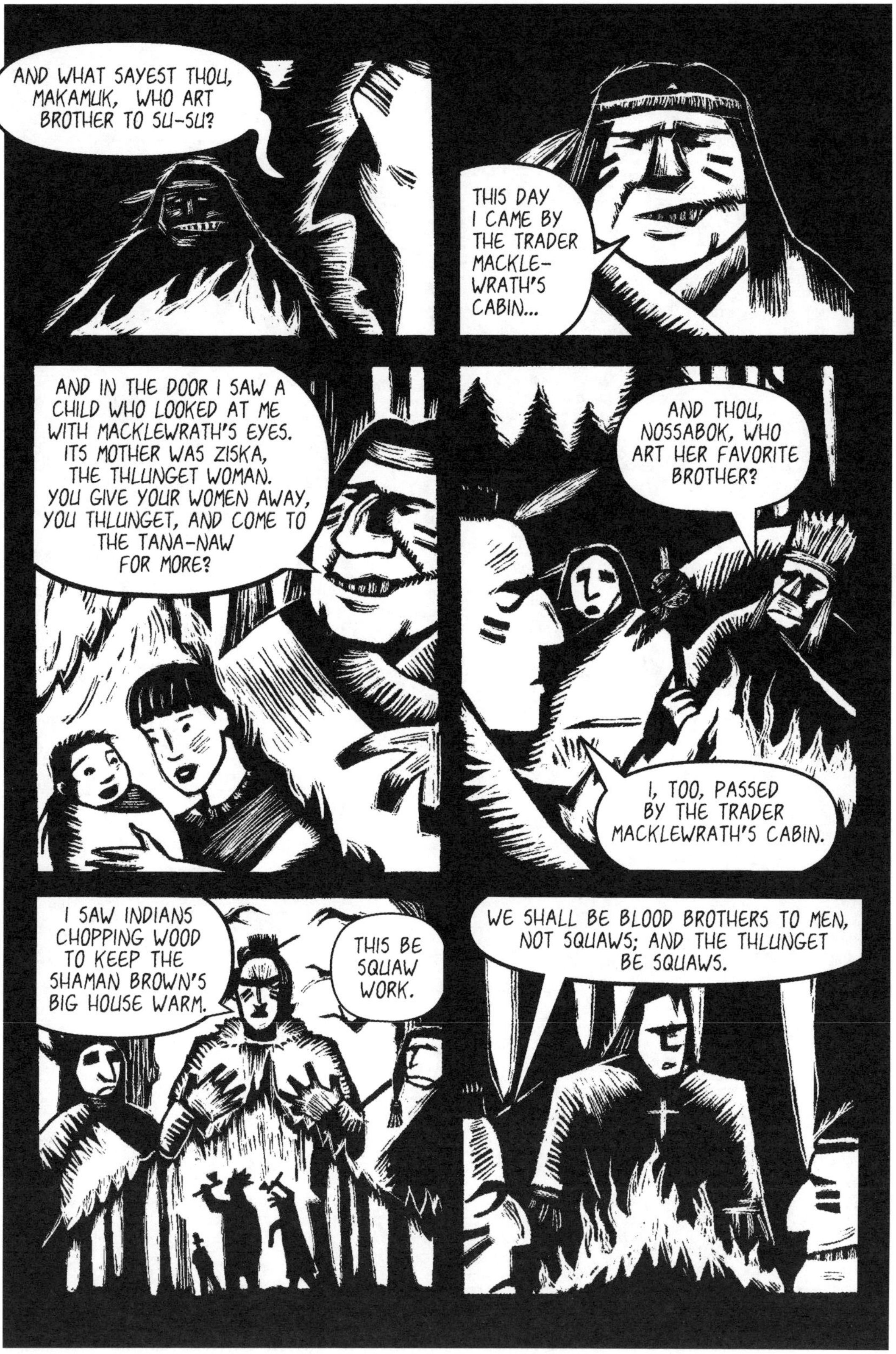
AND WHAT SAYEST THOU, MAKAMUK, WHO ART BROTHER TO SU-SU?
THIS DAY I CAME BY THE TRADER MACKLE-WRATH'S CABIN...
AND IN THE DOOR I SAW A CHILD WHO LOOKED AT ME WITH MACKLEWRATH'S EYES. ITS MOTHER WAS ZISKA, THE THLUNGET WOMAN. YOU GIVE YOUR WOMEN AWAY, YOU THLUNGET, AND COME TO THE TANA-NAW FOR MORE?
AND THOU, NOSSABOK, WHO ART HER FAVORITE BROTHER?
I, TOO, PASSED BY THE TRADER MACKLEWRATH'S CABIN.
I SAW INDIANS CHOPPING WOOD TO KEEP THE SHAMAN BROWN'S BIG HOUSE WARM.
THIS BE SQUAW WORK.
WE SHALL BE BLOOD BROTHERS TO MEN, NOT SQUAWS; AND THE THLUNGET BE SQUAWS.

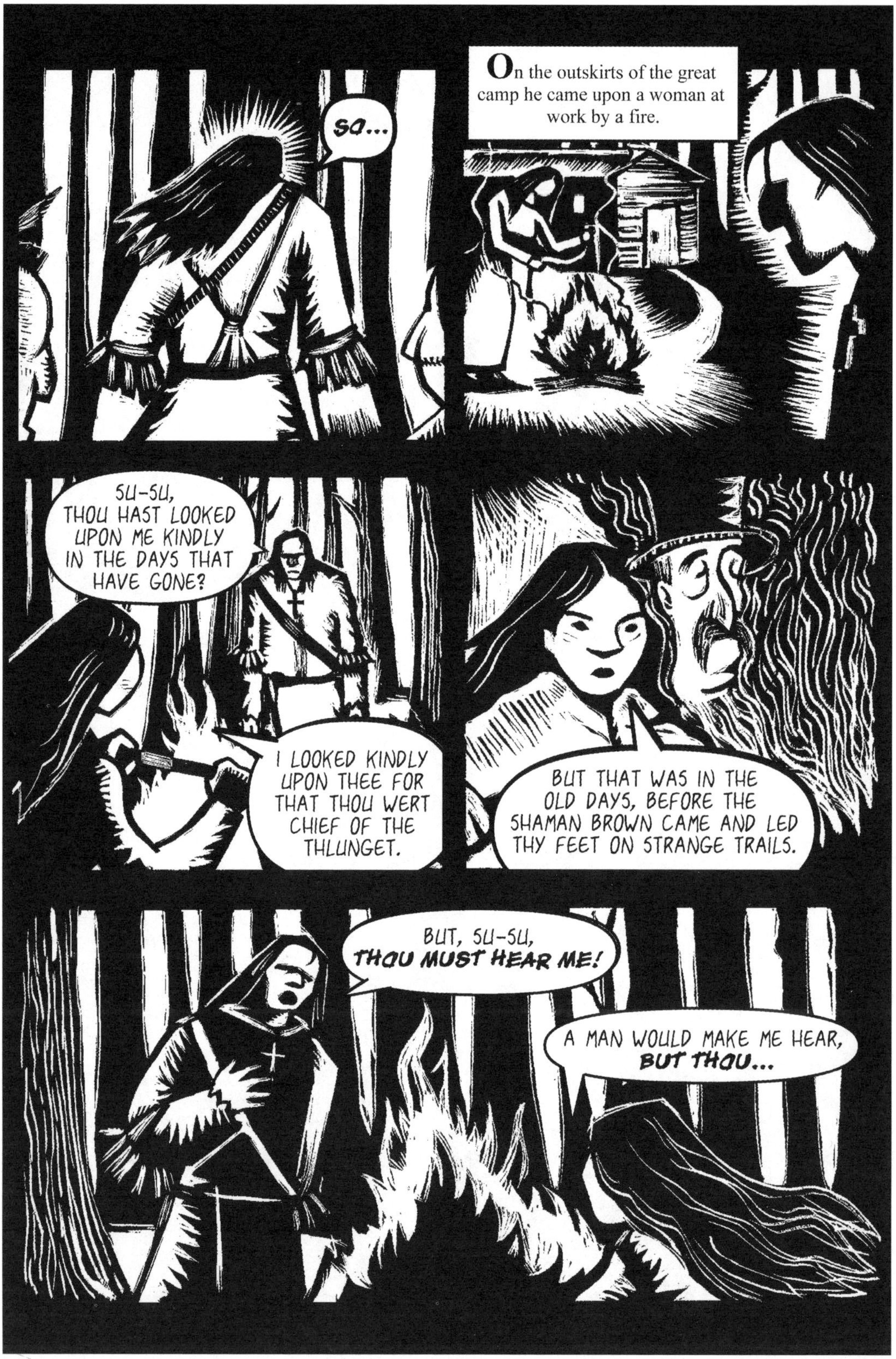
SA...
On the outskirts of the great camp he came upon a woman at work by a fire.
SU-SU, THOU HAST LOOKED UPON ME KINDLY IN THE DAYS THAT HAVE GONE?
I LOOKED KINDLY UPON THEE FOR THAT THOU WERT CHIEF OF THE THLUNGET.
BUT THAT WAS IN THE OLD DAYS, BEFORE THE SHAMAN BROWN CAME AND LED THY FEET ON STRANGE TRAILS.
BUT, SU-SU, THOU MUST HEAR ME!
A MAN WOULD MAKE ME HEAR, BUT THOU...

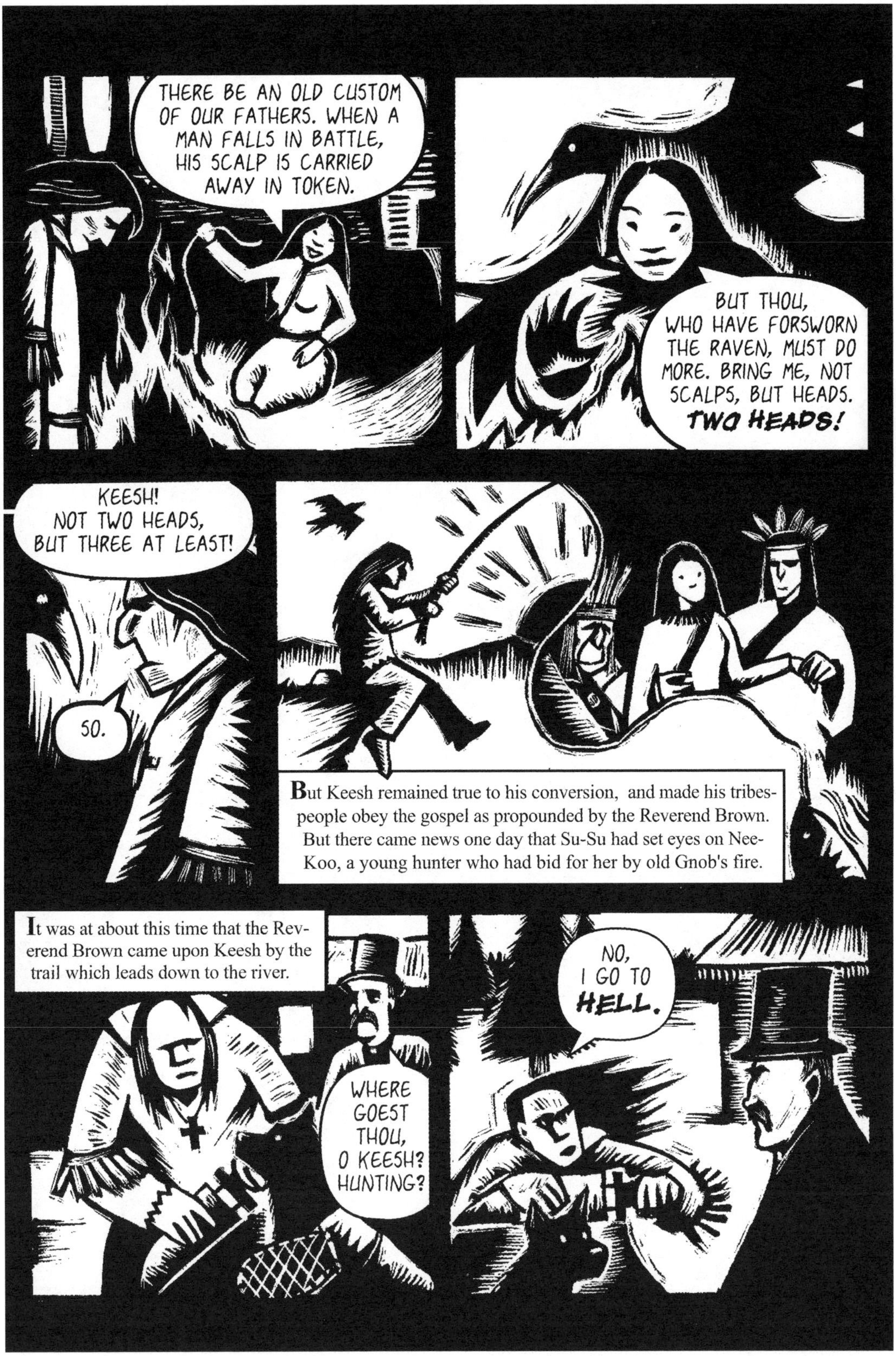
THERE BE AN OLD CUSTOM OF OUR FATHERS. WHEN A MAN FALLS IN BATTLE, HIS SCALP IS CARRIED AWAY IN TOKEN.
BUT THOU, WHO HAVE FORSWORN THE RAVEN, MUST DO MORE. BRING ME, NOT SCALPS, BUT HEADS. TWO HEADS!
KEESH! NOT TWO HEADS, BUT THREE AT LEAST!
SO.
But Keesh remained true to his conversion, and made his tribes-people obey the gospel as propounded by the Reverend Brown. But there came news one day that Su-Su had set eyes on Nee-Koo, a young hunter who had bid for her by old Gnob's fire.
It was at about this time that the Reverend Brown came upon Keesh by the trail which leads down to the river.
WHERE GOEST THOU, O KEESH? HUNTING?
NO, I GO TO HELL.

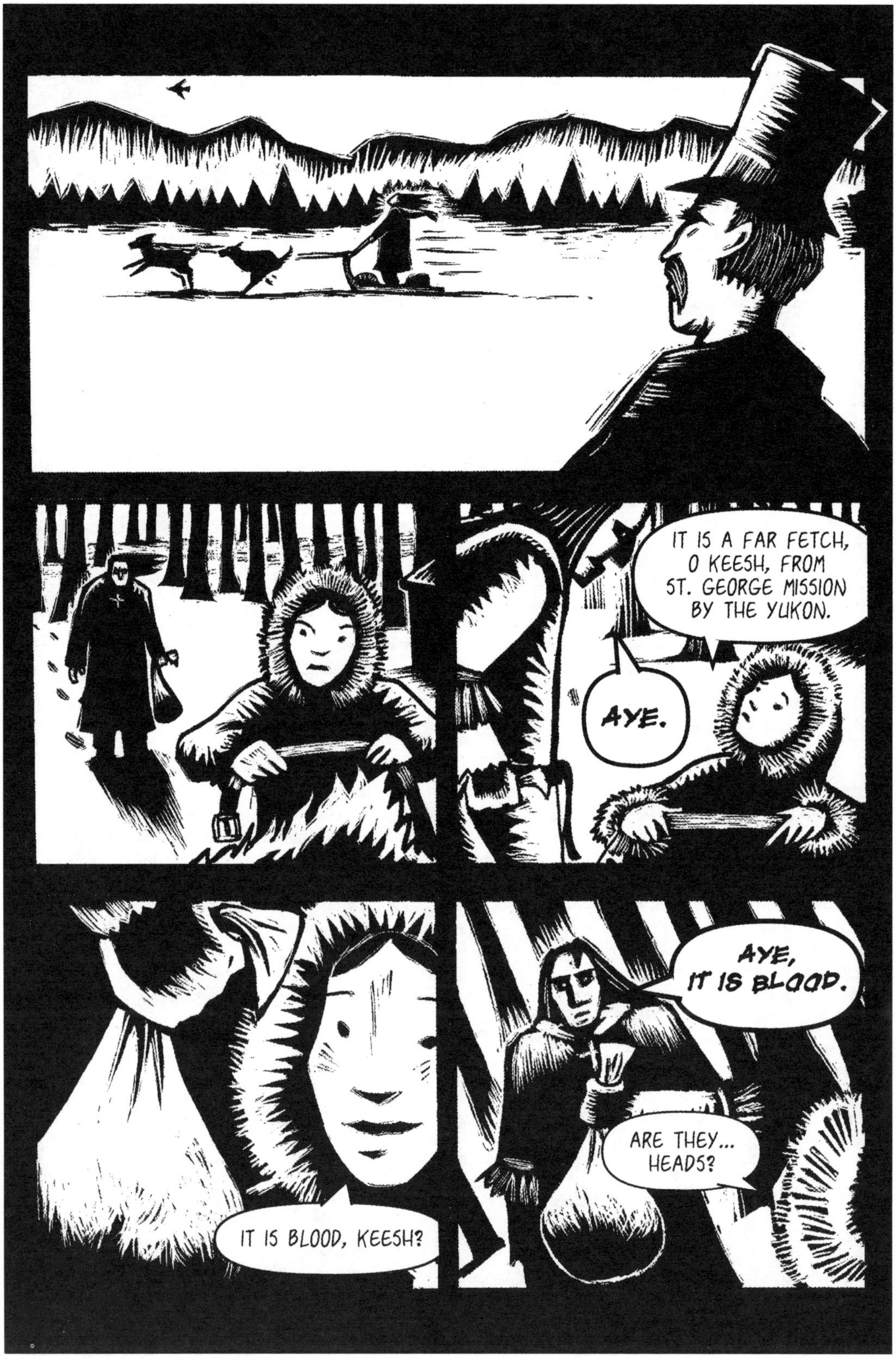
IT IS A FAR FETCH, O KEESH, FROM ST. GEORGE MISSION BY THE YUKON.
AYE.
IT IS BLOOD, KEESH?
AYE, IT IS BLOOD.
ARE THEY... HEADS?

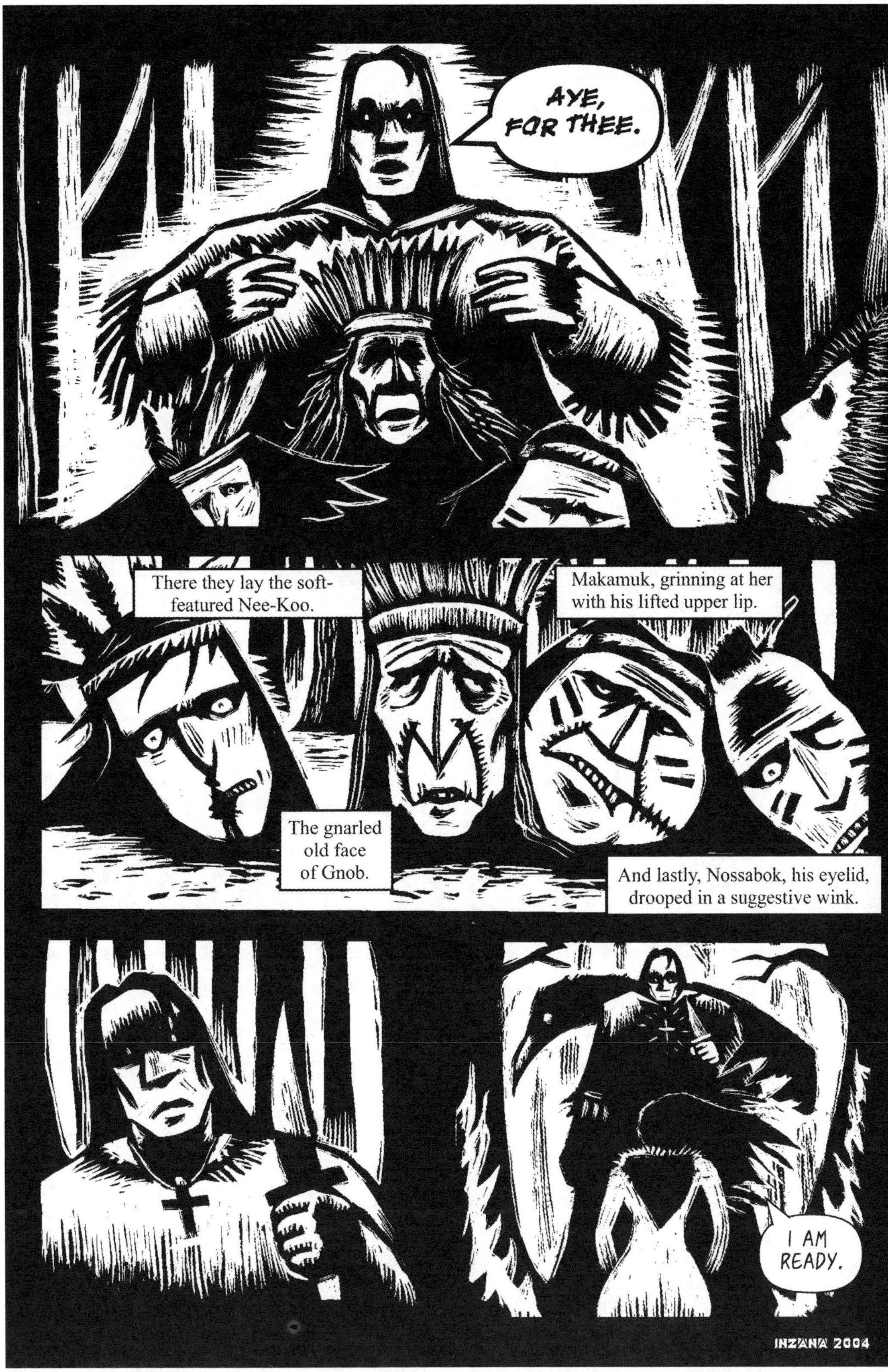
AYE, FOR THEE.
There they lay the soft-featured Nee-Koo.
The gnarled old face of Gnob.
Makamuk, grinning at her with his lifted upper lip.
And lastly, Nossabok, his eyelid, drooped in a suggestive wink.
I AM READY.
INZANA 2004

"PROFESSOR JONKIN'S CANNIBAL PLANT"

BY: HOWARD R. GARIS ~ ADAPTED BY: ONSMITH JEREMI, 2004

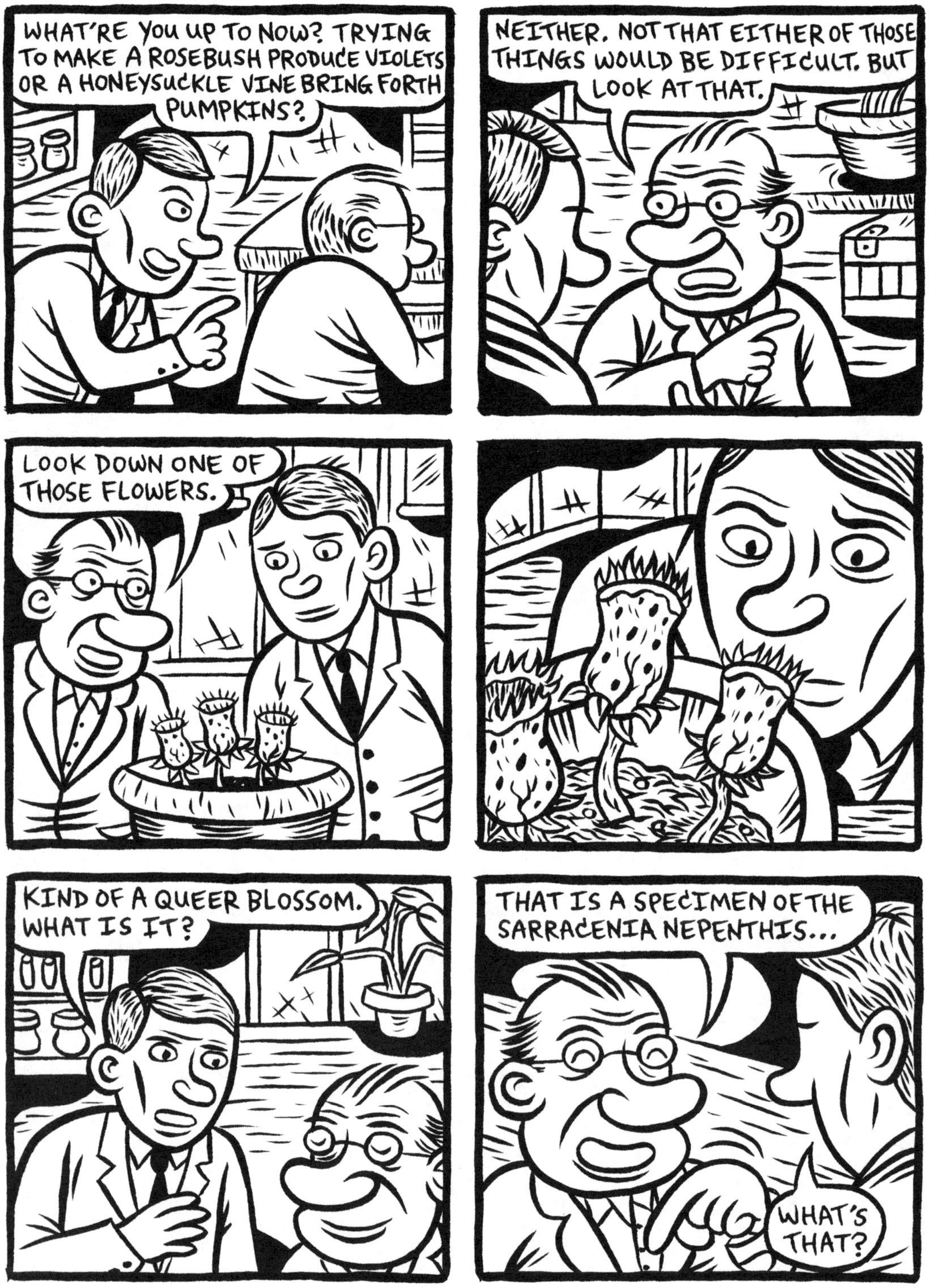
WHAT'RE YOU UP TO NOW? TRYING TO MAKE A ROSEBUSH PRODUCE VIOLETS OR A HONEYSUCKLE VINE BRING FORTH PUMPKINS?
NEITHER. NOT THAT EITHER OF THOSE THINGS WOULD BE DIFFICULT. BUT LOOK AT THAT.
LOOK DOWN ONE OF THOSE FLOWERS.
KIND OF A QUEER BLOSSOM. WHAT IS IT?
THAT IS A SPECIMEN OF THE SARRACENIA NEPENTHIS...
WHAT'S THAT?

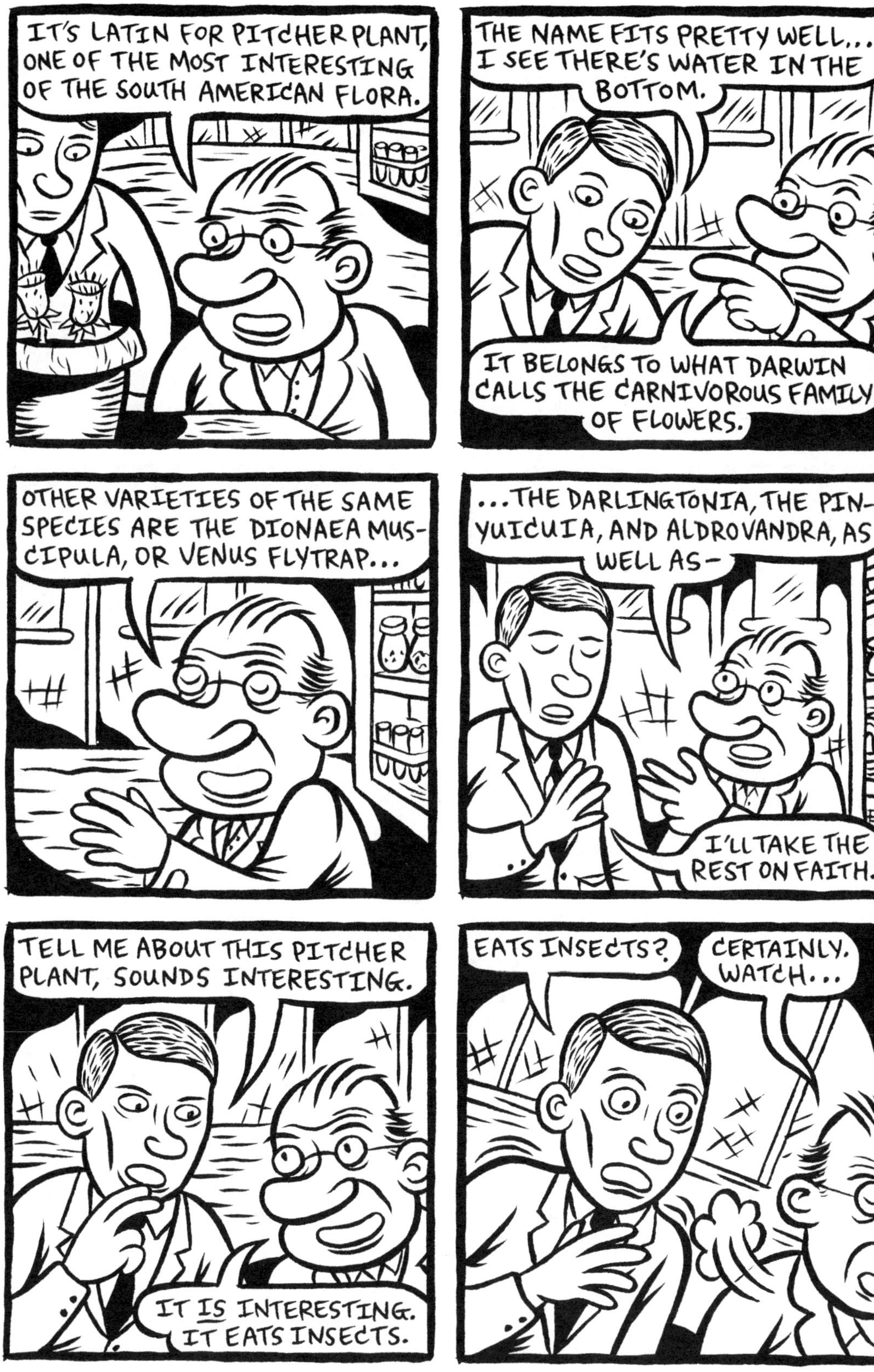
IT'S LATIN FOR PITCHER PLANT, ONE OF THE MOST INTERESTING OF THE SOUTH AMERICAN FLORA.
THE NAME FITS PRETTY WELL... I SEE THERE'S WATER IN THE BOTTOM.
IT BELONGS TO WHAT DARWIN CALLS THE CARNIVOROUS FAMILY OF FLOWERS.
OTHER VARIETIES OF THE SAME SPECIES ARE THE DIONAEA MUSCIPULA, OR VENUS FLYTRAP...
...THE DARLINGTONIA, THE PINYUICUIA, AND ALDROVANDRA, AS WELL AS–
I'LL TAKE THE REST ON FAITH.
TELL ME ABOUT THIS PITCHER PLANT, SOUNDS INTERESTING.
IT IS INTERESTING. IT EATS INSECTS.
EATS INSECTS?
CERTAINLY. WATCH...

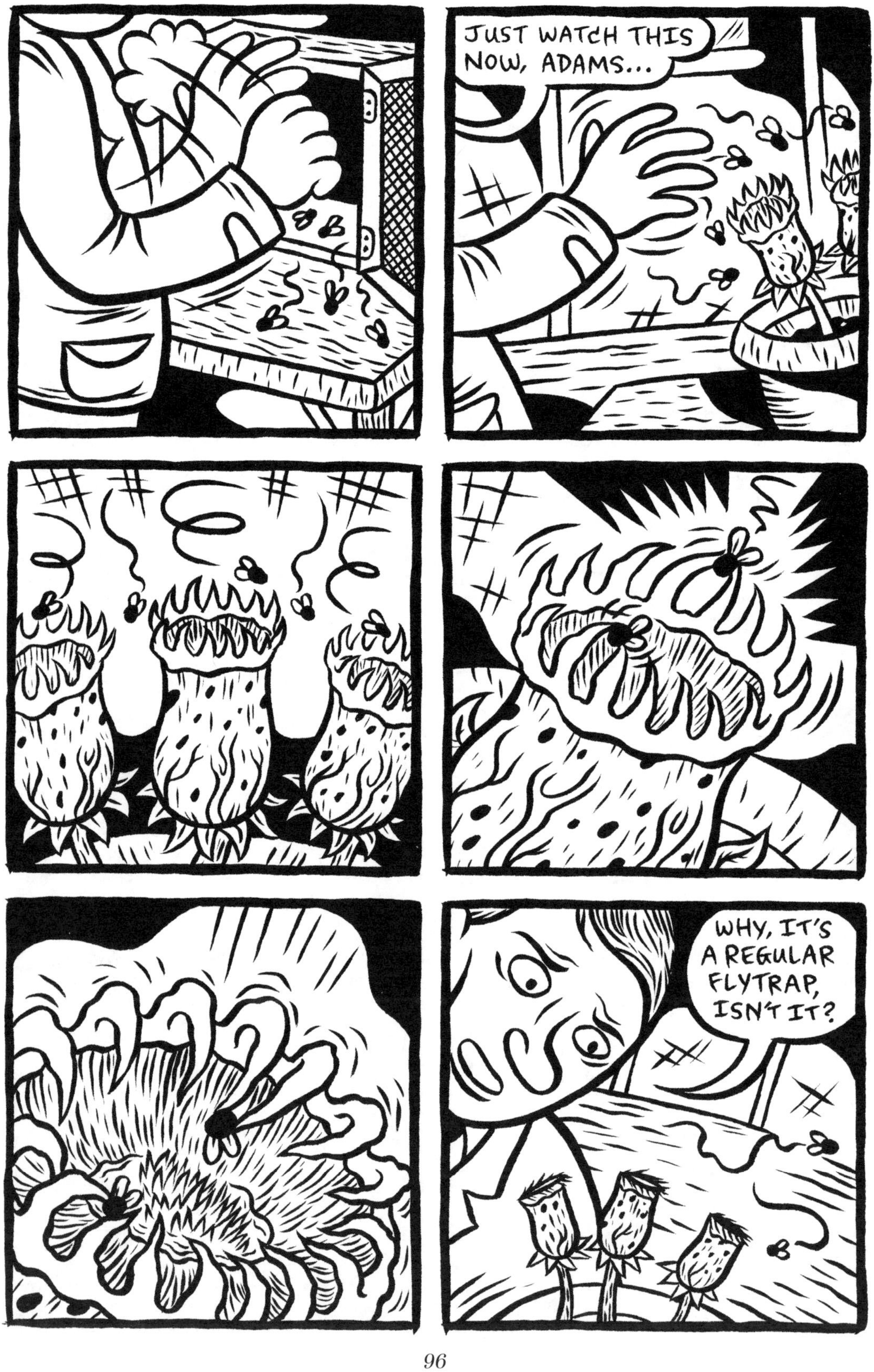
JUST WATCH THIS NOW, ADAMS...
WHY, IT'S A REGULAR FLYTRAP, ISN'T IT?

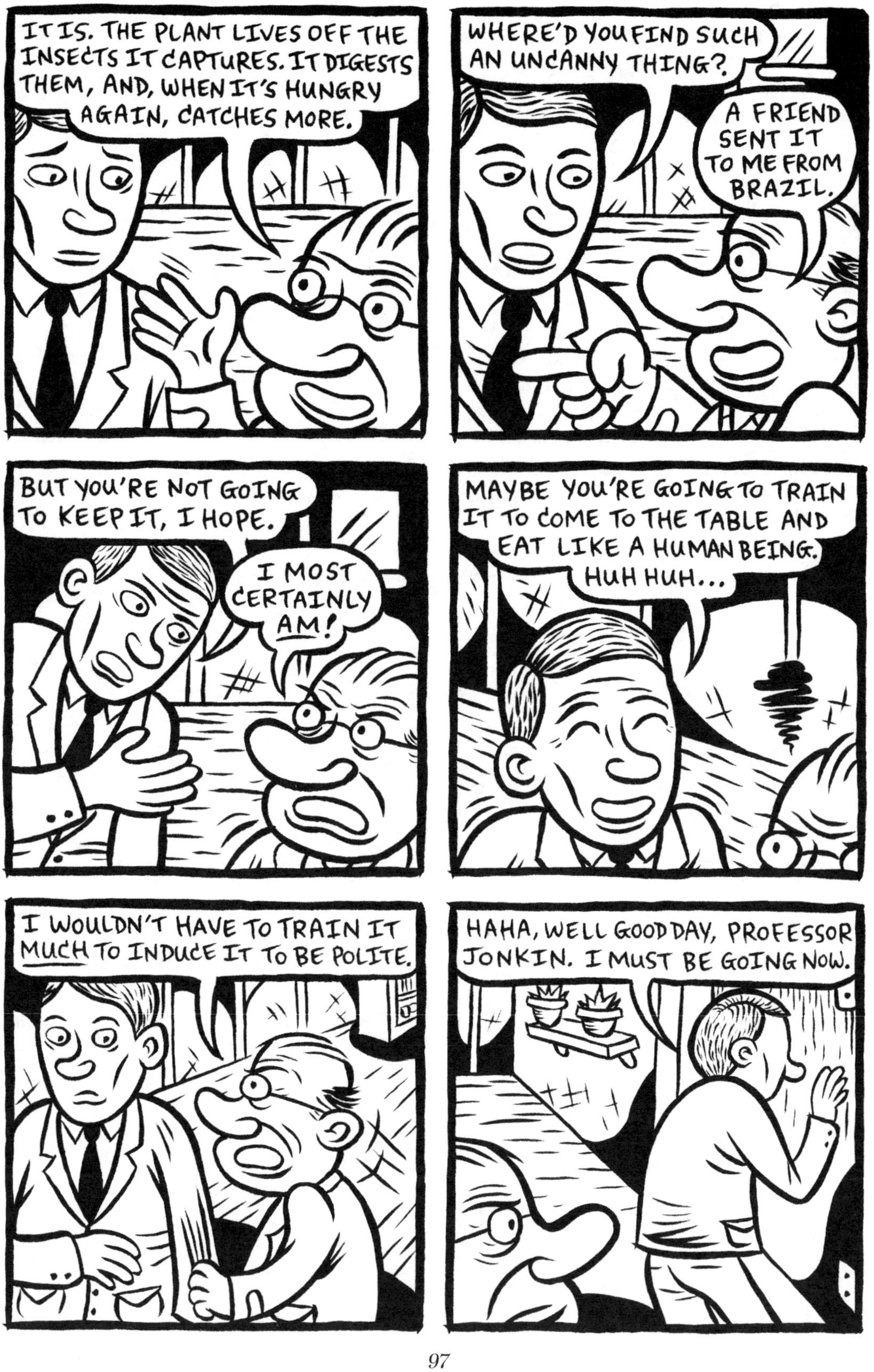
IT IS. THE PLANT LIVES OFF THE INSECTS IT CAPTURES. IT DIGESTS THEM, AND, WHEN IT'S HUNGRY AGAIN, CATCHES MORE.
WHERE'D YOU FIND SUCH AN UNCANNY THING?
A FRIEND SENT IT TO ME FROM BRAZIL.
BUT YOU'RE NOT GOING TO KEEP IT, I HOPE.
I MOST CERTAINLY AM!
MAYBE YOU'RE GOING TO TRAIN IT TO COME TO THE TABLE AND EAT LIKE A HUMAN BEING. HUH HUH...
I WOULDN'T HAVE TO TRAIN IT MUCH TO INDUCE IT TO BE POLITE.
HAHA, WELL GOOD DAY, PROFESSOR JONKIN. I MUST BE GOING NOW.

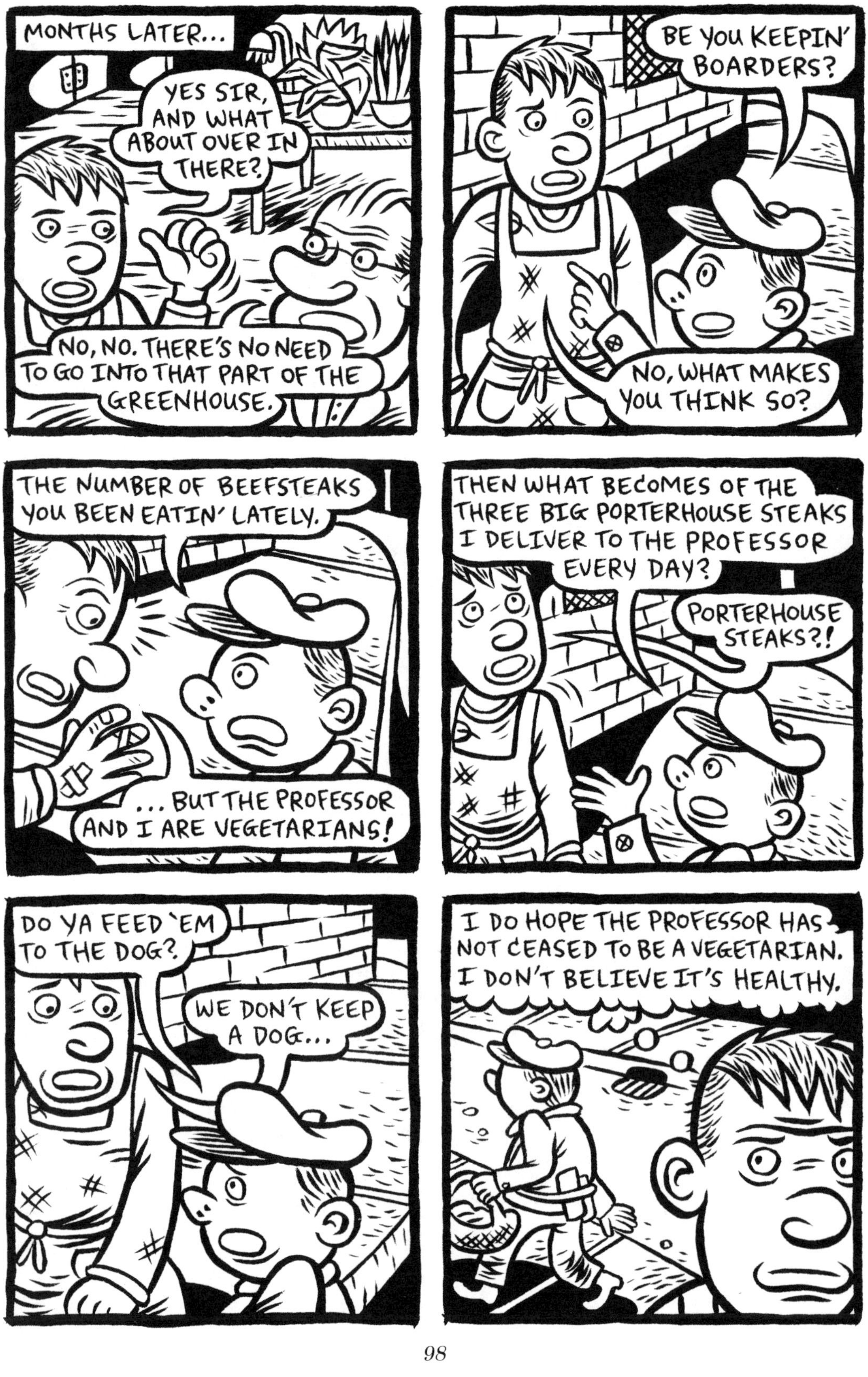
MONTHS LATER...
YES SIR, AND WHAT ABOUT OVER IN THERE?
NO, NO. THERE'S NO NEED TO GO INTO THAT PART OF THE GREENHOUSE.
BE YOU KEEPIN' BOARDERS?
NO, WHAT MAKES YOU THINK SO?
THE NUMBER OF BEEFSTEAKS YOU BEEN EATIN' LATELY.
... BUT THE PROFESSOR AND I ARE VEGETARIANS!
THEN WHAT BECOMES OF THE THREE BIG PORTERHOUSE STEAKS I DELIVER TO THE PROFESSOR EVERY DAY?
PORTERHOUSE STEAKS?!
DO YA FEED 'EM TO THE DOG?
WE DON'T KEEP A DOG...
I DO HOPE THE PROFESSOR HAS NOT CEASED TO BE A VEGETARIAN. I DON'T BELIEVE IT'S HEALTHY.

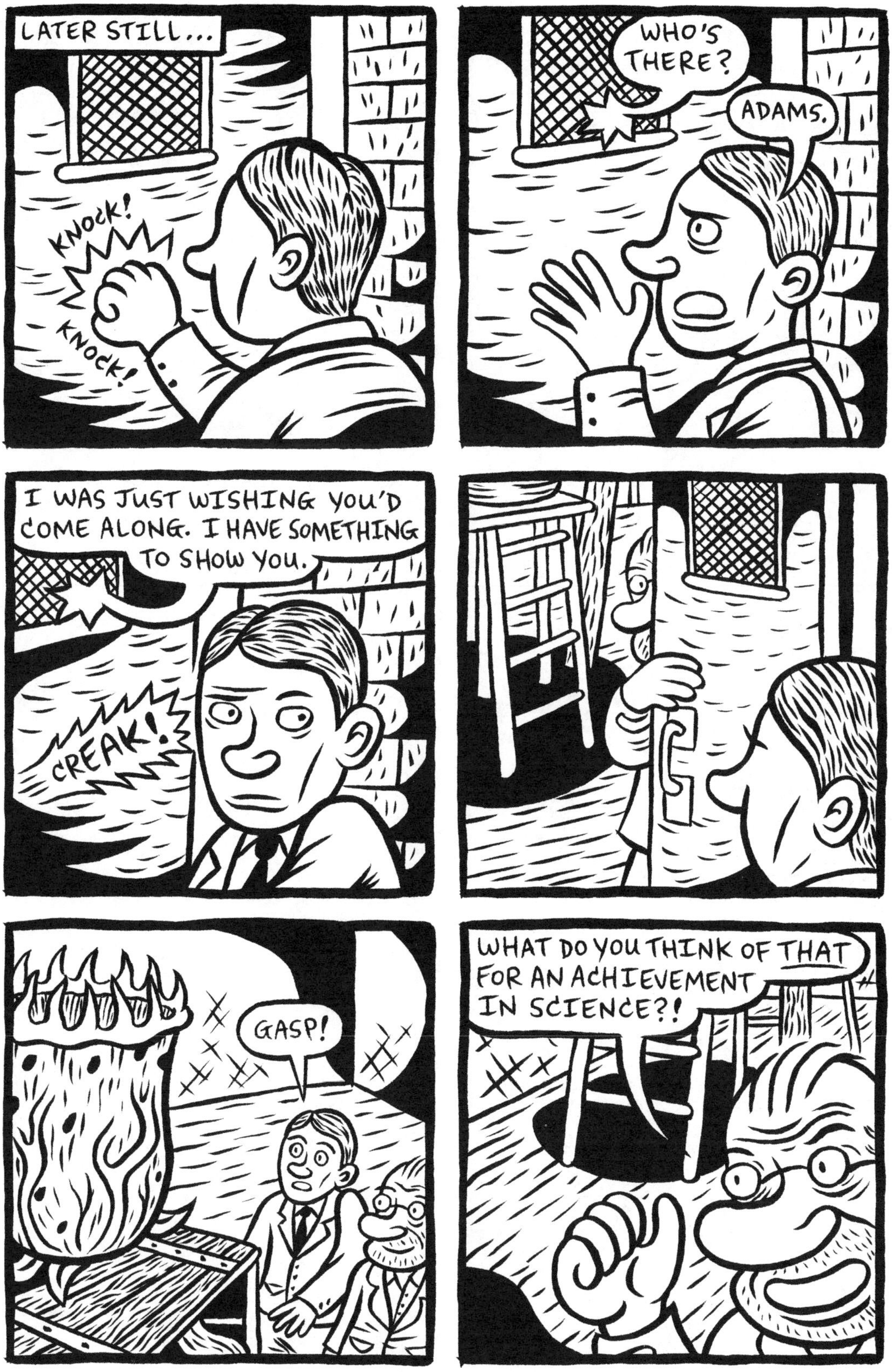
LATER STILL...
KNOCK!
KNOCK!
WHO'S THERE?
ADAMS.
I WAS JUST WISHING YOU'D COME ALONG. I HAVE SOMETHING TO SHOW YOU.
CREAK!
GASP!
WHAT DO YOU THINK OF THAT FOR AN ACHIEVEMENT IN SCIENCE?!

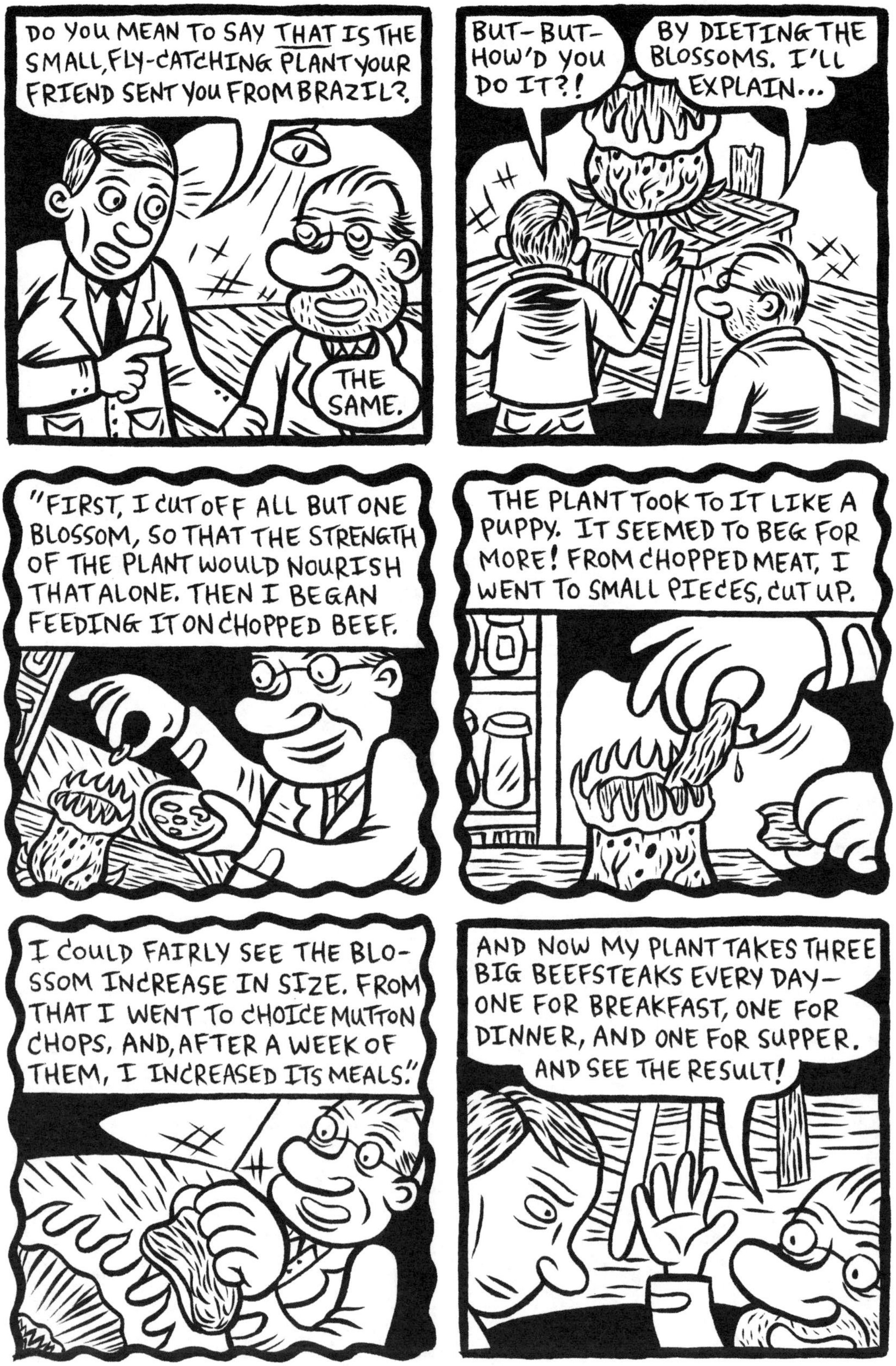
DO YOU MEAN TO SAY THAT IS THE SMALL, FLY-CATCHING PLANT YOUR FRIEND SENT YOU FROM BRAZIL?
THE SAME.
BUT-BUT- HOW'D YOU DO IT?!
BY DIETING THE BLOSSOMS. I'LL EXPLAIN...
"FIRST, I CUT OFF ALL BUT ONE BLOSSOM, SO THAT THE STRENGTH OF THE PLANT WOULD NOURISH THAT ALONE. THEN I BEGAN FEEDING IT ON CHOPPED BEEF.
THE PLANT TOOK TO IT LIKE A PUPPY. IT SEEMED TO BEG FOR MORE! FROM CHOPPED MEAT, I WENT TO SMALL PIECES, CUT UP.
I COULD FAIRLY SEE THE BLOSSOM INCREASE IN SIZE. FROM THAT I WENT TO CHOICE MUTTON CHOPS, AND, AFTER A WEEK OF THEM, I INCREASED ITS MEALS."
AND NOW MY PLANT TAKES THREE BIG BEEFSTEAKS EVERY DAY— ONE FOR BREAKFAST, ONE FOR DINNER, AND ONE FOR SUPPER. AND SEE THE RESULT!

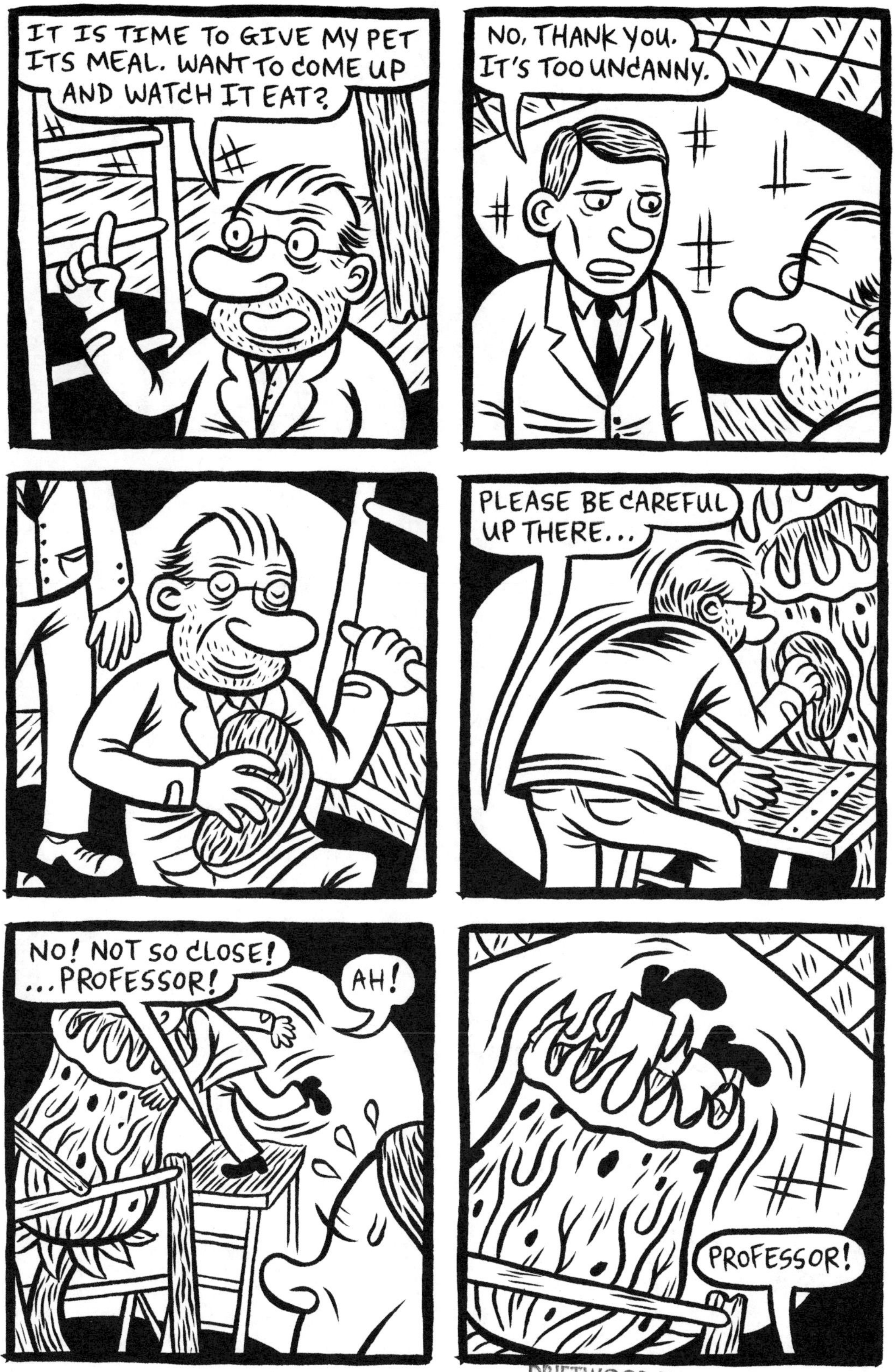
IT IS TIME TO GIVE MY PET ITS MEAL. WANT TO COME UP AND WATCH IT EAT?
NO, THANK YOU. IT'S TOO UNCANNY.
PLEASE BE CAREFUL UP THERE...
NO! NOT SO CLOSE! ...PROFESSOR!
AH!
PROFESSOR!

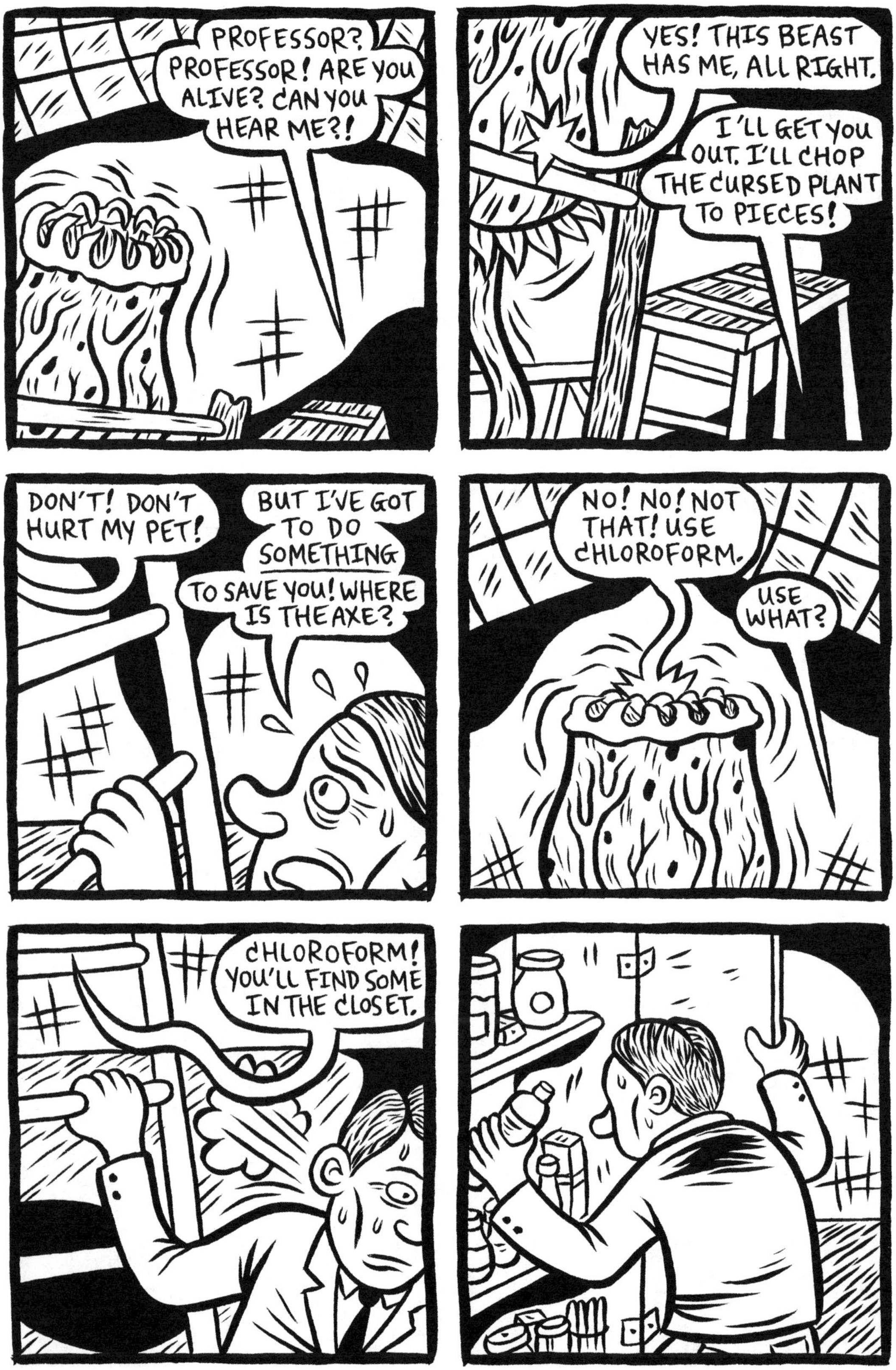
PROFESSOR? PROFESSOR! ARE YOU ALIVE? CAN YOU HEAR ME?!
YES! THIS BEAST HAS ME, ALL RIGHT.
I'LL GET YOU OUT. I'LL CHOP THE CURSED PLANT TO PIECES!
DON'T! DON'T HURT MY PET!
BUT I'VE GOT TO DO SOMETHING
TO SAVE YOU! WHERE IS THE AXE?
NO! NO! NOT THAT! USE CHLOROFORM.
USE WHAT?
CHLOROFORM! YOU'LL FIND SOME IN THE CLOSET.

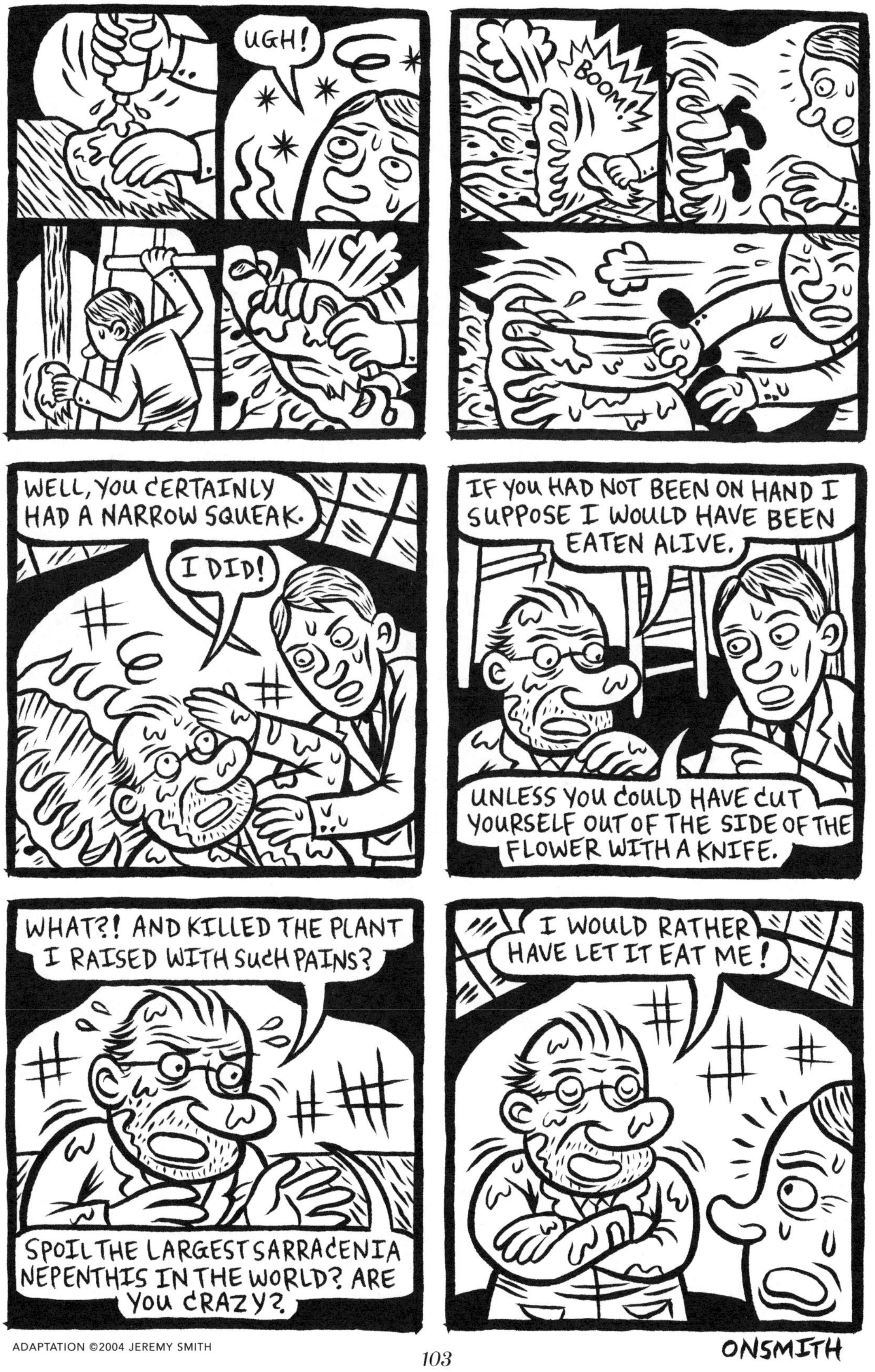
UGH!
BOOM!
WELL, YOU CERTAINLY HAD A NARROW SQUEAK.
I DID!
IF YOU HAD NOT BEEN ON HAND I SUPPOSE I WOULD HAVE BEEN EATEN ALIVE.
UNLESS YOU COULD HAVE CUT YOURSELF OUT OF THE SIDE OF THE FLOWER WITH A KNIFE.
WHAT?! AND KILLED THE PLANT I RAISED WITH SUCH PAINS?
SPOIL THE LARGEST SARRACENIA NEPENTHIS IN THE WORLD? ARE YOU CRAZY?
I WOULD RATHER HAVE LET IT EAT ME!

ONSMITH

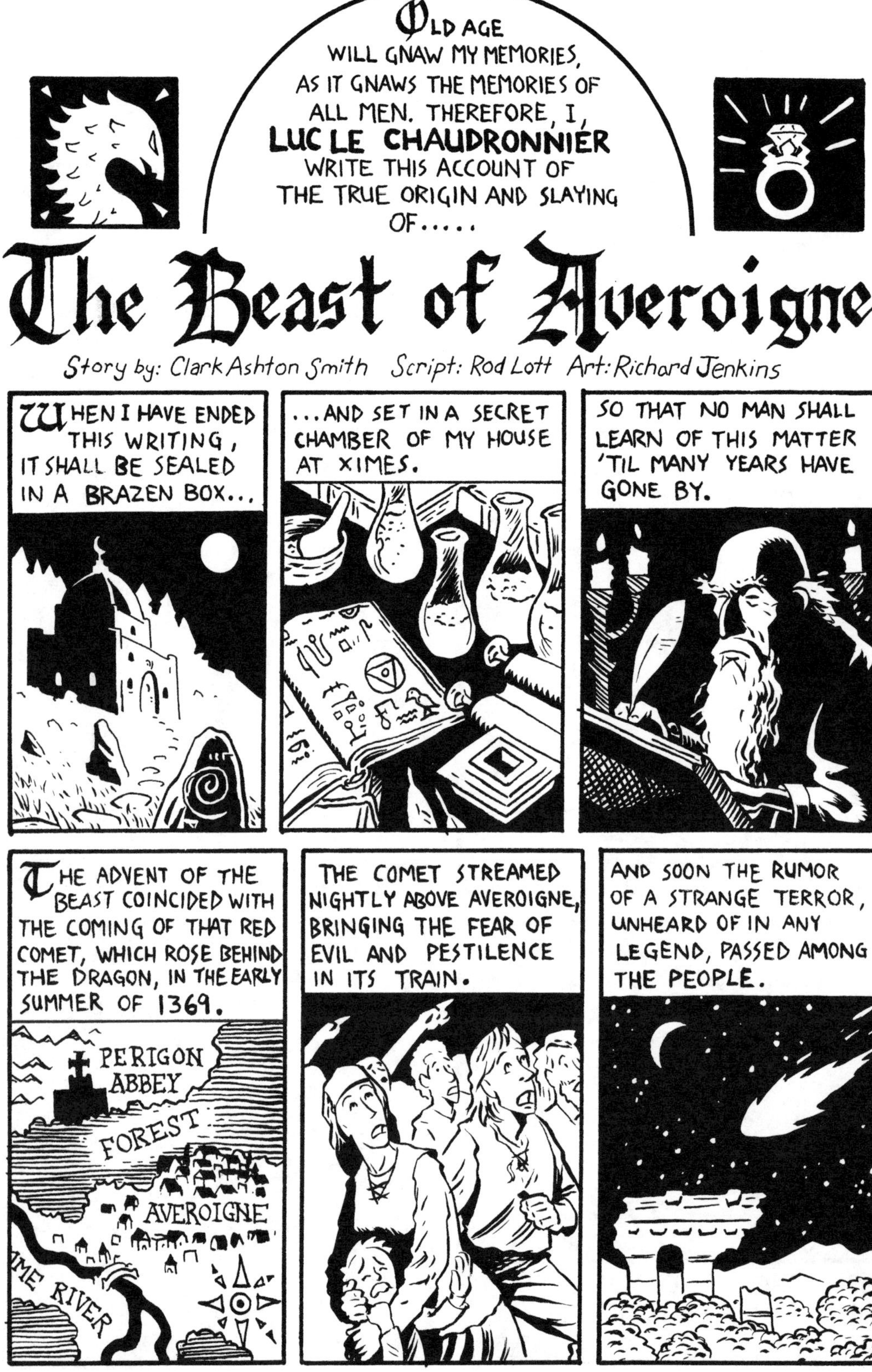
OLD AGE WILL GNAW MY MEMORIES, AS IT GNAWS THE MEMORIES OF ALL MEN. THEREFORE, I, LUC LE CHAUDRONNIER WRITE THIS ACCOUNT OF THE TRUE ORIGIN AND SLAYING OF.....
The Beast of Averoigne
Story by: Clark Ashton Smith Script: Rod Lott Art: Richard Jenkins
WHEN I HAVE ENDED THIS WRITING, IT SHALL BE SEALED IN A BRAZEN BOX...
...AND SET IN A SECRET CHAMBER OF MY HOUSE AT XIMES.
SO THAT NO MAN SHALL LEARN OF THIS MATTER 'TIL MANY YEARS HAVE GONE BY.
THE ADVENT OF THE BEAST COINCIDED WITH THE COMING OF THAT RED COMET, WHICH ROSE BEHIND THE DRAGON, IN THE EARLY SUMMER OF 1369.
PERIGON ABBEY
FOREST
AVEROIGNE
ME RIVER
THE COMET STREAMED NIGHTLY ABOVE AVEROIGNE, BRINGING THE FEAR OF EVIL AND PESTILENCE IN ITS TRAIN.
AND SOON THE RUMOR OF A STRANGE TERROR, UNHEARD OF IN ANY LEGEND, PASSED AMONG THE PEOPLE.

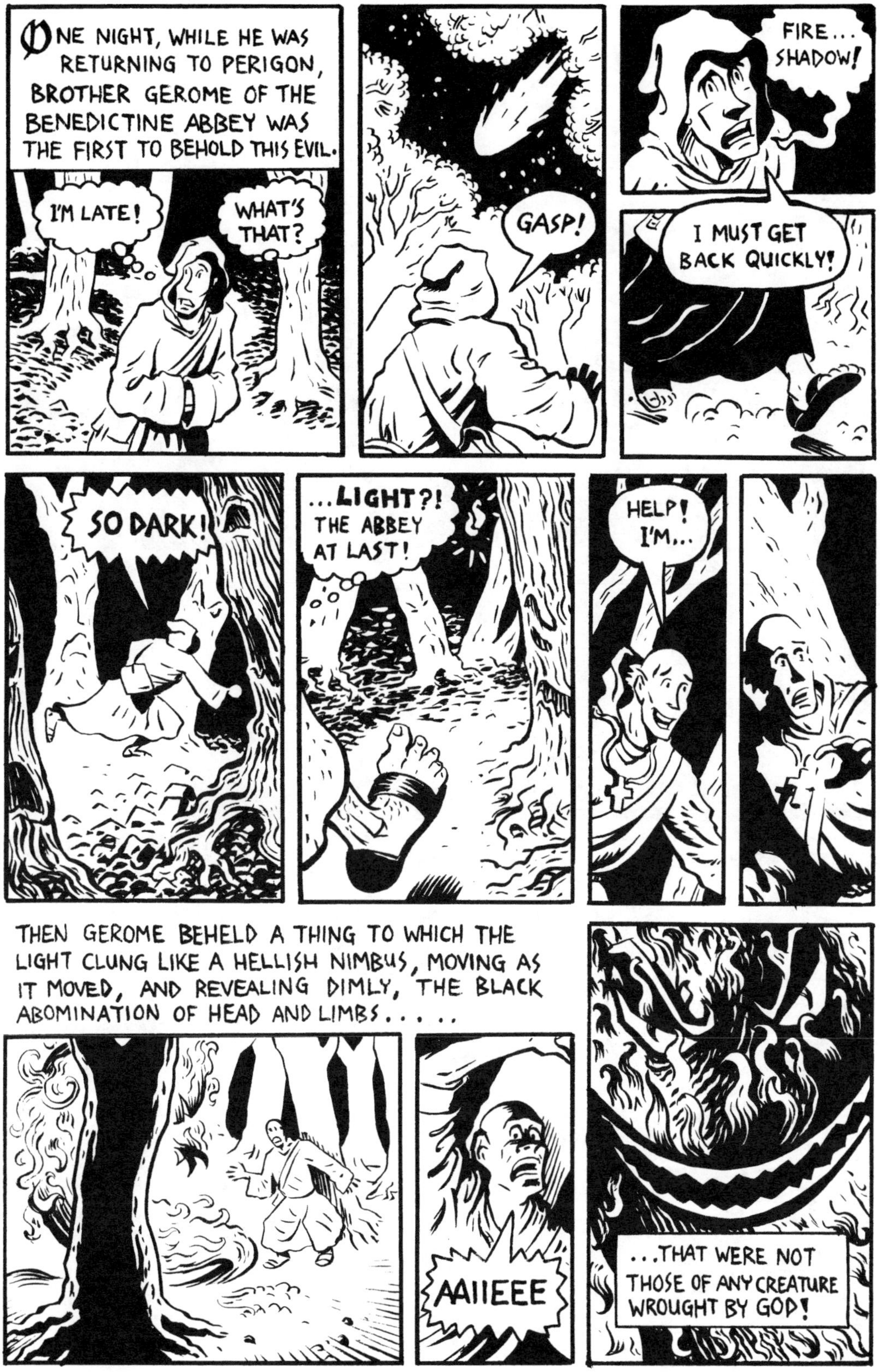
ONE NIGHT, WHILE HE WAS RETURNING TO PERIGON, BROTHER GEROME OF THE BENEDICTINE ABBEY WAS THE FIRST TO BEHOLD THIS EVIL.
I'M LATE!
WHAT'S THAT?
GASP!
FIRE... SHADOW!
I MUST GET BACK QUICKLY!
SO DARK!
...LIGHT?! THE ABBEY AT LAST!
HELP! I'M...
THEN GEROME BEHELD A THING TO WHICH THE LIGHT CLUNG LIKE A HELLISH NIMBUS, MOVING AS IT MOVED, AND REVEALING DIMLY, THE BLACK ABOMINATION OF HEAD AND LIMBS.....
AAIIEEE
...THAT WERE NOT THOSE OF ANY CREATURE WROUGHT BY GOD!

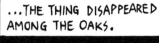

WITH ITS NIMBUS FLARING FROM VENOMOUS GREEN TO A WRATHFUL RED, RUNNING AND SLITHERING RAPIDLY...

NO!

...THE THING DISAPPEARED AMONG THE OAKS.

AND GEROME SAW THE HELLISH LIGHT NO MORE.

On THE MORROW...

LATER, AT THE ABBEY...

A DEAD STAG WAS FOUND UNMARKED BY ANY WOUND OTHER THAN A WIDE GASH THAT LAID OPEN THE SPINE FROM NECK TO TAIL! THE SPINE ITSELF HAD BEEN SHATTERED...

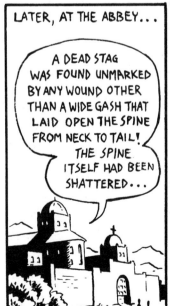

...AND THE..TH.. MARROW SUCKED DRY:

WHAT NATURE OF BEAST WOULD SLAY AND RAVEN SO?!

SOME CREATURE FROM THE **PIT** IS ABROAD IN AVEROIGNE!

NIGHT BY NIGHT THE COMET GREATENS, BURNING LIKE AN EVIL MIST OF BLOOD AND FIRE!

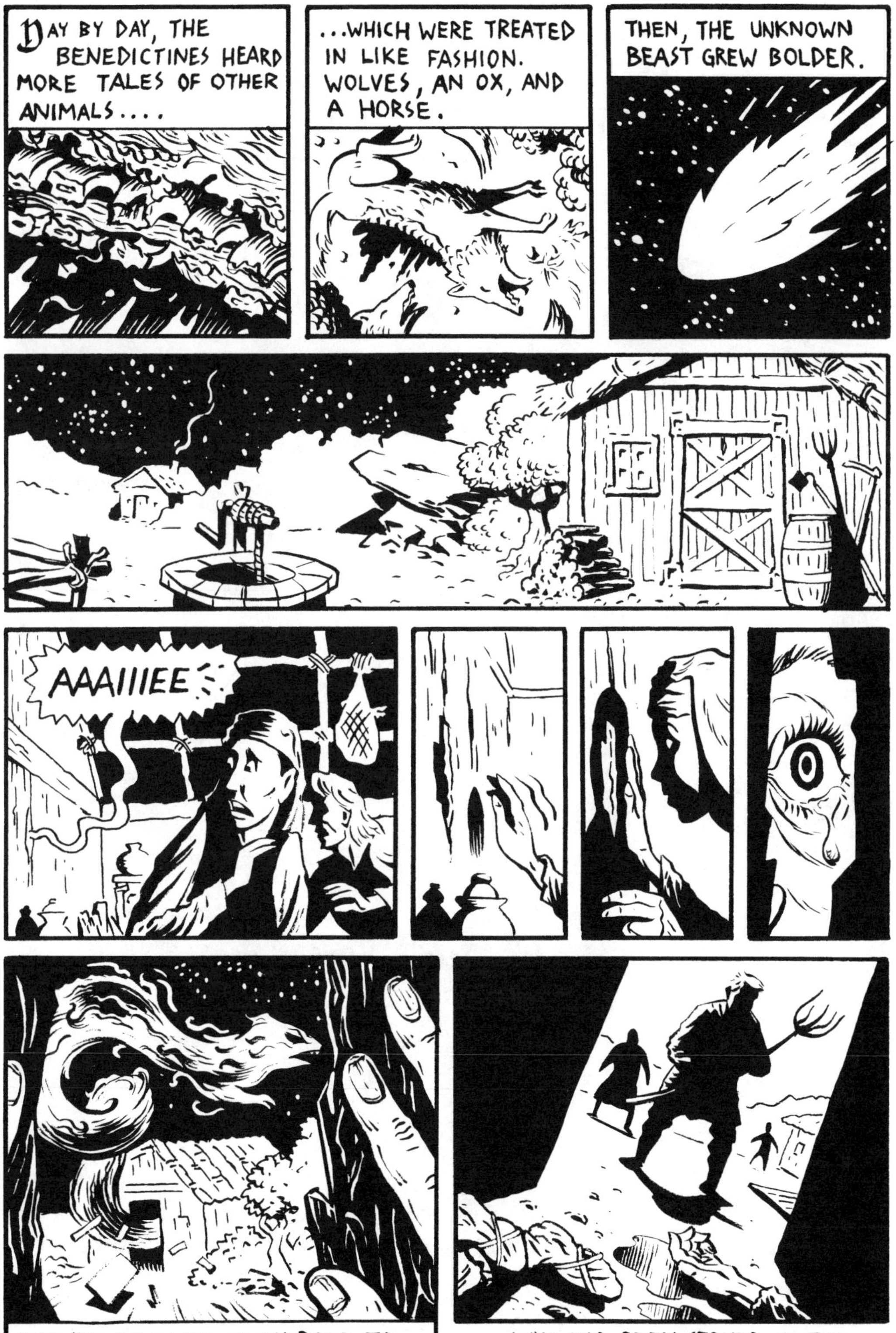
DAY BY DAY, THE BENEDICTINES HEARD MORE TALES OF OTHER ANIMALS....
...WHICH WERE TREATED IN LIKE FASHION. WOLVES, AN OX, AND A HORSE.
THEN, THE UNKNOWN BEAST GREW BOLDER.
AAAIIIEE
NOT 'TIL DAWN DID THEY DARE TO VERIFY THE FATE OF THEIR FELLOWS
...WHO HAD BEEN SERVED IN THE SAME MANNER AS THE ANIMALS.

BROTHER THEOPHILE, THE ABBOT OF PERIGON, WAS MUCH EXERCISED OVER THIS EVIL THAT HAD CHOSEN TO MANIFEST ITSELF IN THE NEIGHBORHOOD OF THE ABBEY. HE CALLED THE MONKS BEFORE HIM IN ASSEMBLY.

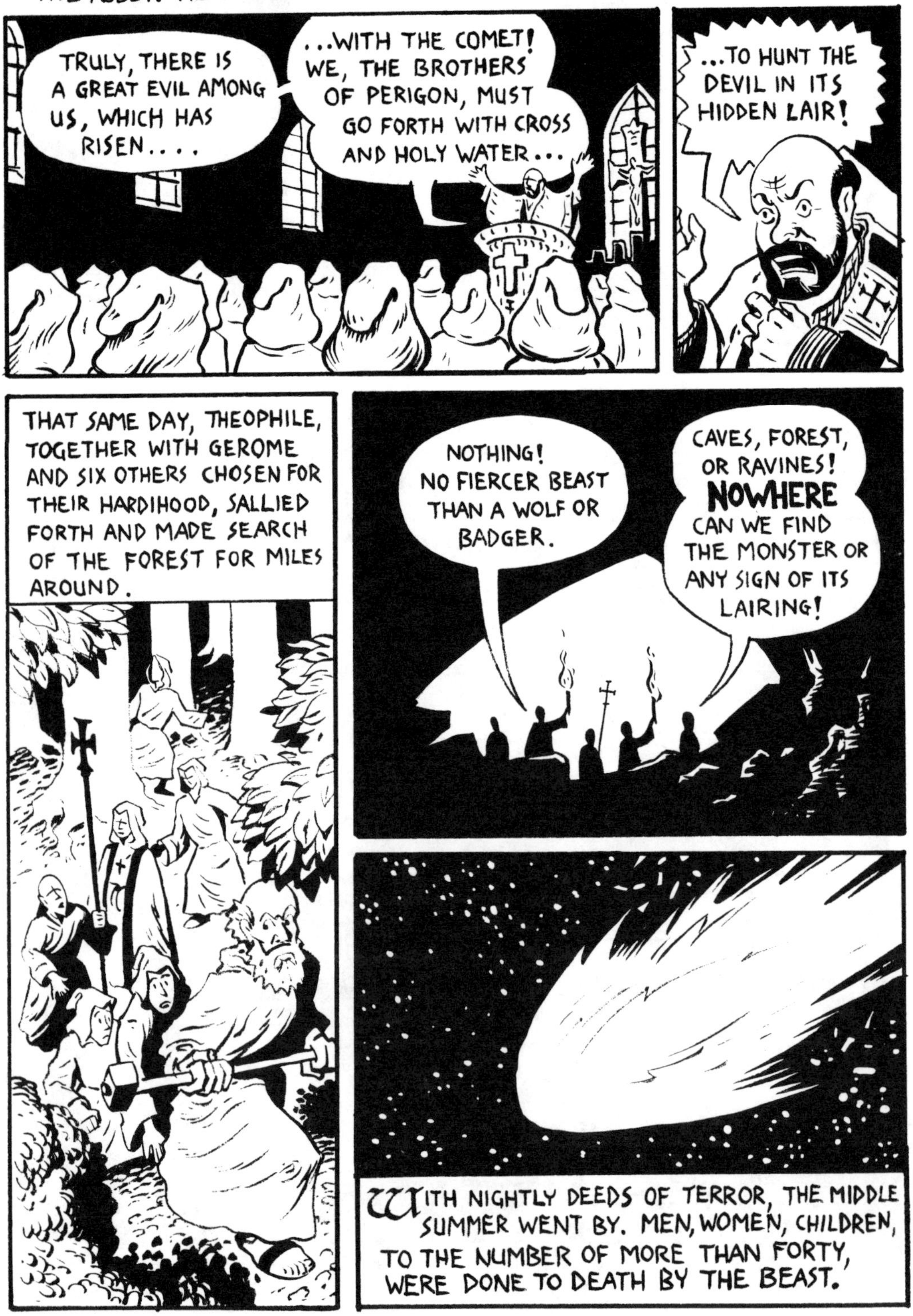
TRULY, THERE IS A GREAT EVIL AMONG US, WHICH HAS RISEN....
...WITH THE COMET! WE, THE BROTHERS OF PERIGON, MUST GO FORTH WITH CROSS AND HOLY WATER...
...TO HUNT THE DEVIL IN ITS HIDDEN LAIR!
THAT SAME DAY, THEOPHILE, TOGETHER WITH GEROME AND SIX OTHERS CHOSEN FOR THEIR HARDIHOOD, SALLIED FORTH AND MADE SEARCH OF THE FOREST FOR MILES AROUND.
NOTHING! NO FIERCER BEAST THAN A WOLF OR BADGER.
CAVES, FOREST, OR RAVINES! NOWHERE CAN WE FIND THE MONSTER OR ANY SIGN OF ITS LAIRING!
WITH NIGHTLY DEEDS OF TERROR, THE MIDDLE SUMMER WENT BY. MEN, WOMEN, CHILDREN, TO THE NUMBER OF MORE THAN FORTY, WERE DONE TO DEATH BY THE BEAST.

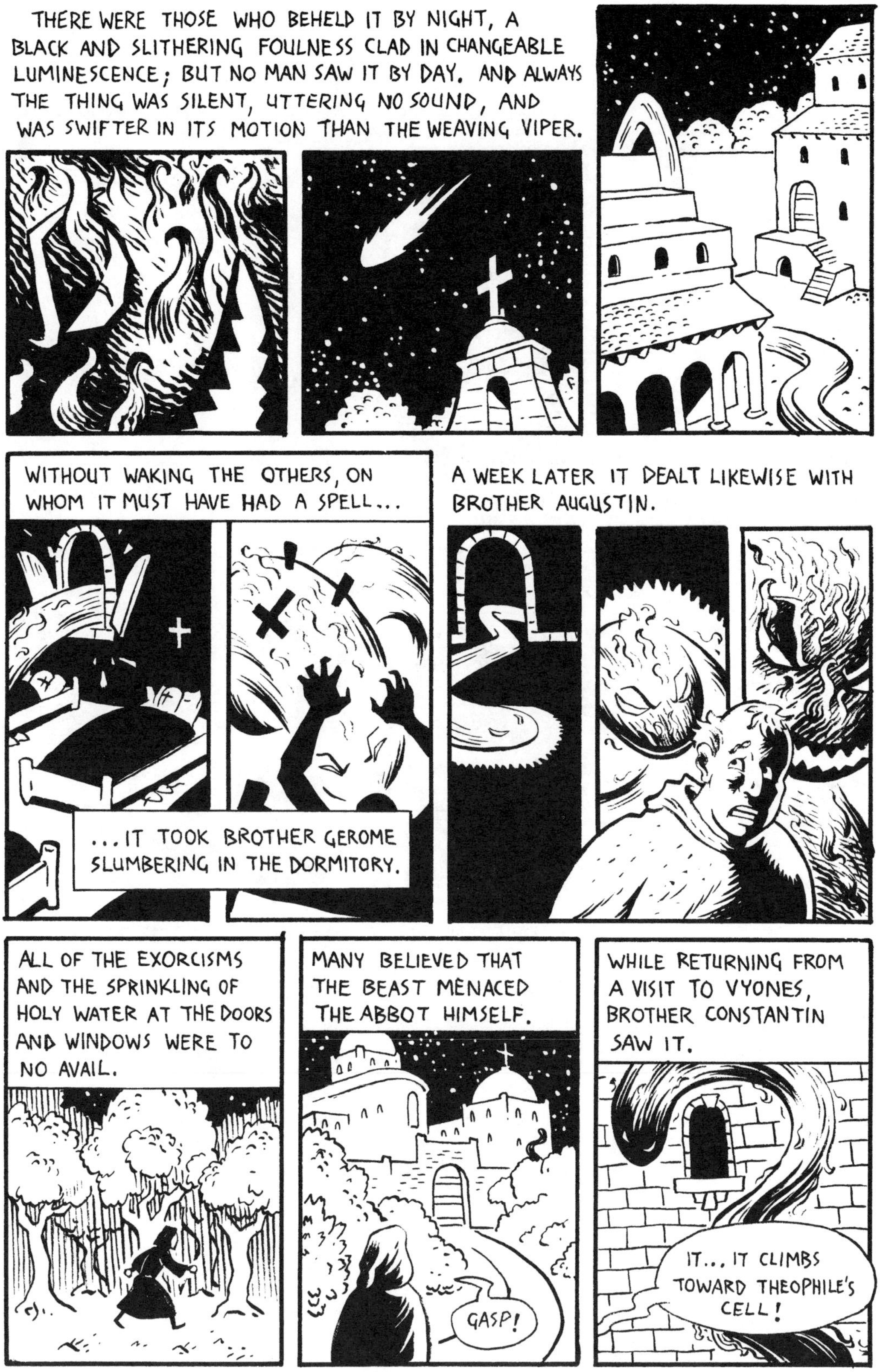
THERE WERE THOSE WHO BEHELD IT BY NIGHT, A BLACK AND SLITHERING FOULNESS CLAD IN CHANGEABLE LUMINESCENCE; BUT NO MAN SAW IT BY DAY. AND ALWAYS THE THING WAS SILENT, UTTERING NO SOUND, AND WAS SWIFTER IN ITS MOTION THAN THE WEAVING VIPER.
WITHOUT WAKING THE OTHERS, ON WHOM IT MUST HAVE HAD A SPELL...
...IT TOOK BROTHER GEROME SLUMBERING IN THE DORMITORY.
A WEEK LATER IT DEALT LIKEWISE WITH BROTHER AUGUSTIN.
ALL OF THE EXORCISMS AND THE SPRINKLING OF HOLY WATER AT THE DOORS AND WINDOWS WERE TO NO AVAIL.
MANY BELIEVED THAT THE BEAST MENACED THE ABBOT HIMSELF.
GASP!
WHILE RETURNING FROM A VISIT TO VYONES, BROTHER CONSTANTIN SAW IT.
IT... IT CLIMBS TOWARD THEOPHILE'S CELL!

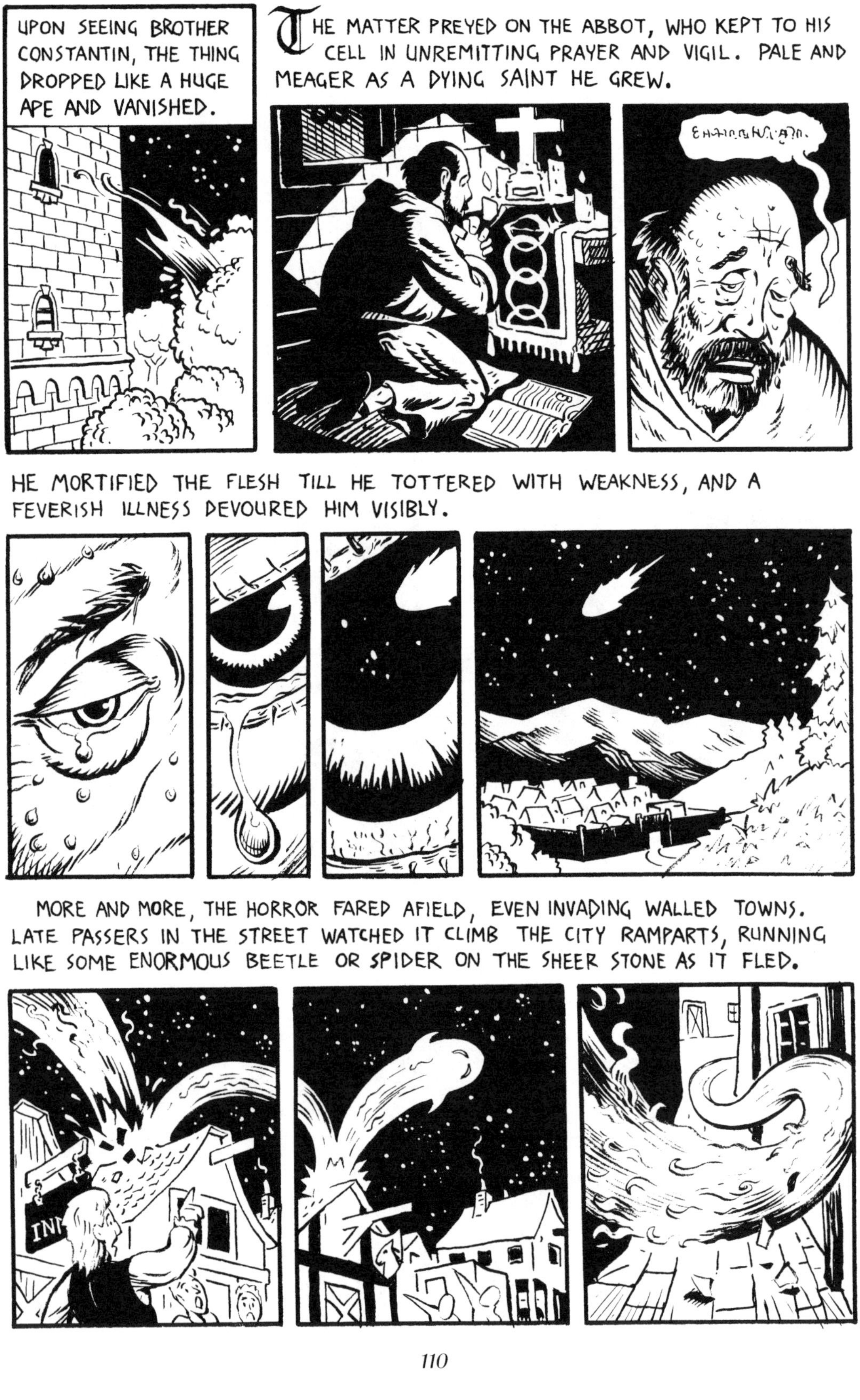
UPON SEEING BROTHER CONSTANTIN, THE THING DROPPED LIKE A HUGE APE AND VANISHED.
THE MATTER PREYED ON THE ABBOT, WHO KEPT TO HIS CELL IN UNREMITTING PRAYER AND VIGIL. PALE AND MEAGER AS A DYING SAINT HE GREW.
HE MORTIFIED THE FLESH TILL HE TOTTERED WITH WEAKNESS, AND A FEVERISH ILLNESS DEVOURED HIM VISIBLY.
MORE AND MORE, THE HORROR FARED AFIELD, EVEN INVADING WALLED TOWNS. LATE PASSERS IN THE STREET WATCHED IT CLIMB THE CITY RAMPARTS, RUNNING LIKE SOME ENORMOUS BEETLE OR SPIDER ON THE SHEER STONE AS IT FLED.

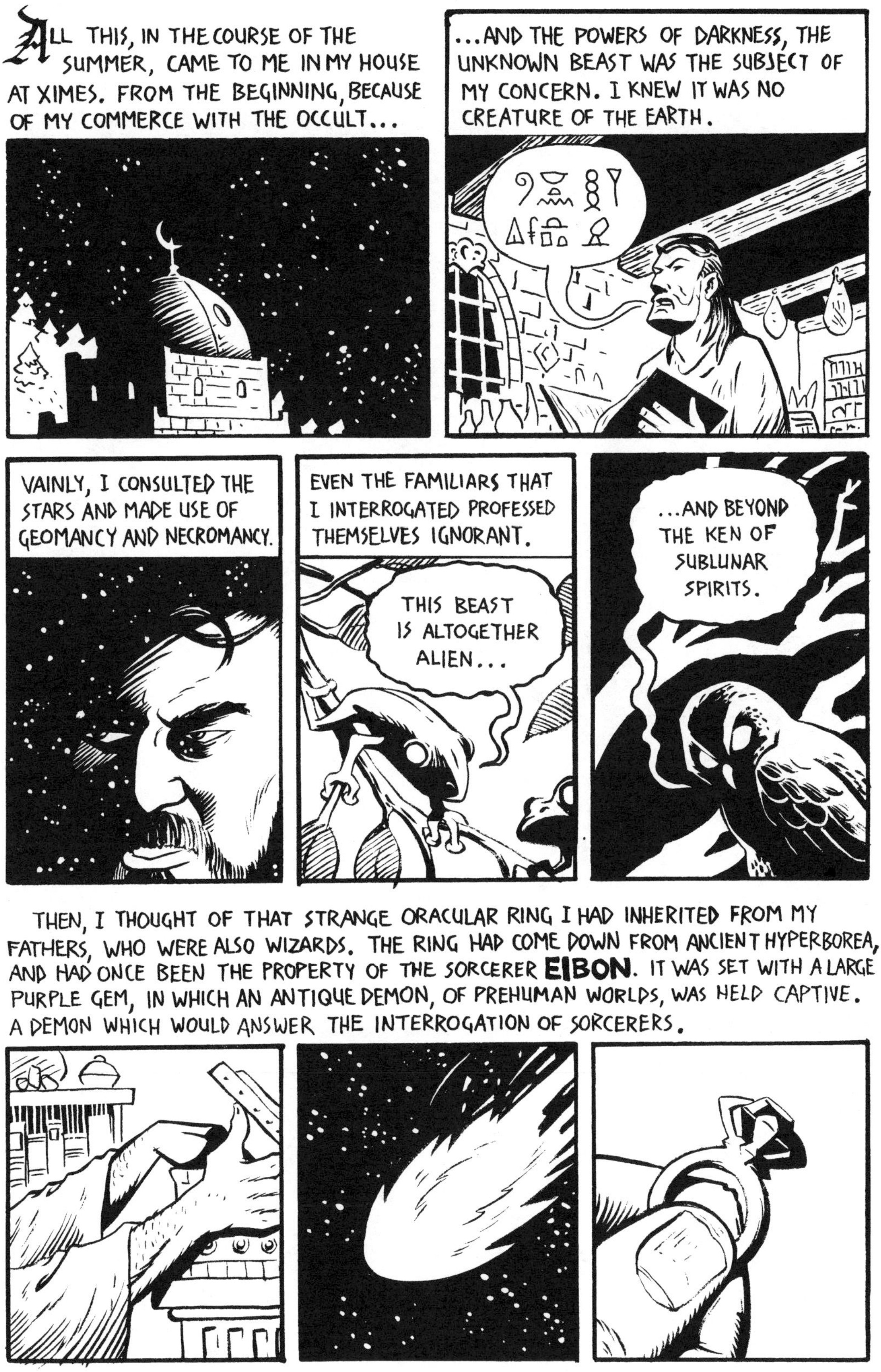
ALL THIS, IN THE COURSE OF THE SUMMER, CAME TO ME IN MY HOUSE AT XIMES. FROM THE BEGINNING, BECAUSE OF MY COMMERCE WITH THE OCCULT...
...AND THE POWERS OF DARKNESS, THE UNKNOWN BEAST WAS THE SUBJECT OF MY CONCERN. I KNEW IT WAS NO CREATURE OF THE EARTH.
VAINLY, I CONSULTED THE STARS AND MADE USE OF GEOMANCY AND NECROMANCY.
EVEN THE FAMILIARS THAT I INTERROGATED PROFESSED THEMSELVES IGNORANT.
THIS BEAST IS ALTOGETHER ALIEN...
...AND BEYOND THE KEN OF SUBLUNAR SPIRITS.
THEN, I THOUGHT OF THAT STRANGE ORACULAR RING I HAD INHERITED FROM MY FATHERS, WHO WERE ALSO WIZARDS. THE RING HAD COME DOWN FROM ANCIENT HYPERBOREA, AND HAD ONCE BEEN THE PROPERTY OF THE SORCERER EIBON. IT WAS SET WITH A LARGE PURPLE GEM, IN WHICH AN ANTIQUE DEMON, OF PREHUMAN WORLDS, WAS HELD CAPTIVE. A DEMON WHICH WOULD ANSWER THE INTERROGATION OF SORCERERS.

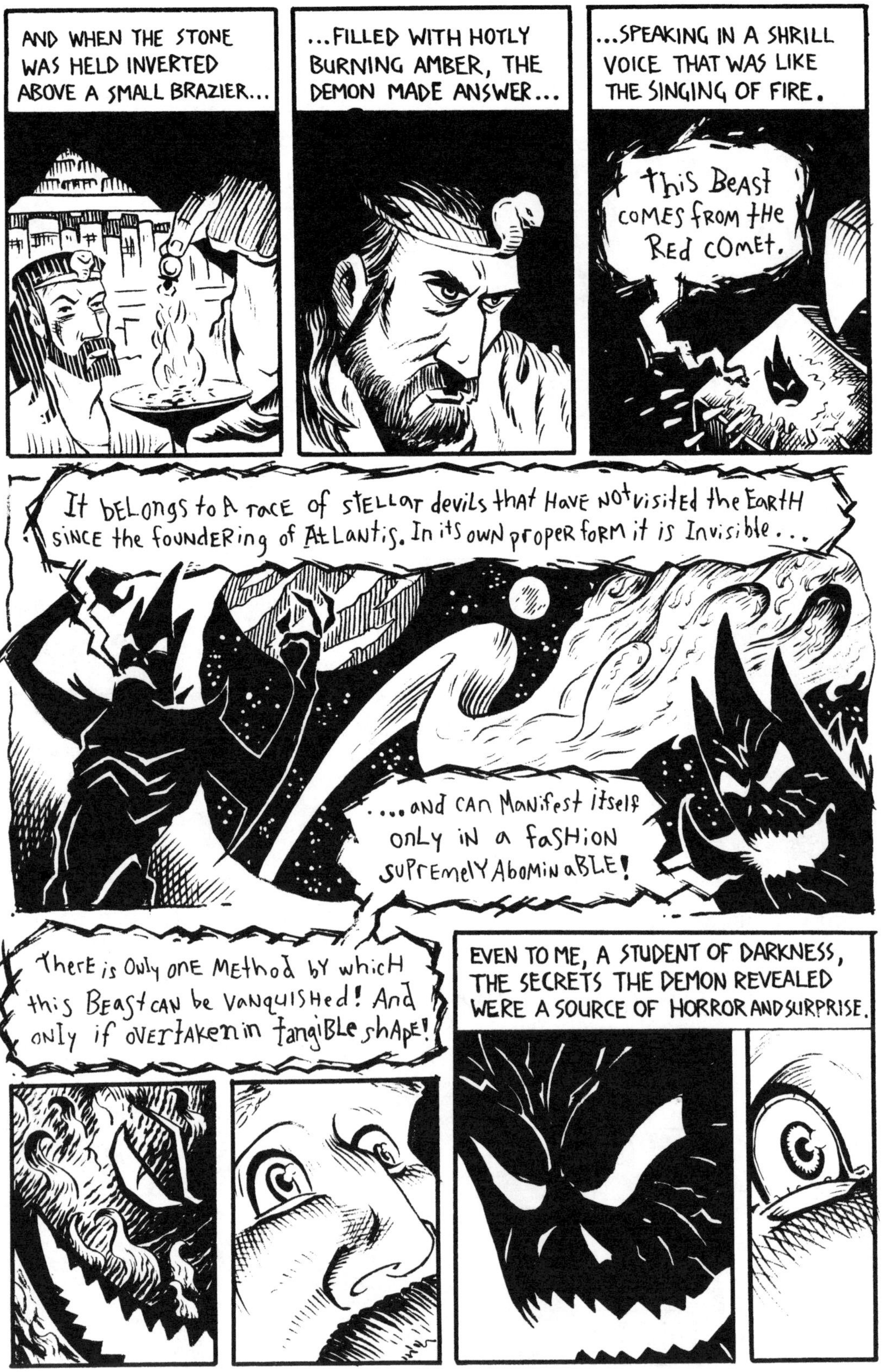
AND WHEN THE STONE WAS HELD INVERTED ABOVE A SMALL BRAZIER...
...FILLED WITH HOTLY BURNING AMBER, THE DEMON MADE ANSWER...
...SPEAKING IN A SHRILL VOICE THAT WAS LIKE THE SINGING OF FIRE.
This Beast comes from the Red comet.
It belongs to a race of stellar devils that have not visited the Earth since the foundering of Atlantis. In its own proper form it is invisible...
...and can manifest itself only in a fashion supremely abominable!
There is only one method by which this Beast can be vanquished! And only if overtaken in tangible shape!
EVEN TO ME, A STUDENT OF DARKNESS, THE SECRETS THE DEMON REVEALED WERE A SOURCE OF HORROR AND SURPRISE.

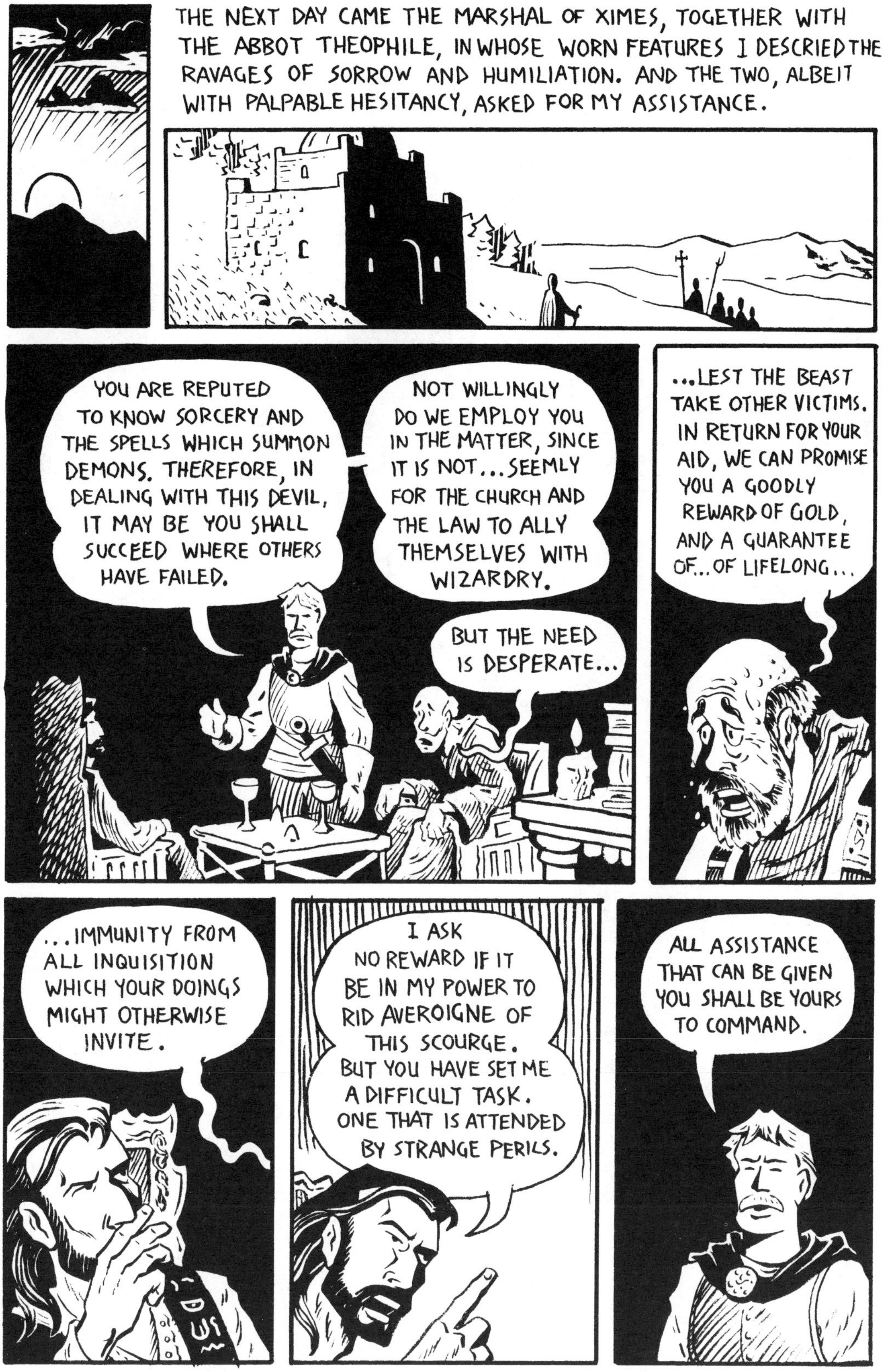
THE NEXT DAY CAME THE MARSHAL OF XIMES, TOGETHER WITH THE ABBOT THEOPHILE, IN WHOSE WORN FEATURES I DESCRIED THE RAVAGES OF SORROW AND HUMILIATION. AND THE TWO, ALBEIT WITH PALPABLE HESITANCY, ASKED FOR MY ASSISTANCE.
YOU ARE REPUTED TO KNOW SORCERY AND THE SPELLS WHICH SUMMON DEMONS. THEREFORE, IN DEALING WITH THIS DEVIL, IT MAY BE YOU SHALL SUCCEED WHERE OTHERS HAVE FAILED.
NOT WILLINGLY DO WE EMPLOY YOU IN THE MATTER, SINCE IT IS NOT... SEEMLY FOR THE CHURCH AND THE LAW TO ALLY THEMSELVES WITH WIZARDRY.
BUT THE NEED IS DESPERATE...
...LEST THE BEAST TAKE OTHER VICTIMS. IN RETURN FOR YOUR AID, WE CAN PROMISE YOU A GOODLY REWARD OF GOLD, AND A GUARANTEE OF... OF LIFELONG...
...IMMUNITY FROM ALL INQUISITION WHICH YOUR DOINGS MIGHT OTHERWISE INVITE.
I ASK NO REWARD IF IT BE IN MY POWER TO RID AVEROIGNE OF THIS SCOURGE. BUT YOU HAVE SET ME A DIFFICULT TASK. ONE THAT IS ATTENDED BY STRANGE PERILS.
ALL ASSISTANCE THAT CAN BE GIVEN YOU SHALL BE YOURS TO COMMAND.

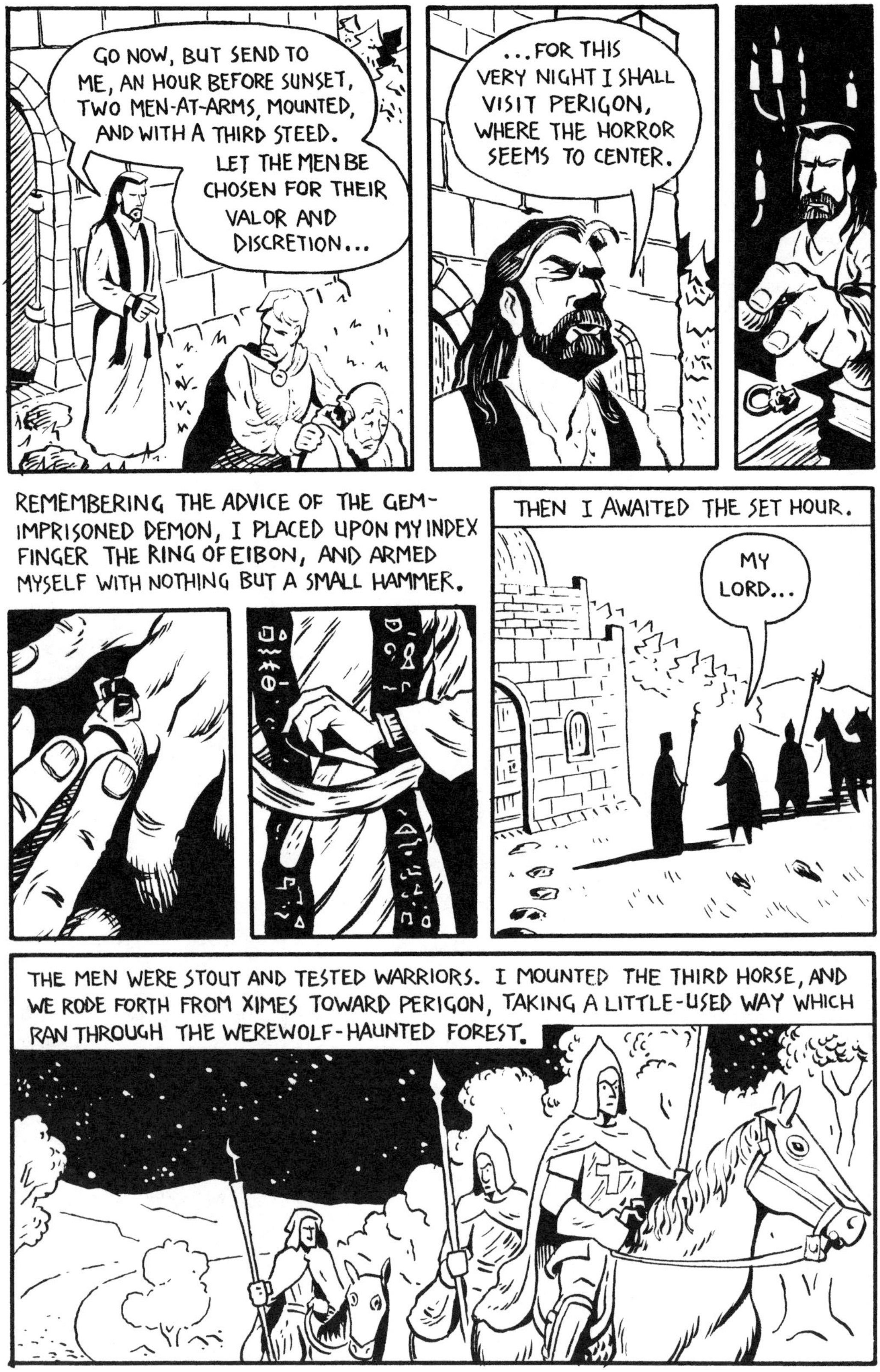
GO NOW, BUT SEND TO ME, AN HOUR BEFORE SUNSET, TWO MEN-AT-ARMS, MOUNTED, AND WITH A THIRD STEED.
LET THE MEN BE CHOSEN FOR THEIR VALOR AND DISCRETION...
...FOR THIS VERY NIGHT I SHALL VISIT PERIGON, WHERE THE HORROR SEEMS TO CENTER.
REMEMBERING THE ADVICE OF THE GEM-IMPRISONED DEMON, I PLACED UPON MY INDEX FINGER THE RING OF EIBON, AND ARMED MYSELF WITH NOTHING BUT A SMALL HAMMER.
THEN I AWAITED THE SET HOUR.
MY LORD...
THE MEN WERE STOUT AND TESTED WARRIORS. I MOUNTED THE THIRD HORSE, AND WE RODE FORTH FROM XIMES TOWARD PERIGON, TAKING A LITTLE-USED WAY WHICH RAN THROUGH THE WEREWOLF-HAUNTED FOREST.

WE CAME TO THE ABBEY AT LATE MOONRISE, WHEN ALL THE MONKS, EXCEPT THE AGED PORTER, HAD RETIRED TO THEIR DORMITORY.

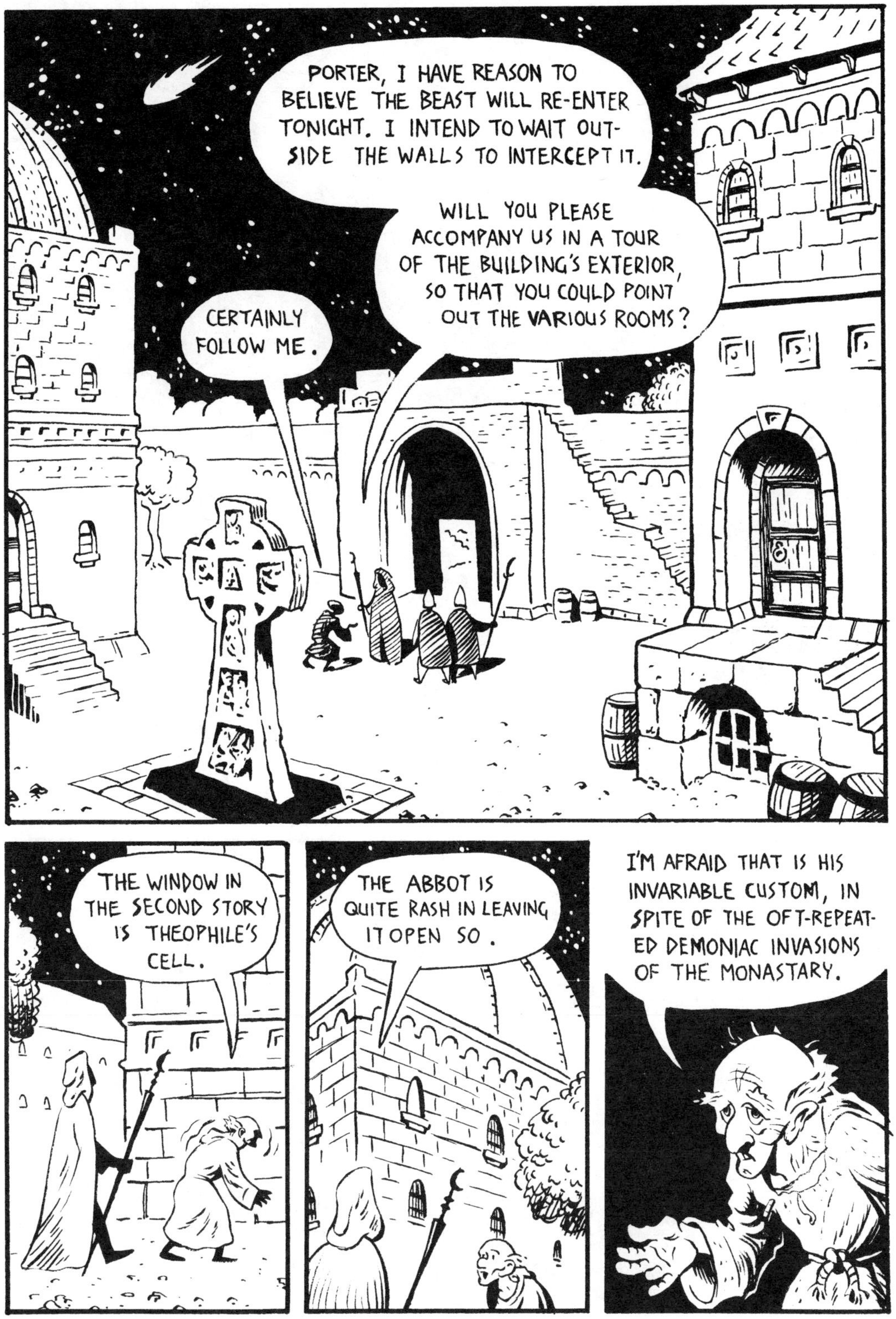
PORTER, I HAVE REASON TO BELIEVE THE BEAST WILL RE-ENTER TONIGHT. I INTEND TO WAIT OUTSIDE THE WALLS TO INTERCEPT IT.
WILL YOU PLEASE ACCOMPANY US IN A TOUR OF THE BUILDING'S EXTERIOR, SO THAT YOU COULD POINT OUT THE VARIOUS ROOMS?
CERTAINLY FOLLOW ME.
THE WINDOW IN THE SECOND STORY IS THEOPHILE'S CELL.
THE ABBOT IS QUITE RASH IN LEAVING IT OPEN SO.
I'M AFRAID THAT IS HIS INVARIABLE CUSTOM, IN SPITE OF THE OFT-REPEATED DEMONIAC INVASIONS OF THE MONASTARY.

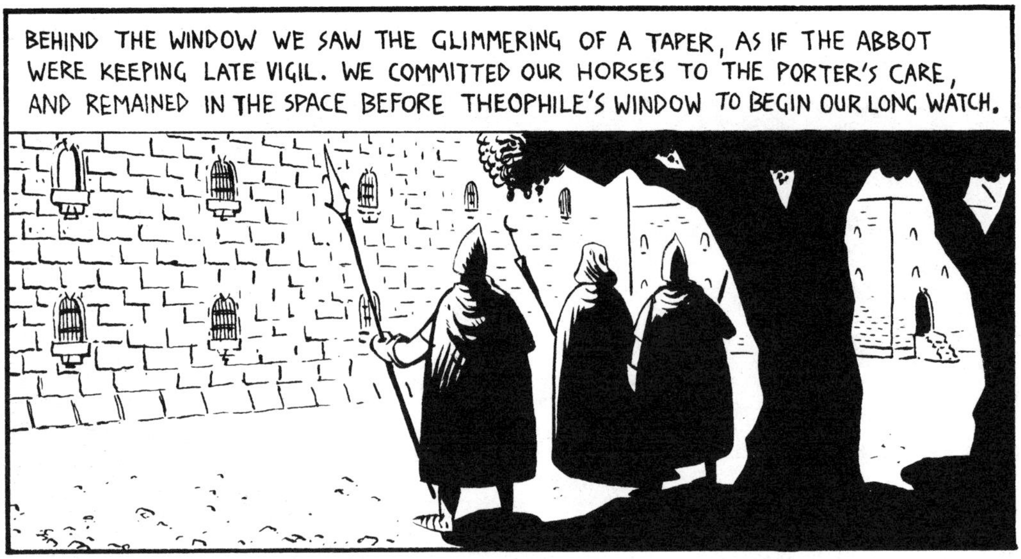
BEHIND THE WINDOW WE SAW THE GLIMMERING OF A TAPER, AS IF THE ABBOT WERE KEEPING LATE VIGIL. WE COMMITTED OUR HORSES TO THE PORTER'S CARE, AND REMAINED IN THE SPACE BEFORE THEOPHILE'S WINDOW TO BEGIN OUR LONG WATCH.

WE WAITED HOUR BY HOUR IN THE SHADOW OF A TALL OAK, WHERE NONE COULD SEE US FROM THE WINDOWS. WHEN THE MOON HAD PASSED OVER, THE SHADOW BEGAN TO LENGTHEN.

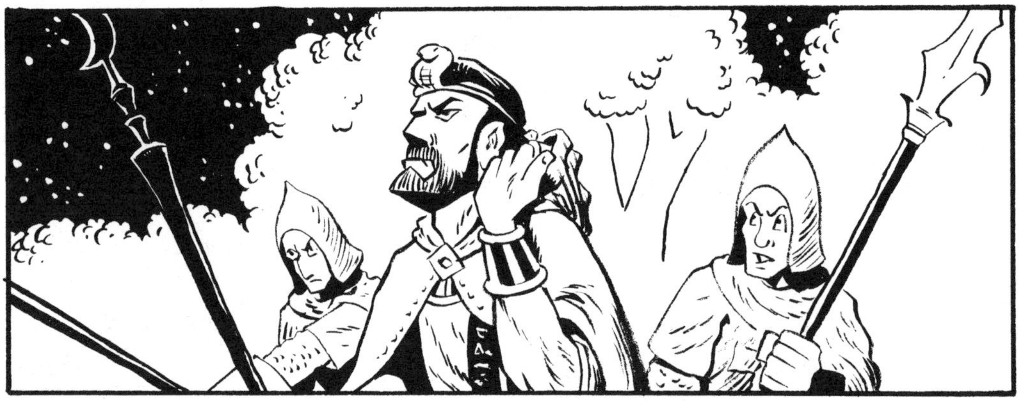

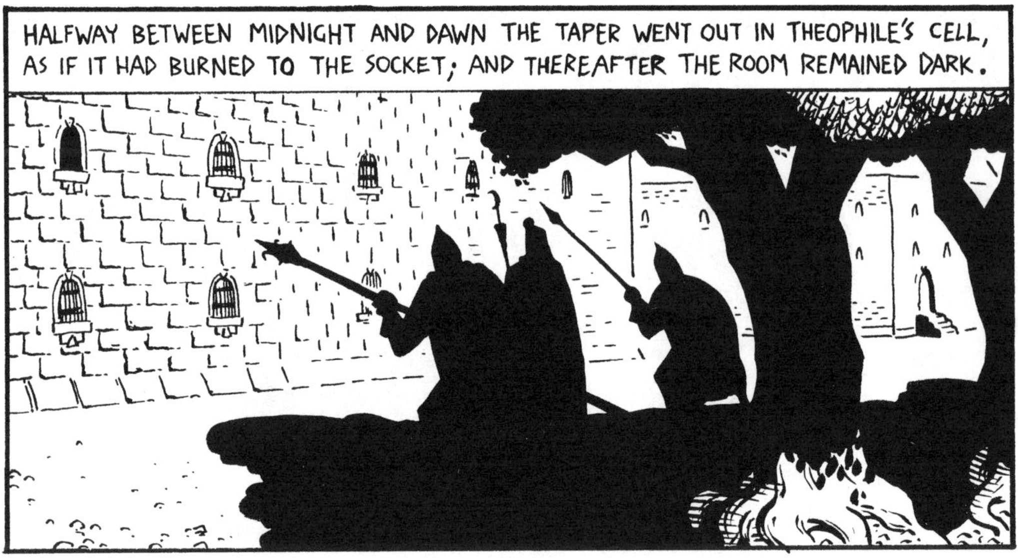
HALFWAY BETWEEN MIDNIGHT AND DAWN THE TAPER WENT OUT IN THEOPHILE'S CELL, AS IF IT HAD BURNED TO THE SOCKET; AND THEREAFTER THE ROOM REMAINED DARK.

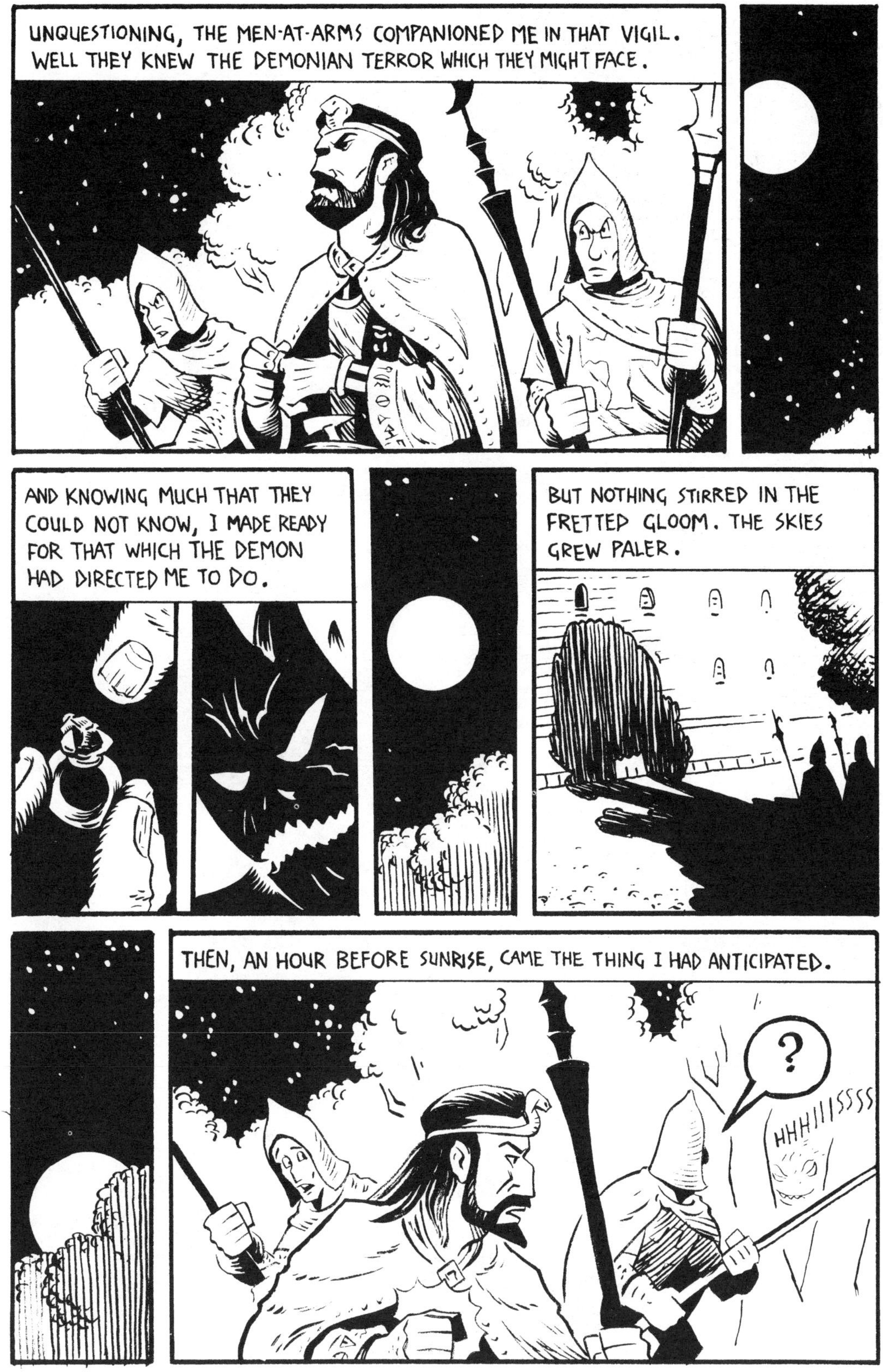
UNQUESTIONING, THE MEN-AT-ARMS COMPANIONED ME IN THAT VIGIL. WELL THEY KNEW THE DEMONIAN TERROR WHICH THEY MIGHT FACE.
AND KNOWING MUCH THAT THEY COULD NOT KNOW, I MADE READY FOR THAT WHICH THE DEMON HAD DIRECTED ME TO DO.
BUT NOTHING STIRRED IN THE FRETTED GLOOM. THE SKIES GREW PALER.
THEN, AN HOUR BEFORE SUNRISE, CAME THE THING I HAD ANTICIPATED.
?
HHH||||SSSS

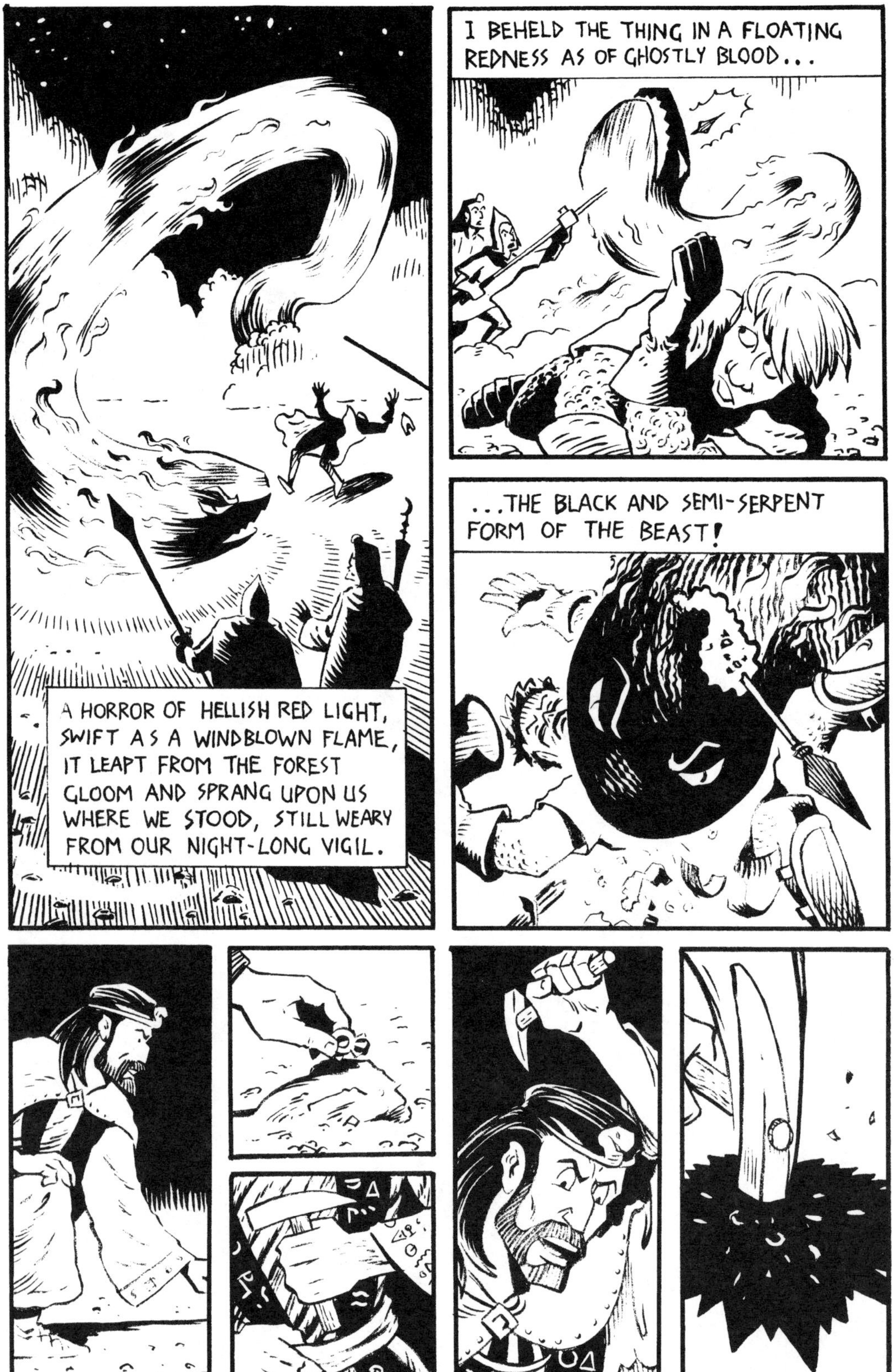
A HORROR OF HELLISH RED LIGHT, SWIFT AS A WINDBLOWN FLAME, IT LEAPT FROM THE FOREST GLOOM AND SPRANG UPON US WHERE WE STOOD, STILL WEARY FROM OUR NIGHT-LONG VIGIL.
I BEHELD THE THING IN A FLOATING REDNESS AS OF GHOSTLY BLOOD...
...THE BLACK AND SEMI-SERPENT FORM OF THE BEAST!

FROM THE PIECES OF ITS SHATTERED PRISON, THE DEMON ROSE, HISSING WITH THE VOICE OF FIRE AND BRIGHTENING TO A WRATHFUL, TERRIBLE GOLD!

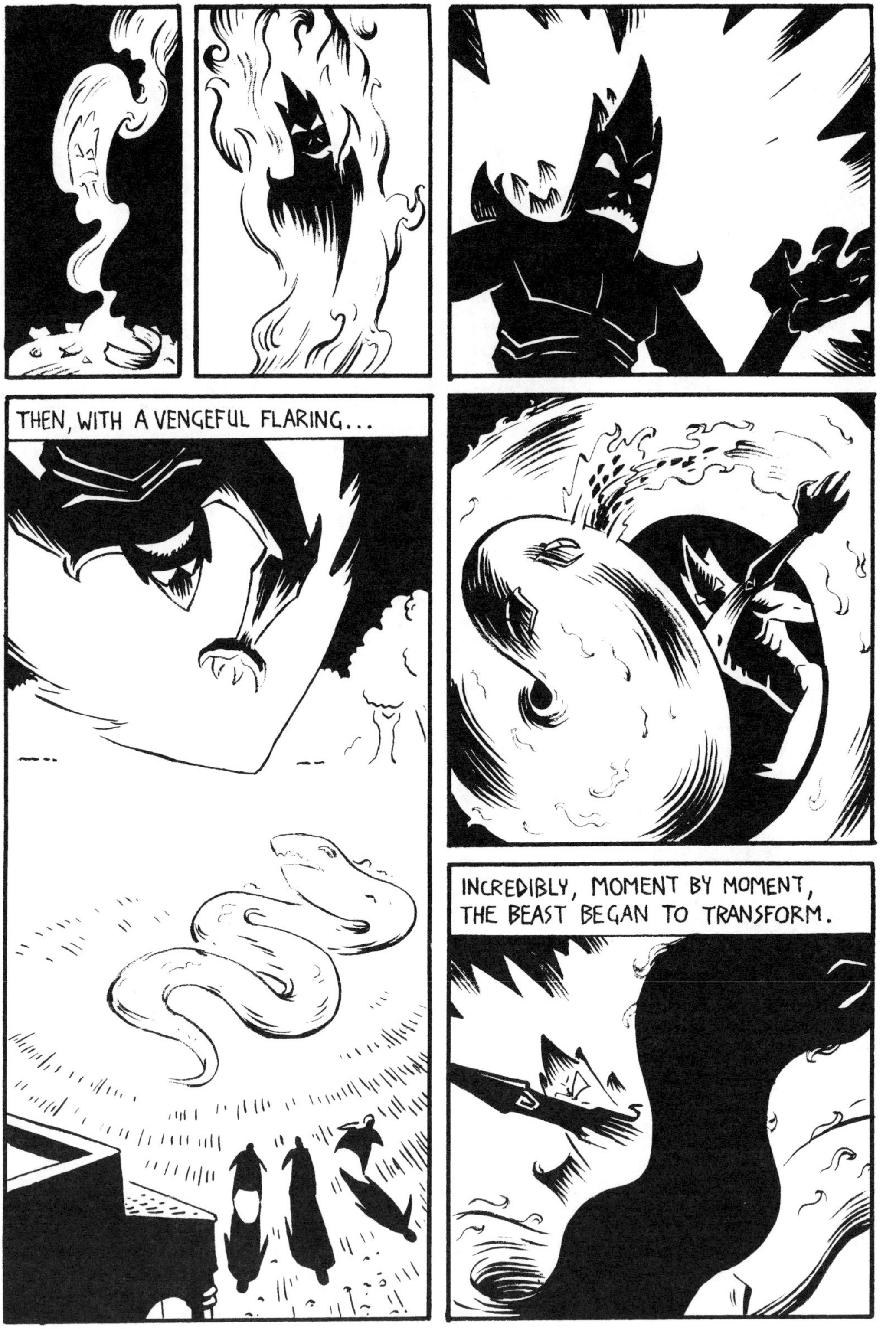
THEN, WITH A VENGEFUL FLARING...
INCREDIBLY, MOMENT BY MOMENT, THE BEAST BEGAN TO TRANSFORM.

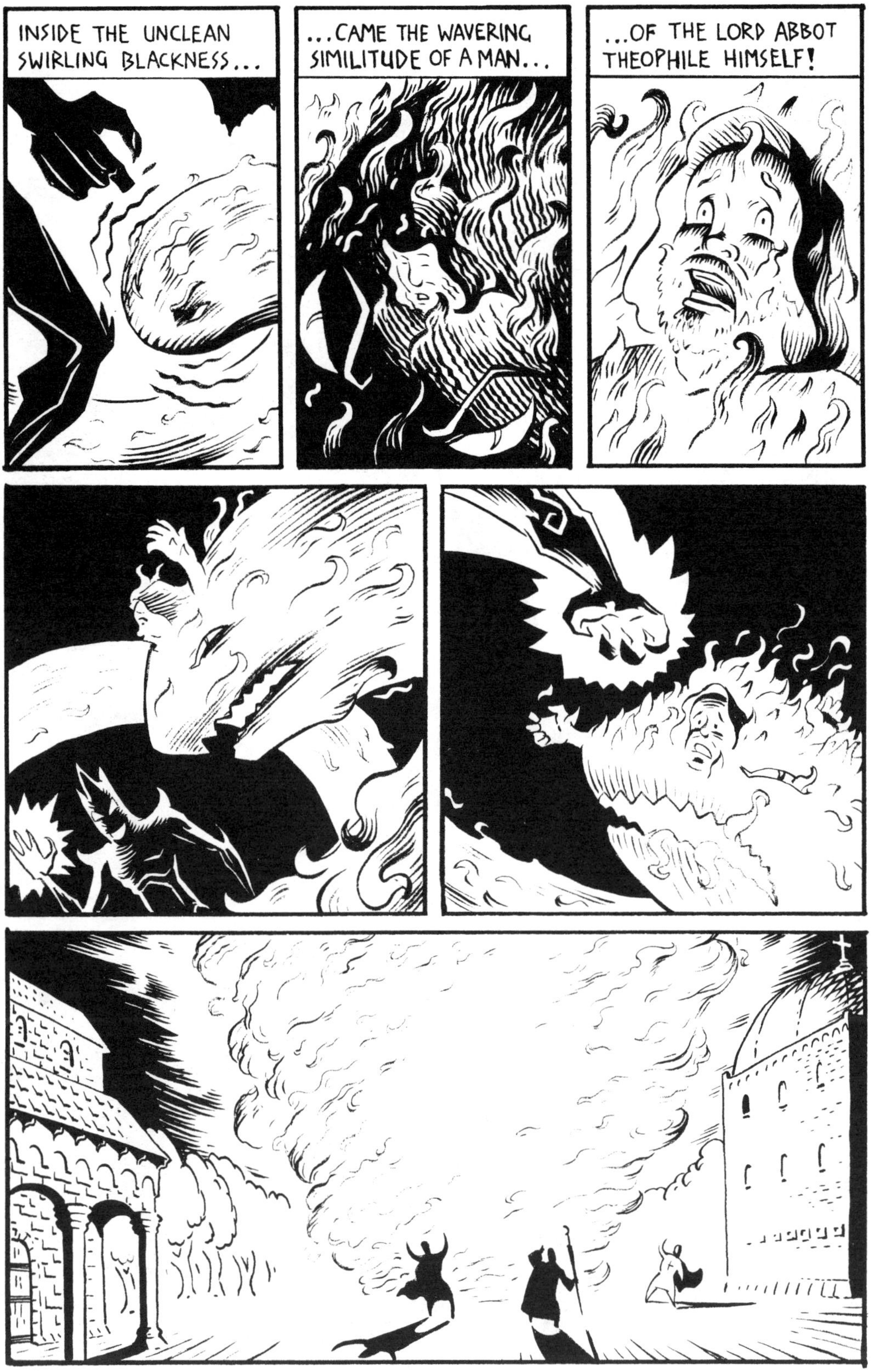
INSIDE THE UNCLEAN SWIRLING BLACKNESS...
...CAME THE WAVERING SIMILITUDE OF A MAN...
...OF THE LORD ABBOT THEOPHILE HIMSELF!

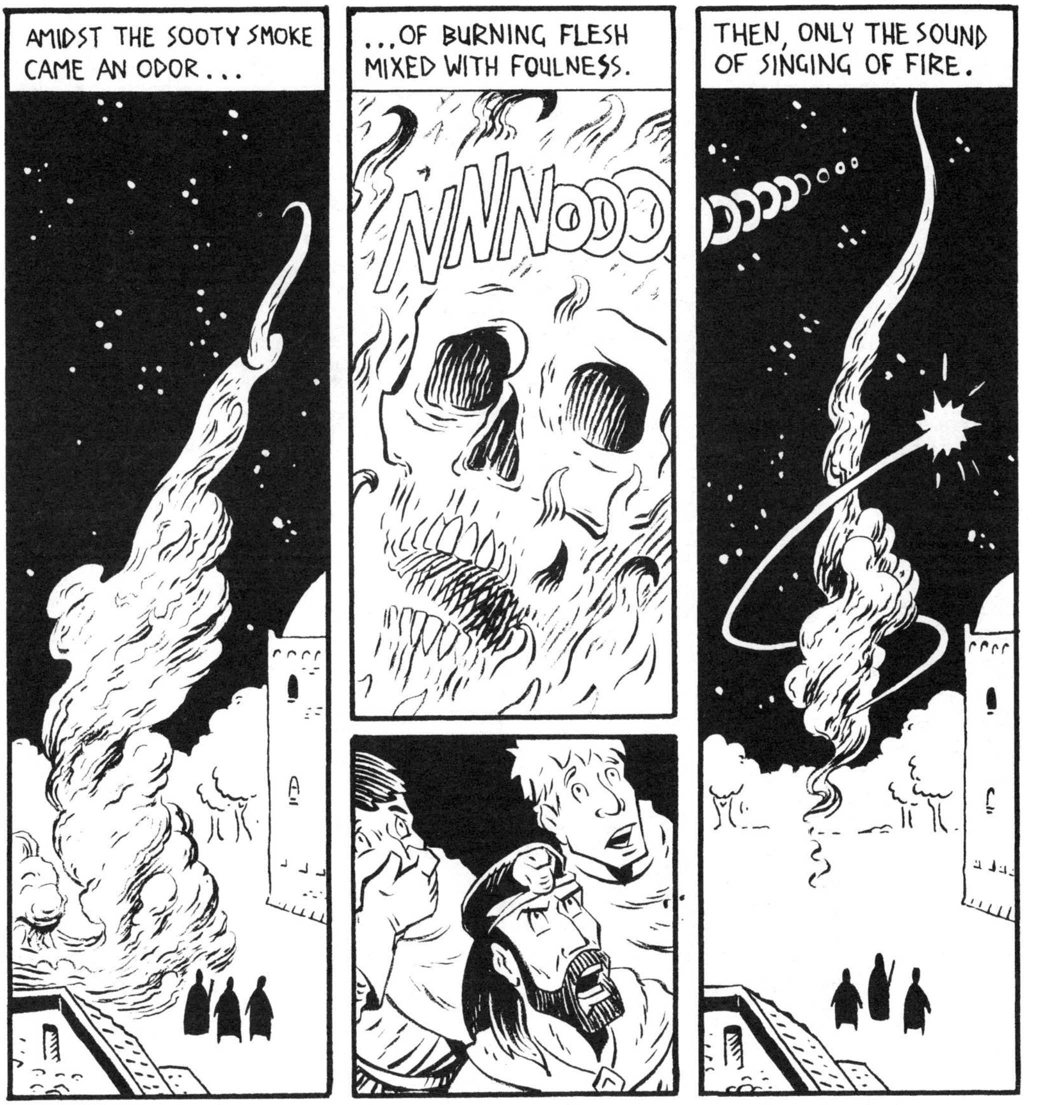
AMIDST THE SOOTY SMOKE CAME AN ODOR...
...OF BURNING FLESH MIXED WITH FOULNESS.
NNNOOO
THEN, ONLY THE SOUND OF SINGING OF FIRE.

I KNEW THAT THE DEMON OF THE RING HAD FULFILLED ITS PROMISE. NOW IT HAD GONE BACK TO THOSE REMOTE DEEPS FROM WHICH THE SORCERER EIBON HAD DRAWN IT DOWN TO BECOME THE CAPTIVE OF THE PURPLE GEM.

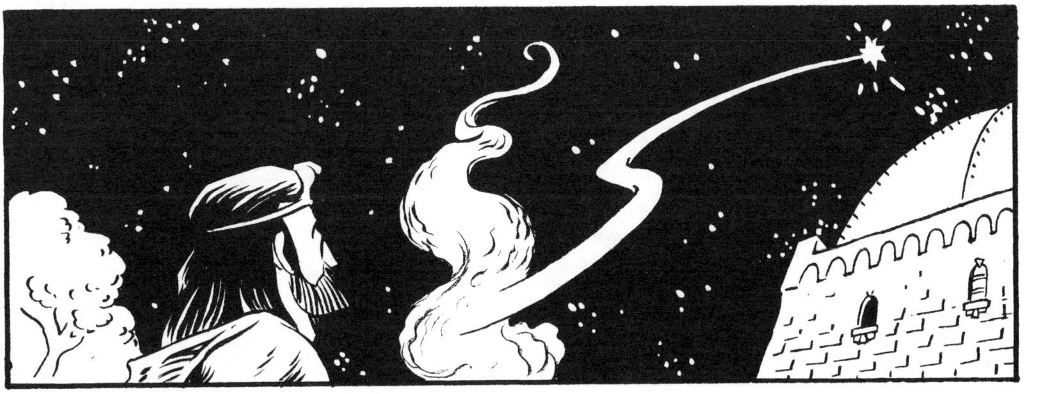

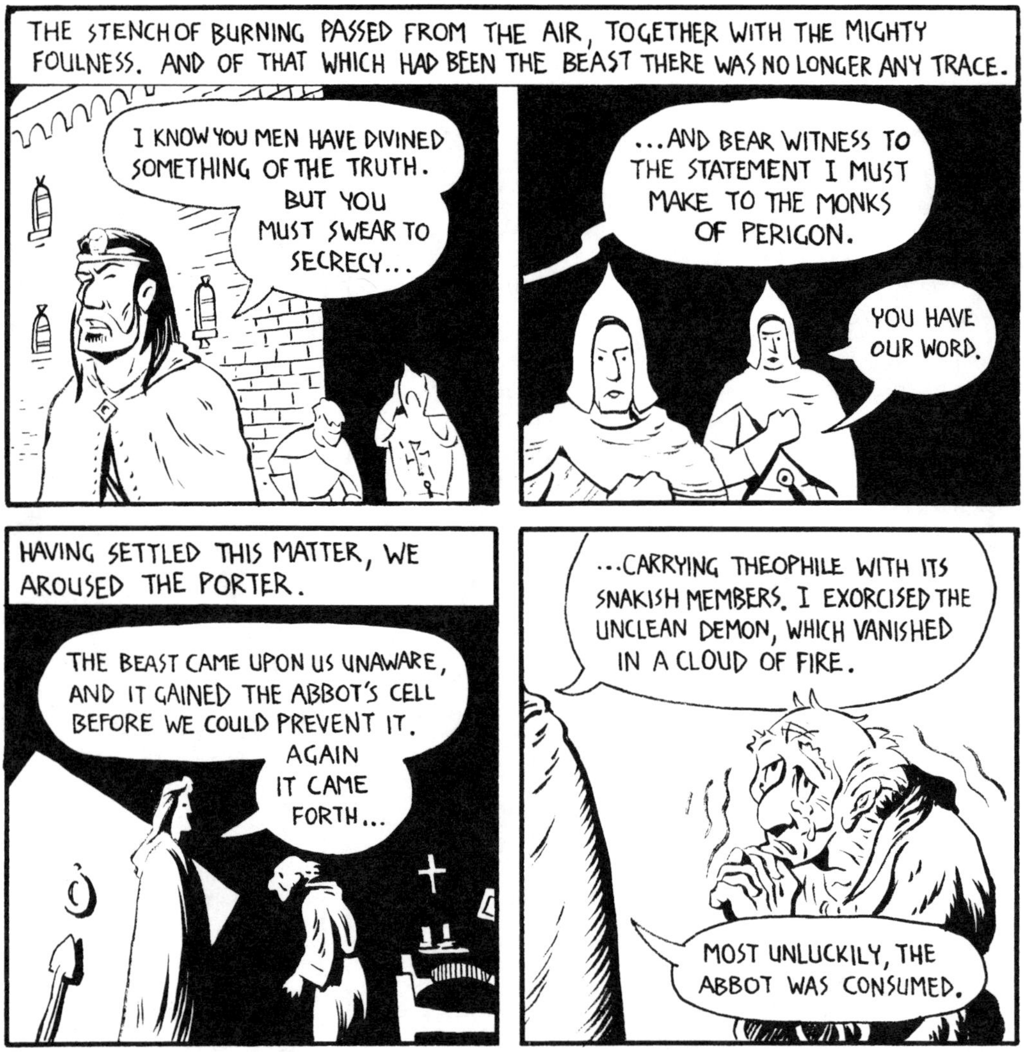
THE STENCH OF BURNING PASSED FROM THE AIR, TOGETHER WITH THE MIGHTY FOULNESS. AND OF THAT WHICH HAD BEEN THE BEAST THERE WAS NO LONGER ANY TRACE.
I KNOW YOU MEN HAVE DIVINED SOMETHING OF THE TRUTH. BUT YOU MUST SWEAR TO SECRECY...
...AND BEAR WITNESS TO THE STATEMENT I MUST MAKE TO THE MONKS OF PERIGON.
YOU HAVE OUR WORD.
HAVING SETTLED THIS MATTER, WE AROUSED THE PORTER.
THE BEAST CAME UPON US UNAWARE, AND IT GAINED THE ABBOT'S CELL BEFORE WE COULD PREVENT IT. AGAIN IT CAME FORTH...
...CARRYING THEOPHILE WITH ITS SNAKISH MEMBERS. I EXORCISED THE UNCLEAN DEMON, WHICH VANISHED IN A CLOUD OF FIRE.
MOST UNLUCKILY, THE ABBOT WAS CONSUMED.

THIS TALE WAS ACCEPTED WITHOUT QUESTION BY THE BROTHERS, WHO GRIEVED MIGHTILY. IT WAS TRUE ENOUGH, FOR THEOPHILE HAD BEEN WHOLLY IGNORANT OF THE FOUL CHANGE THAT CAME UPON HIM NIGHTLY IN HIS CELL, AND THE DEEDS DONE BY THE BEAST THROUGH HIS LOATHFULLY TRANSFIGURED BODY.

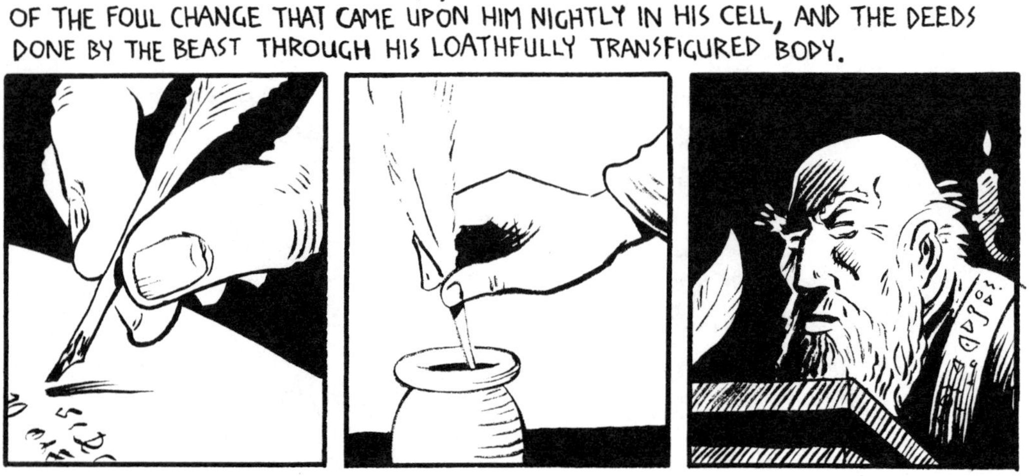

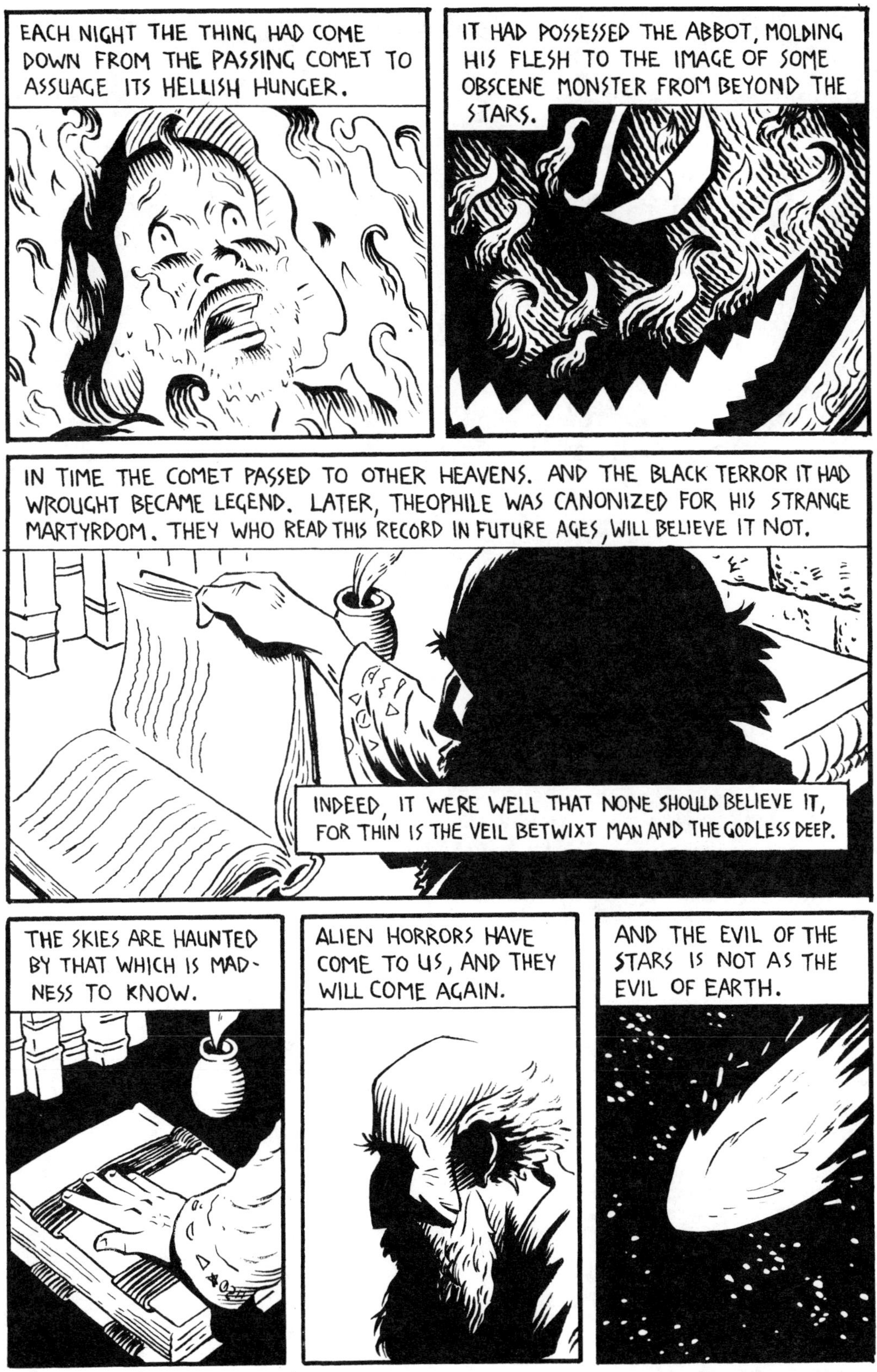
EACH NIGHT THE THING HAD COME DOWN FROM THE PASSING COMET TO ASSUAGE ITS HELLISH HUNGER.
IT HAD POSSESSED THE ABBOT, MOLDING HIS FLESH TO THE IMAGE OF SOME OBSCENE MONSTER FROM BEYOND THE STARS.
IN TIME THE COMET PASSED TO OTHER HEAVENS. AND THE BLACK TERROR IT HAD WROUGHT BECAME LEGEND. LATER, THEOPHILE WAS CANONIZED FOR HIS STRANGE MARTYRDOM. THEY WHO READ THIS RECORD IN FUTURE AGES, WILL BELIEVE IT NOT.
INDEED, IT WERE WELL THAT NONE SHOULD BELIEVE IT, FOR THIN IS THE VEIL BETWIXT MAN AND THE GODLESS DEEP.
THE SKIES ARE HAUNTED BY THAT WHICH IS MADNESS TO KNOW.
ALIEN HORRORS HAVE COME TO US, AND THEY WILL COME AGAIN.
AND THE EVIL OF THE STARS IS NOT AS THE EVIL OF EARTH.

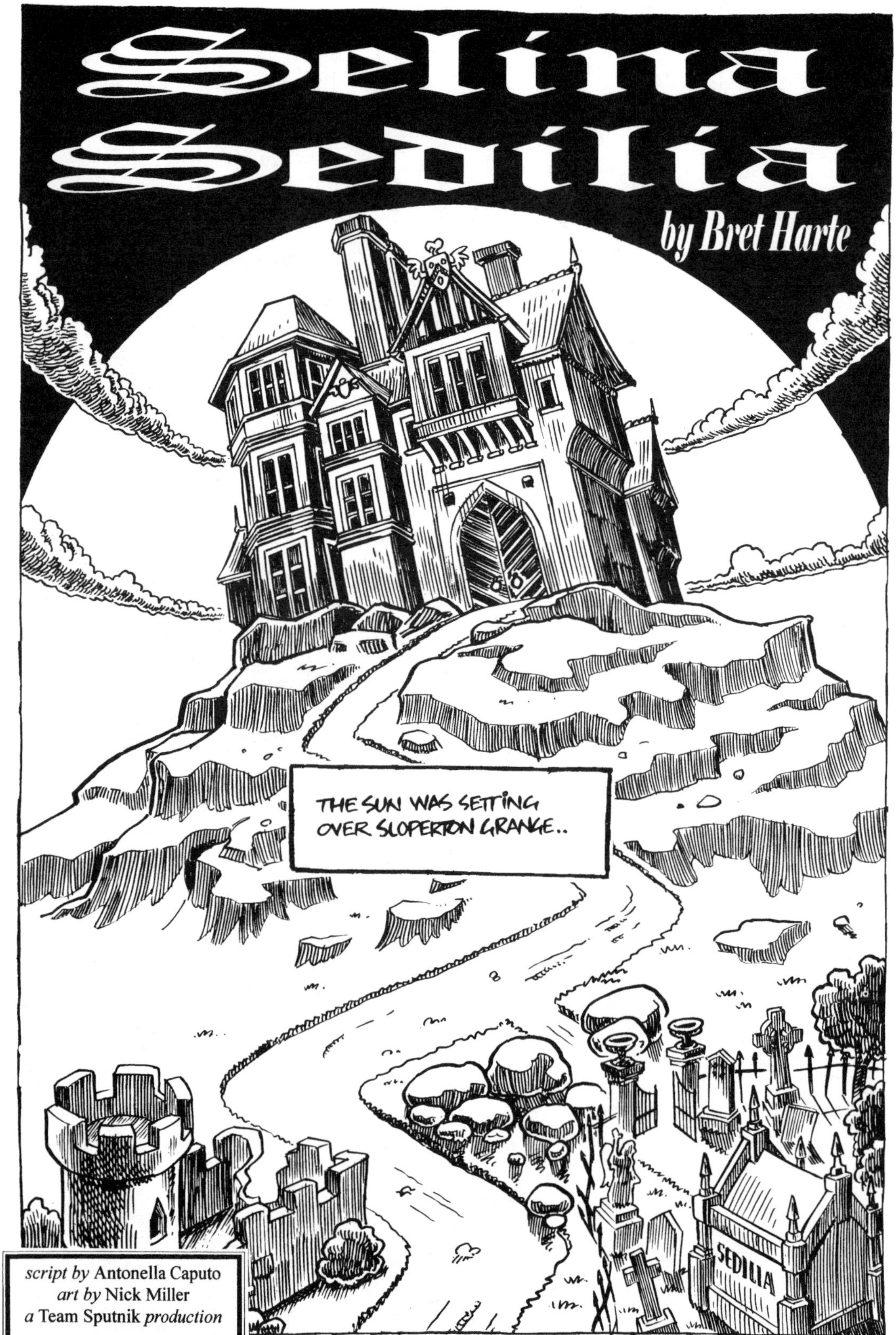
Selina Sedilia
by Bret Harte
THE SUN WAS SETTING OVER SLOPERTON GRANGE..
SEDILIA
script by Antonella Caputo
art by Nick Miller
a Team Sputnik *production*

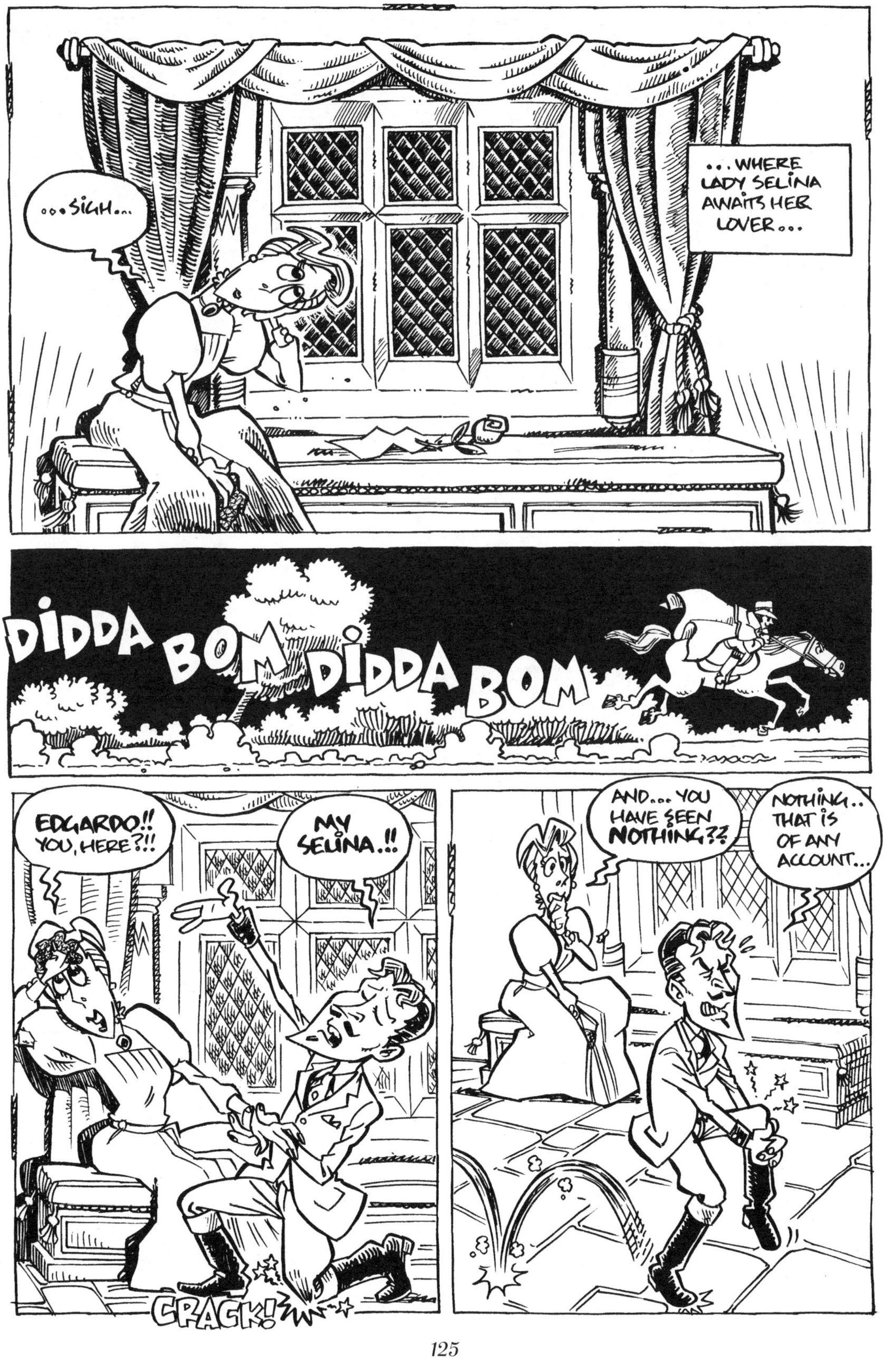
...SIGH...
...WHERE LADY SELINA AWAITS HER LOVER...
DIDDA BOM DIDDA BOM
EDGARDO!! YOU, HERE?!!
MY SELINA..!!
CRACK!
AND... YOU HAVE SEEN NOTHING??
NOTHING.. THAT IS OF ANY ACCOUNT...

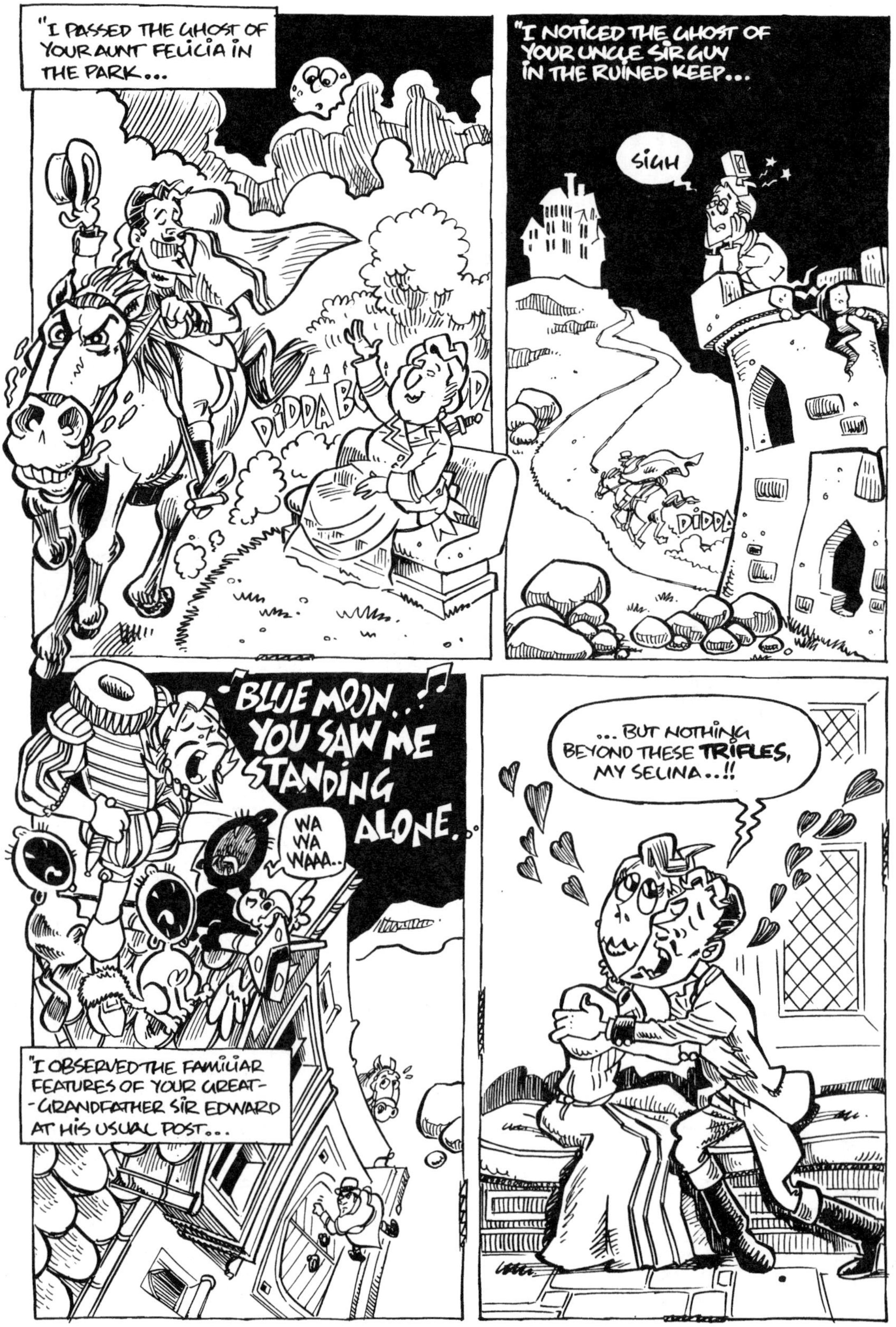
"I PASSED THE GHOST OF YOUR AUNT FELICIA IN THE PARK...
DIDDA BO
"I NOTICED THE GHOST OF YOUR UNCLE SIR GUY IN THE RUINED KEEP...
SIGH
DIDDA
BLUE MOON... YOU SAW ME STANDING ALONE.
WA WA WAAA...
"I OBSERVED THE FAMILIAR FEATURES OF YOUR GREAT-GRANDFATHER SIR EDWARD AT HIS USUAL POST...
... BUT NOTHING BEYOND THESE TRIFLES, MY SELINA..!!

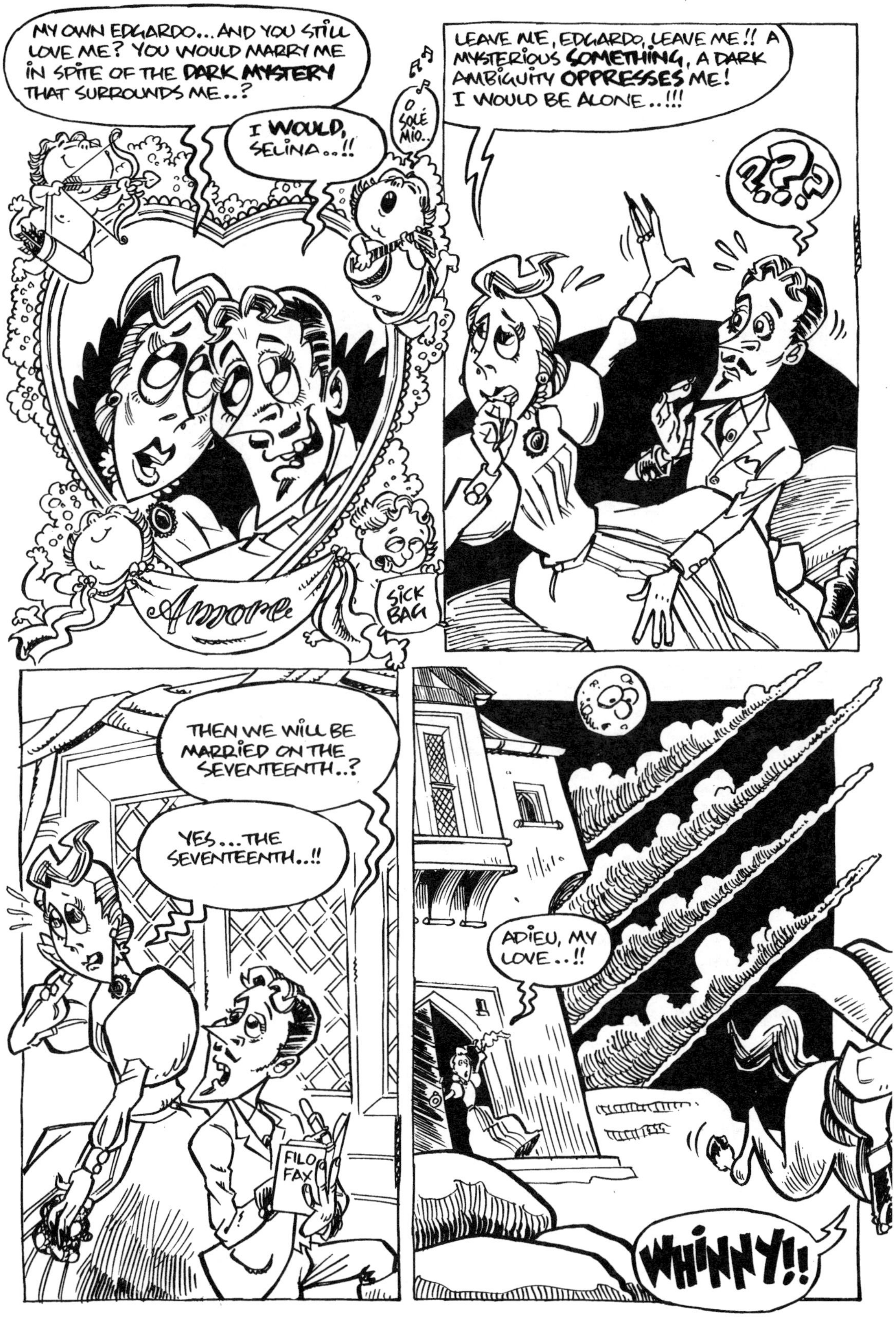
MY OWN EDGARDO... AND YOU STILL LOVE ME? YOU WOULD MARRY ME IN SPITE OF THE DARK MYSTERY THAT SURROUNDS ME..?
I WOULD, SELINA..!!
O SOLÉ MIO..
Amore
SICK BAG
LEAVE ME, EDGARDO, LEAVE ME!! A MYSTERIOUS SOMETHING, A DARK AMBIGUITY OPPRESSES ME! I WOULD BE ALONE..!!!
???
THEN WE WILL BE MARRIED ON THE SEVENTEENTH..?
YES...THE SEVENTEENTH..!!
FILO FAX
ADIEU, MY LOVE..!!
WHINNY!!

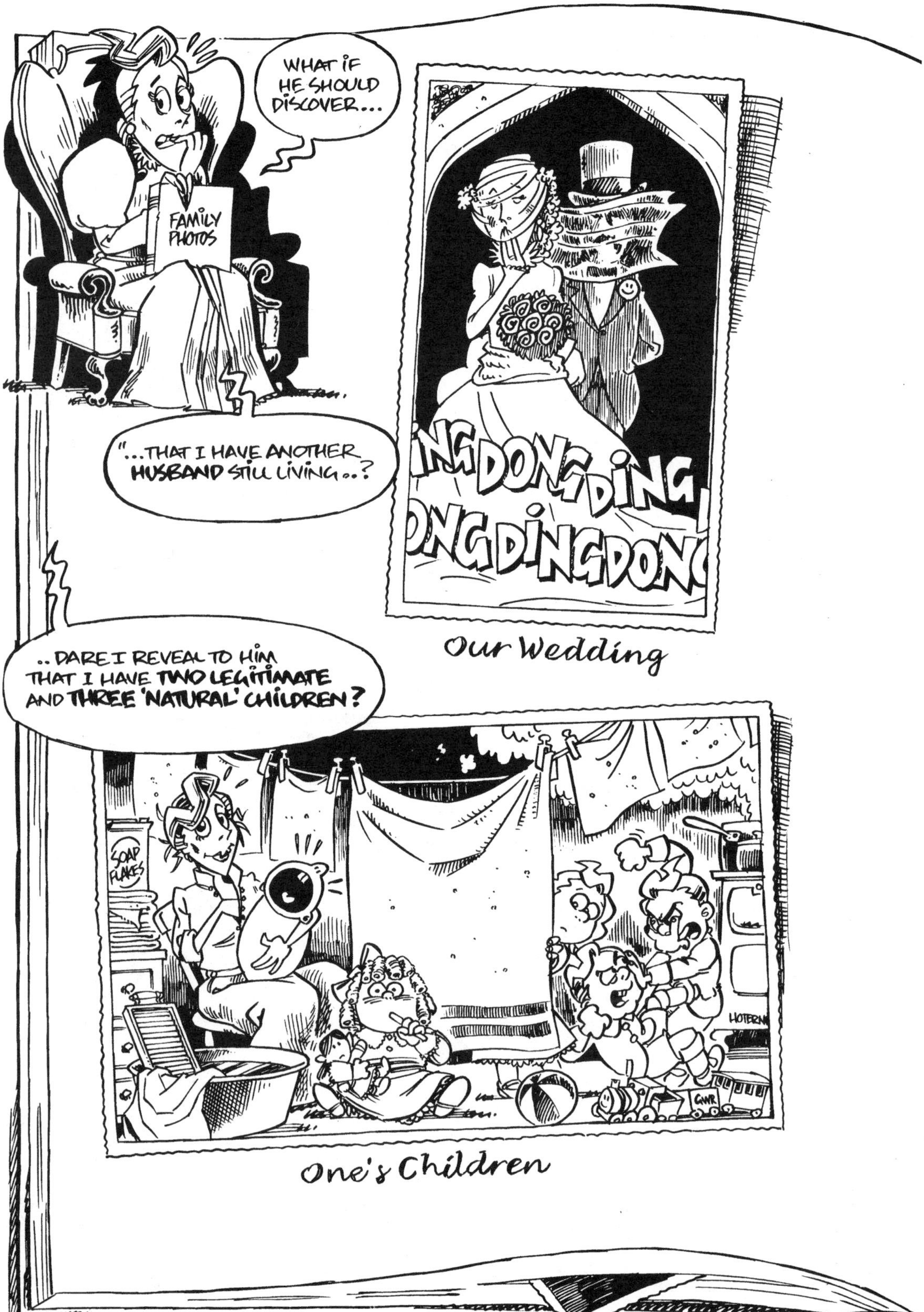
WHAT IF HE SHOULD DISCOVER...
FAMILY PHOTOS
"...THAT I HAVE ANOTHER HUSBAND STILL LIVING..?
INGDONGDING
ONGDINGDONG
Our Wedding
..DARE I REVEAL TO HIM THAT I HAVE TWO LEGITIMATE AND THREE 'NATURAL' CHILDREN?
SOAP FLAKES
GWR
One's Children

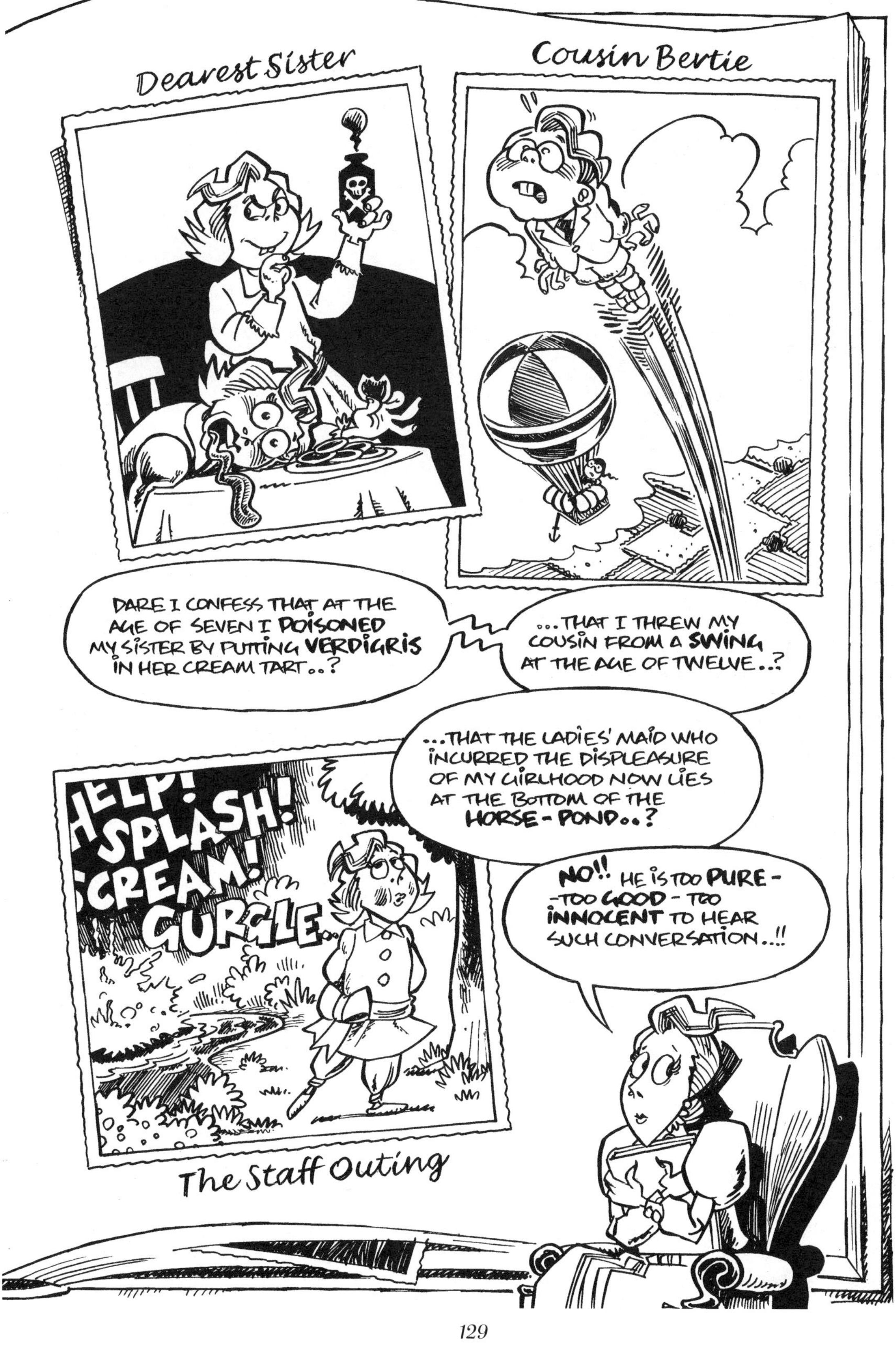
Dearest Sister
Cousin Bertie
DARE I CONFESS THAT AT THE AGE OF SEVEN I POISONED MY SISTER BY PUTTING VERDIGRIS IN HER CREAM TART..?
...THAT I THREW MY COUSIN FROM A SWING AT THE AGE OF TWELVE..?
...THAT THE LADIES' MAID WHO INCURRED THE DISPLEASURE OF MY GIRLHOOD NOW LIES AT THE BOTTOM OF THE HORSE-POND..?
HELP! SPLASH! SCREAM! GURGLE..
The Staff Outing
NO!! HE IS TOO PURE - TOO GOOD - TOO INNOCENT TO HEAR SUCH CONVERSATION..!!

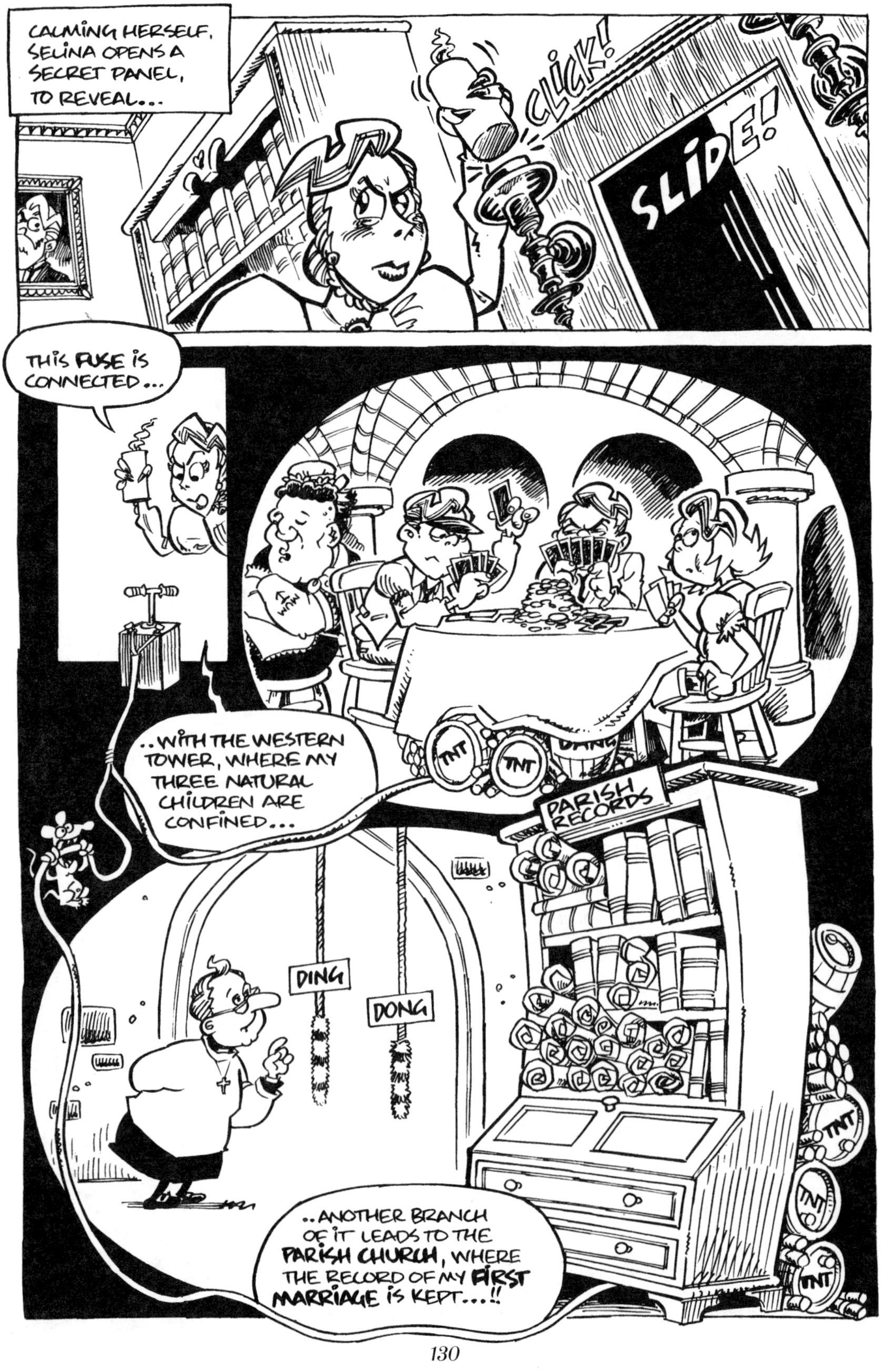
CALMING HERSELF, SELINA OPENS A SECRET PANEL, TO REVEAL...
CLICK!
SLIDE!
THIS FUSE IS CONNECTED...
..WITH THE WESTERN TOWER, WHERE MY THREE NATURAL CHILDREN ARE CONFINED...
TNT
TNT
PARISH RECORDS
DING
DONG
TNT
TNT
TNT
..ANOTHER BRANCH OF IT LEADS TO THE PARISH CHURCH, WHERE THE RECORD OF MY FIRST MARRIAGE IS KEPT...!!

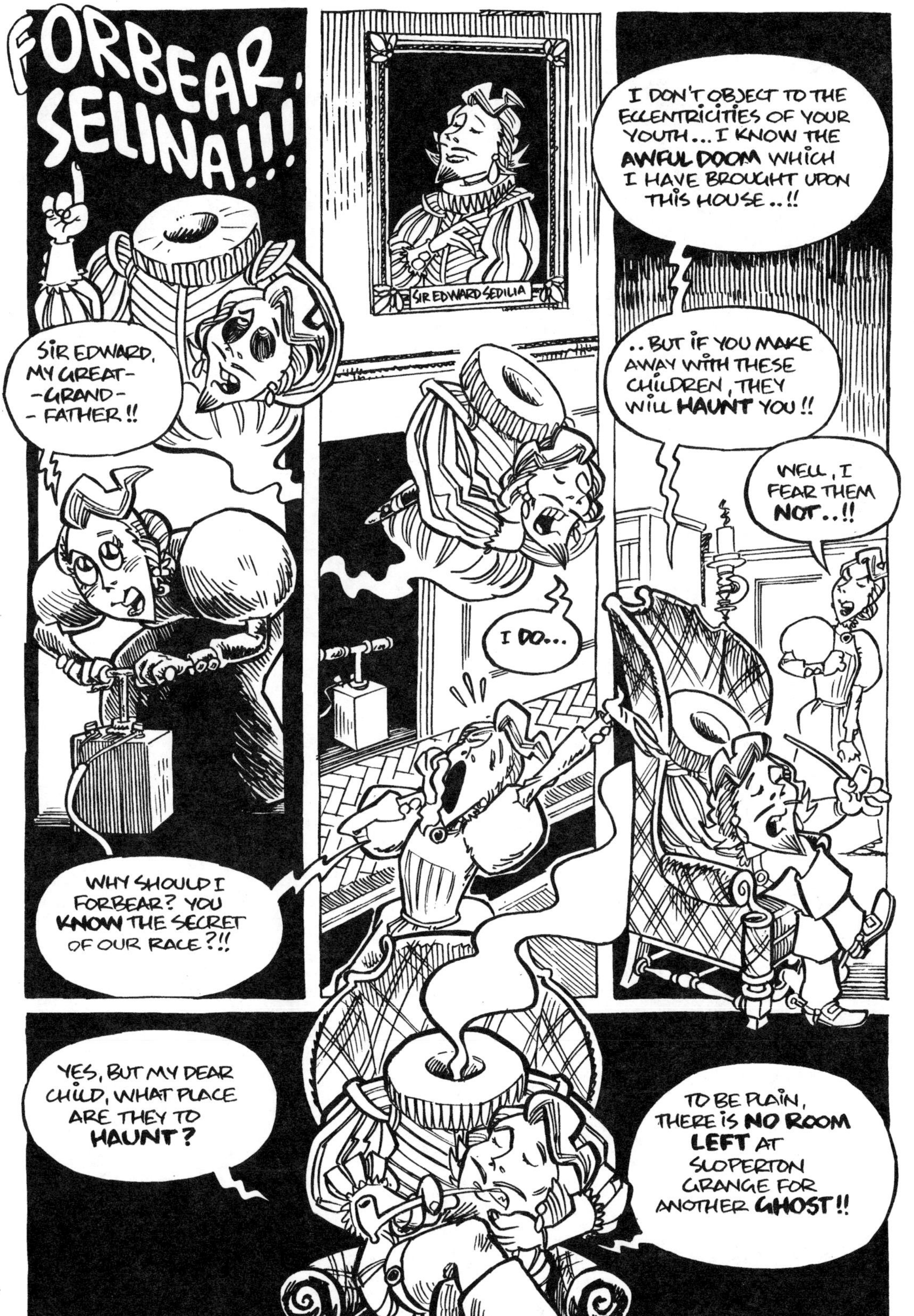
FORBEAR, SELINA!!!
SIR EDWARD, MY GREAT--GRAND--FATHER!!
WHY SHOULD I FORBEAR? YOU KNOW THE SECRET OF OUR RACE?!!
SIR EDWARD SEDILIA
I DO...
I DON'T OBJECT TO THE ECCENTRICITIES OF YOUR YOUTH... I KNOW THE AWFUL DOOM WHICH I HAVE BROUGHT UPON THIS HOUSE..!!
..BUT IF YOU MAKE AWAY WITH THESE CHILDREN, THEY WILL HAUNT YOU!!
WELL, I FEAR THEM NOT..!!
YES, BUT MY DEAR CHILD, WHAT PLACE ARE THEY TO HAUNT?
TO BE PLAIN, THERE IS NO ROOM LEFT AT SLOPERTON GRANGE FOR ANOTHER GHOST!!

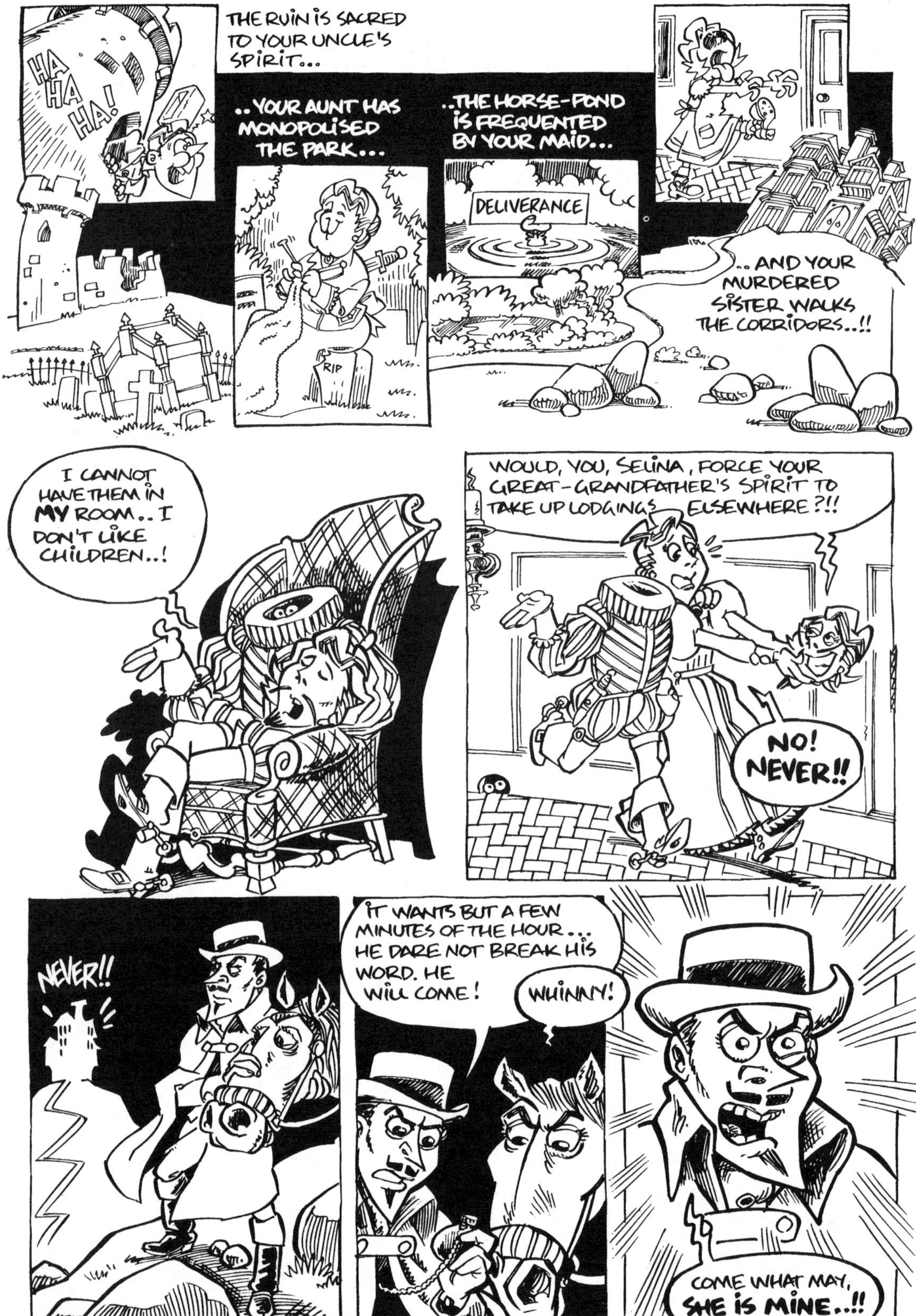
HA HA HA!
THE RUIN IS SACRED TO YOUR UNCLE'S SPIRIT...
..YOUR AUNT HAS MONOPOLISED THE PARK...
RIP
..THE HORSE-POND IS FREQUENTED BY YOUR MAID...
DELIVERANCE
..AND YOUR MURDERED SISTER WALKS THE CORRIDORS..!!
I CANNOT HAVE THEM IN MY ROOM.. I DON'T LIKE CHILDREN..!
WOULD, YOU, SELINA, FORCE YOUR GREAT-GRANDFATHER'S SPIRIT TO TAKE UP LODGINGS ELSEWHERE?!!
NO! NEVER!!
NEVER!!
IT WANTS BUT A FEW MINUTES OF THE HOUR... HE DARE NOT BREAK HIS WORD. HE WILL COME!
WHINNY!
COME WHAT MAY, SHE IS MINE..!!

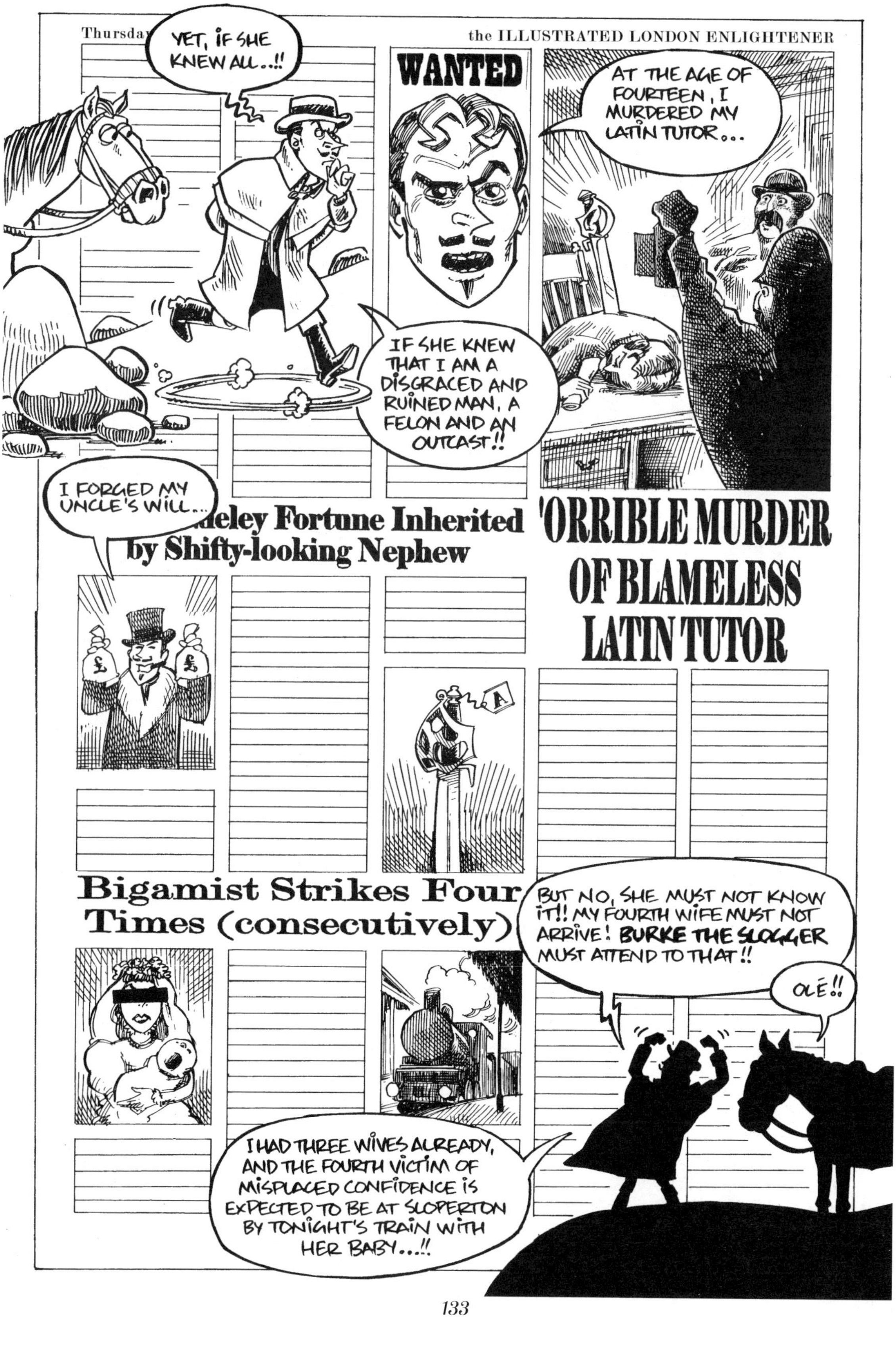
Thursday
the ILLUSTRATED LONDON ENLIGHTENER
YET, IF SHE KNEW ALL..!!
WANTED
AT THE AGE OF FOURTEEN, I MURDERED MY LATIN TUTOR...
IF SHE KNEW THAT I AM A DISGRACED AND RUINED MAN, A FELON AND AN OUTCAST!!
I FORGED MY UNCLE'S WILL...
meley Fortune Inherited by Shifty-looking Nephew
'ORRIBLE MURDER OF BLAMELESS LATIN TUTOR
A
Bigamist Strikes Four Times (consecutively)
BUT NO, SHE MUST NOT KNOW IT!! MY FOURTH WIFE MUST NOT ARRIVE! BURKE THE SLOGGER MUST ATTEND TO THAT!!
OLÉ!!
I HAD THREE WIVES ALREADY, AND THE FOURTH VICTIM OF MISPLACED CONFIDENCE IS EXPECTED TO BE AT SLOPERTON BY TONIGHT'S TRAIN WITH HER BABY...!!

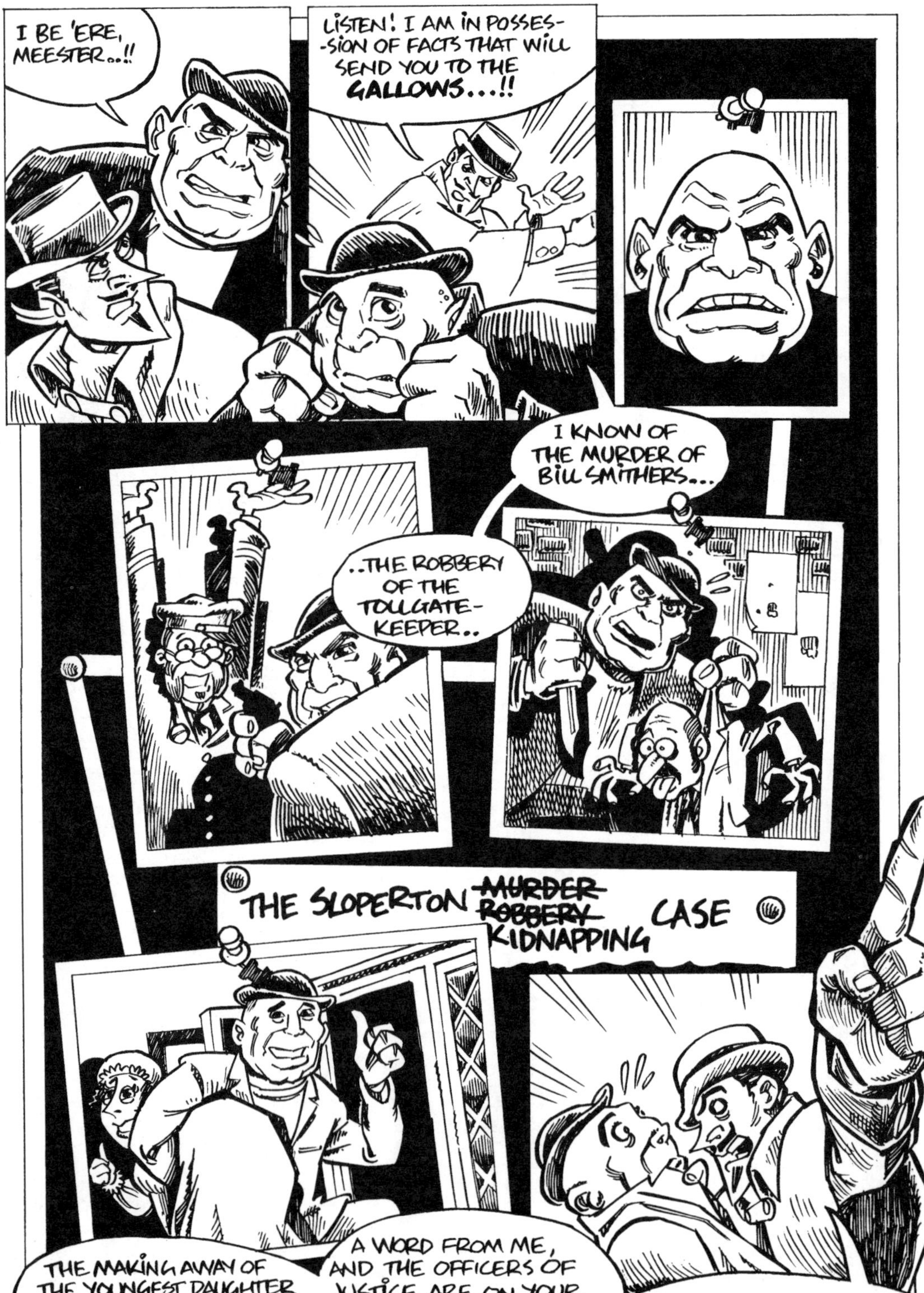
I BE 'ERE, MEESTER..!!
LISTEN! I AM IN POSSESSION OF FACTS THAT WILL SEND YOU TO THE GALLOWS...!!
I KNOW OF THE MURDER OF BILL SMITHERS...
..THE ROBBERY OF THE TOLLGATE-KEEPER..
THE SLOPERTON MURDER ROBBERY KIDNAPPING CASE
THE MAKING AWAY OF THE YOUNGEST DAUGHTER OF SIR REGINALD DE WALTON..!!
A WORD FROM ME, AND THE OFFICERS OF JUSTICE ARE ON YOUR TRACK, BUT SERVE ME, AND I MAY SERVE YOU..!!
THE 5:30 TRAIN FROM CLAPHAM IS DUE AT SLOPERTON AT 9:25! IT MUST NOT ARRIVE!!

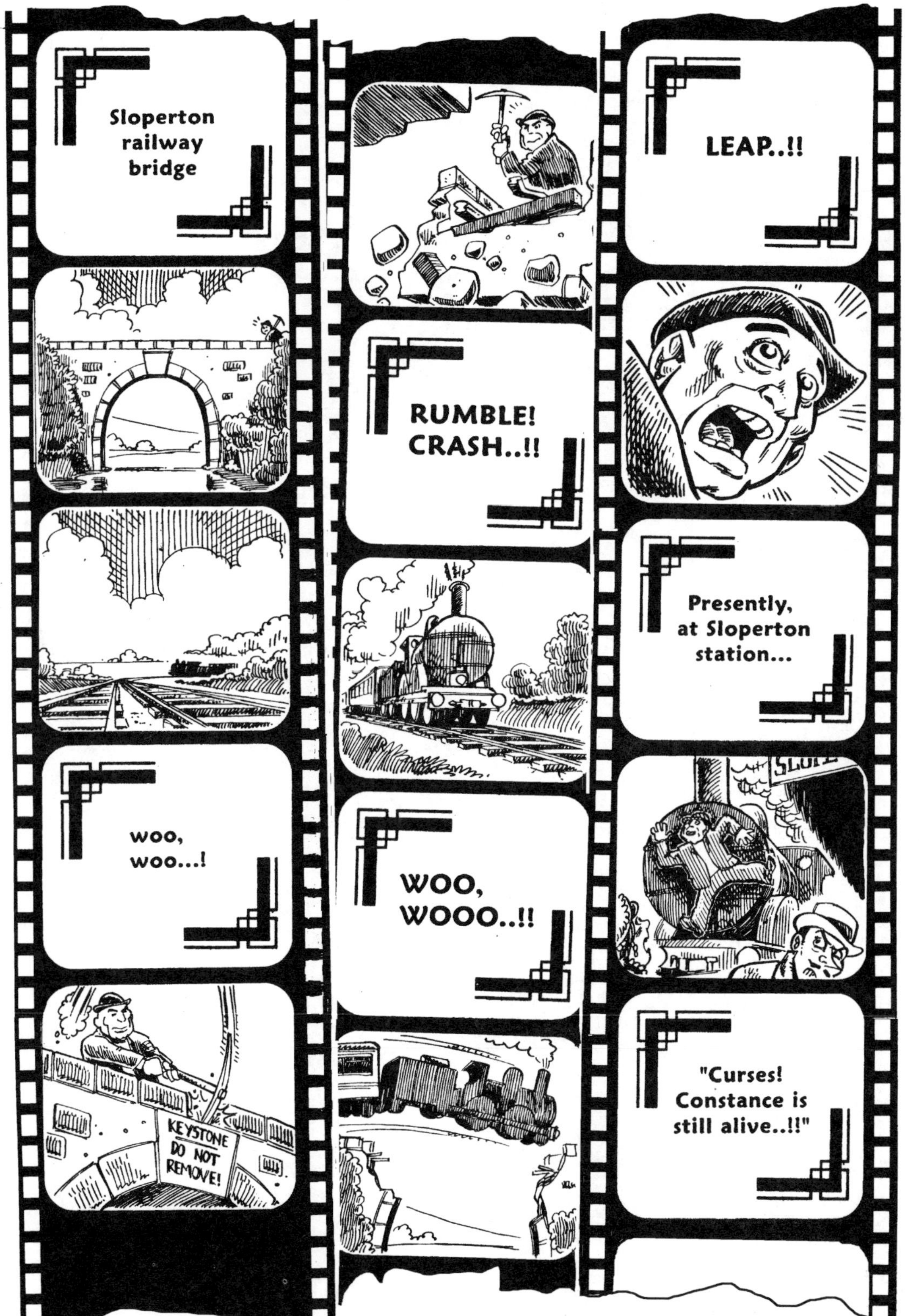
Sloperton
railway
bridge
woo,
woo...!
KEYSTONE
DO NOT
REMOVE!
RUMBLE!
CRASH..!!
WOO,
WOOO..!!
LEAP..!!
Presently,
at Sloperton
station...
"Curses!
Constance is
still alive..!!"

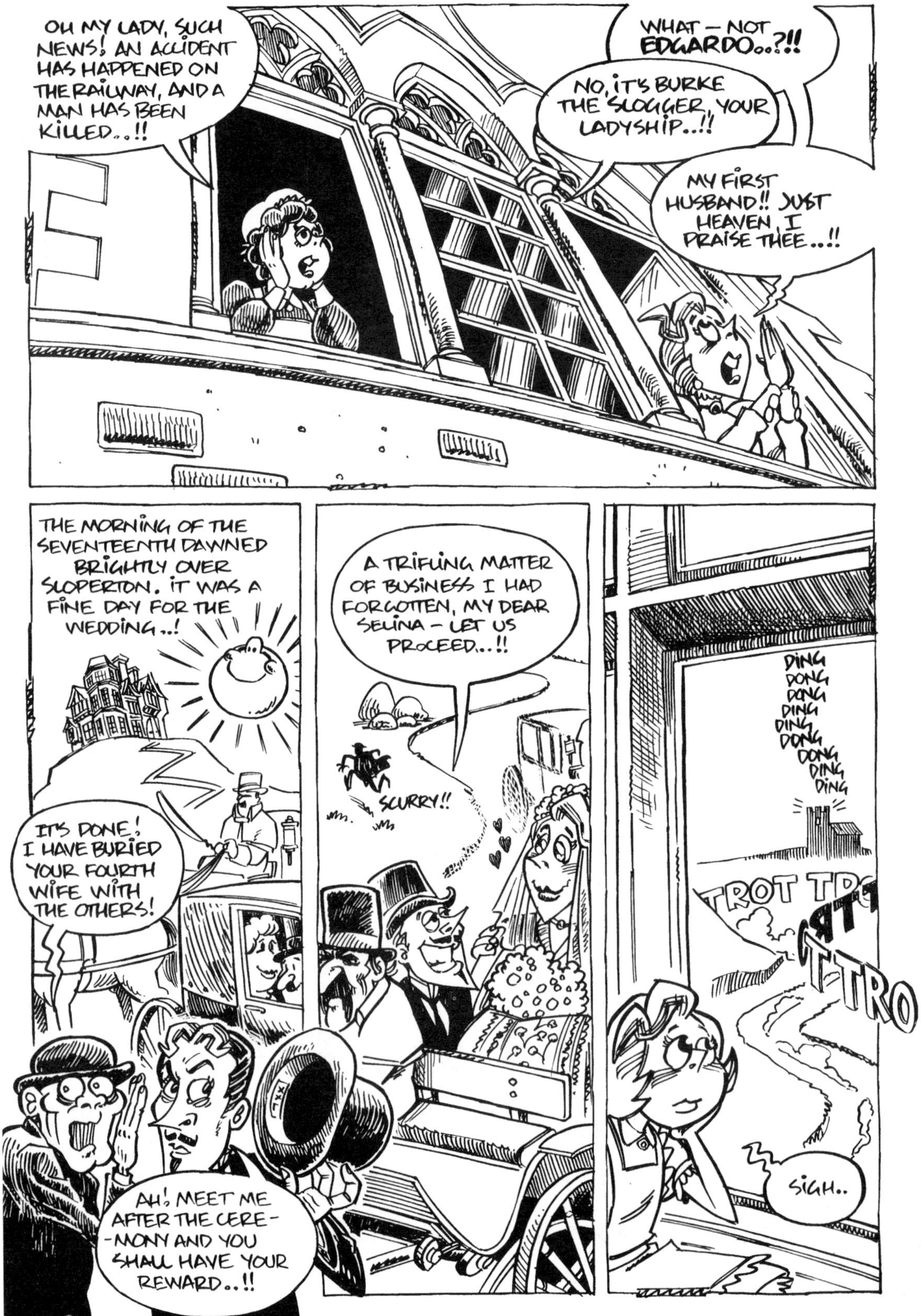
OH MY LADY, SUCH NEWS! AN ACCIDENT HAS HAPPENED ON THE RAILWAY, AND A MAN HAS BEEN KILLED..!!
WHAT — NOT EDGARDO..?!!
NO, IT'S BURKE THE 'SLOGGER,' YOUR LADYSHIP..!!
MY FIRST HUSBAND!! JUST HEAVEN I PRAISE THEE..!!
THE MORNING OF THE SEVENTEENTH DAWNED BRIGHTLY OVER SLOPERTON. IT WAS A FINE DAY FOR THE WEDDING..!
IT'S DONE! I HAVE BURIED YOUR FOURTH WIFE WITH THE OTHERS!
AH! MEET ME AFTER THE CERE-MONY AND YOU SHALL HAVE YOUR REWARD..!!
A TRIFLING MATTER OF BUSINESS I HAD FORGOTTEN, MY DEAR SELINA — LET US PROCEED..!!
SCURRY!!
DING DONG DONG DING DING DONG DONG DING DING
TROT TROT
TROT TROT
SIGH..

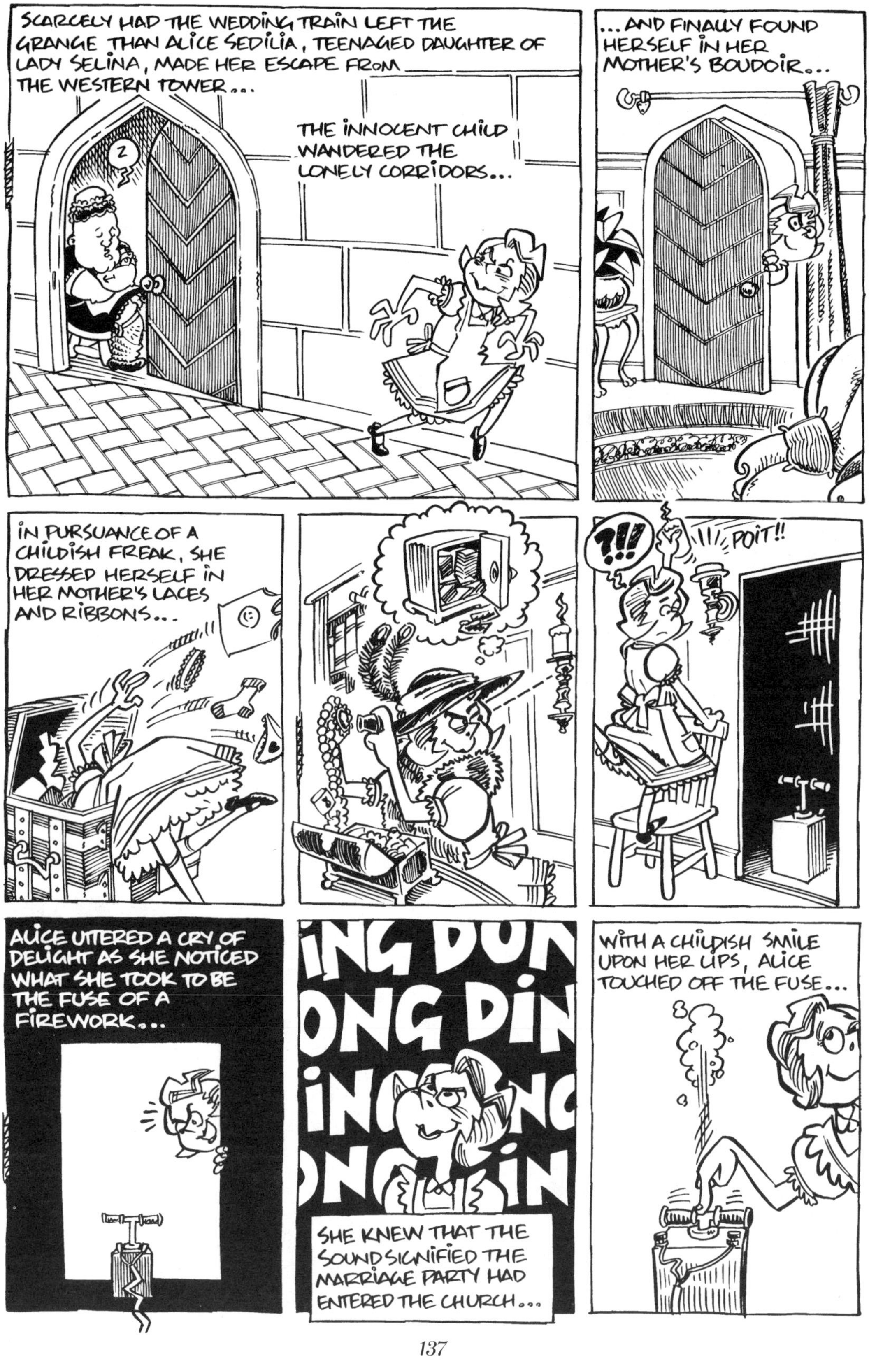
SCARCELY HAD THE WEDDING TRAIN LEFT THE GRANGE THAN ALICE SEDILIA, TEENAGED DAUGHTER OF LADY SELINA, MADE HER ESCAPE FROM THE WESTERN TOWER...
Z
THE INNOCENT CHILD WANDERED THE LONELY CORRIDORS...
...AND FINALLY FOUND HERSELF IN HER MOTHER'S BOUDOIR...
IN PURSUANCE OF A CHILDISH FREAK, SHE DRESSED HERSELF IN HER MOTHER'S LACES AND RIBBONS...
?!!
POIT!!
ALICE UTTERED A CRY OF DELIGHT AS SHE NOTICED WHAT SHE TOOK TO BE THE FUSE OF A FIREWORK...
ING DON
ONG DIN
ING NG
ONG IN
SHE KNEW THAT THE SOUND SIGNIFIED THE MARRIAGE PARTY HAD ENTERED THE CHURCH...
WITH A CHILDISH SMILE UPON HER LIPS, ALICE TOUCHED OFF THE FUSE...

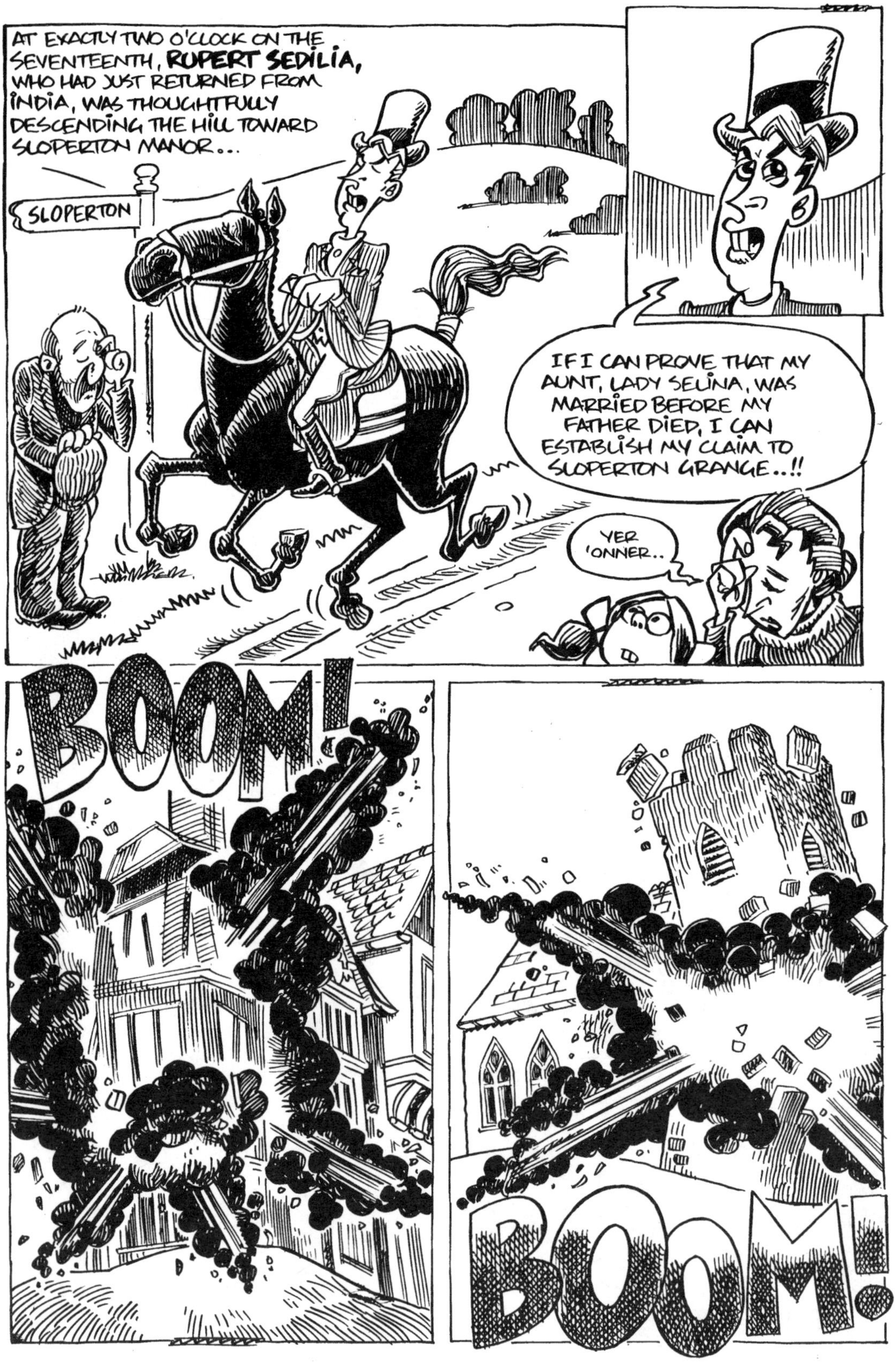
AT EXACTLY TWO O'CLOCK ON THE SEVENTEENTH, RUPERT SEDILIA, WHO HAD JUST RETURNED FROM INDIA, WAS THOUGHTFULLY DESCENDING THE HILL TOWARD SLOPERTON MANOR...
SLOPERTON
IF I CAN PROVE THAT MY AUNT, LADY SELINA, WAS MARRIED BEFORE MY FATHER DIED, I CAN ESTABLISH MY CLAIM TO SLOPERTON GRANGE..!!
YER 'ONNER...
BOOM!
BOOM!

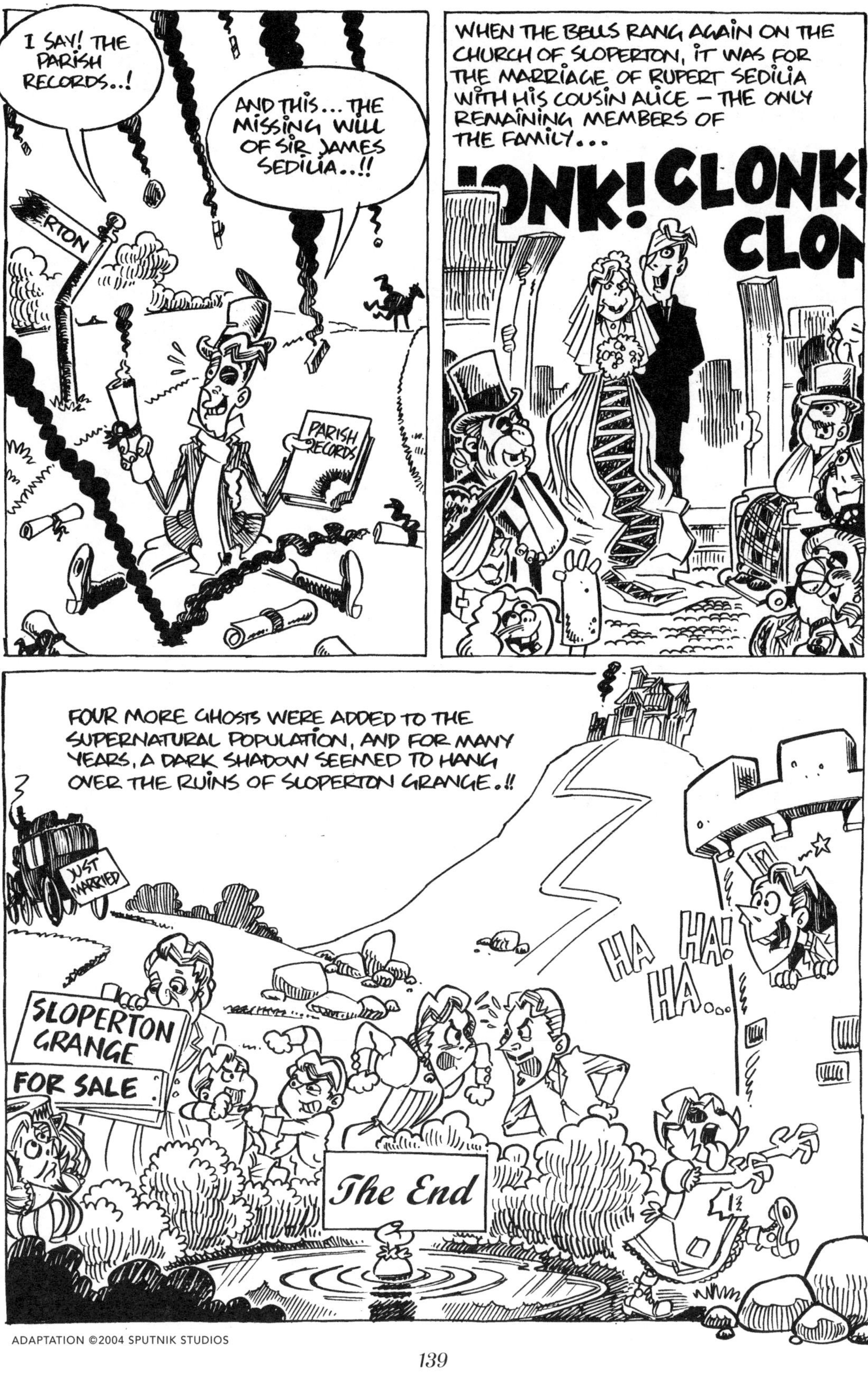
I SAY! THE PARISH RECORDS..!
AND THIS... THE MISSING WILL OF SIR JAMES SEDILIA..!!
RTON
PARISH RECORDS
WHEN THE BELLS RANG AGAIN ON THE CHURCH OF SLOPERTON, IT WAS FOR THE MARRIAGE OF RUPERT SEDILIA WITH HIS COUSIN ALICE – THE ONLY REMAINING MEMBERS OF THE FAMILY...
ONK! CLONK! CLON
FOUR MORE GHOSTS WERE ADDED TO THE SUPERNATURAL POPULATION, AND FOR MANY YEARS, A DARK SHADOW SEEMED TO HANG OVER THE RUINS OF SLOPERTON GRANGE..!!
JUST MARRIED
HA HA! HA...
SLOPERTON GRANGE
FOR SALE
The End

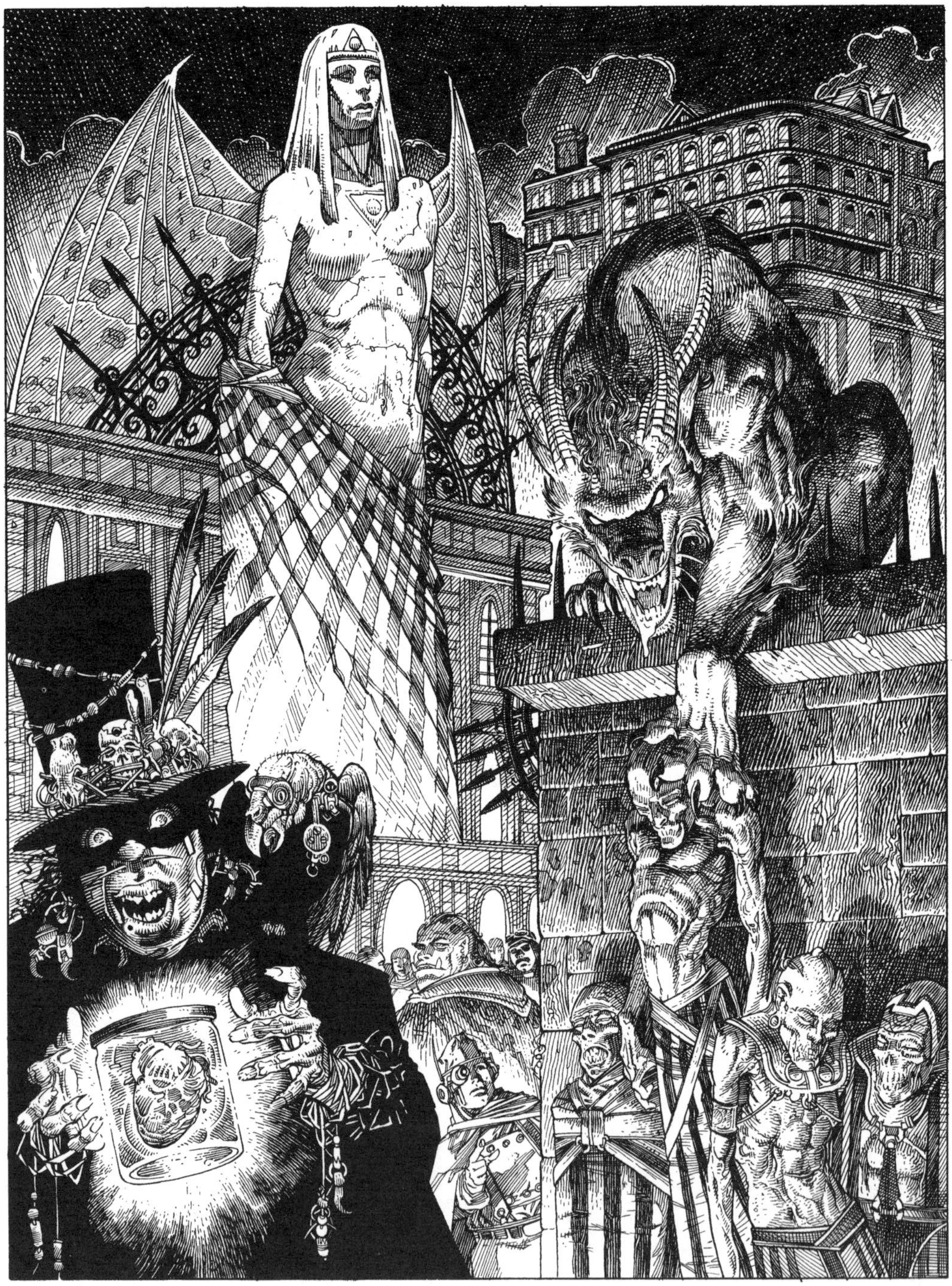

MARK A. NELSON *(cover, page 140)*

Cover artist Mark Nelson was a professor of art at Northern Illinois University for twenty years. He is currently a staff artist at Raven Software, doing conceptual work, painting digital skins and creating textures for computer games. His comics credits include *Blood and Shadows* for DC, *Aliens* for Dark Horse Comics, and *Feud* for Marvel. He has worked for numerous publishers, and his art is represented in *Spectrum #4, 5, 6, 8* and *From Pencils to Inks: The Art of Mark A. Nelson* (2004 Baron Publishing). Mark's comics and illustrations have appeared in *Graphic Classics: Edgar Allan Poe, Graphic Classics: Arthur Conan Doyle, Graphic Classics: H.P. Lovecraft,*

Graphic Classics: Jack London, Graphic Classics: Ambrose Bierce, Rosebud 18 and *The Best of Rosebud*, all from Eureka Productions.

AMBROSE BIERCE *(page 2)*

Born in rural Ohio in 1842, Bierce became a printer's apprentice for a small Indiana newspaper until 1860, when he enlisted in the Union army and witnessed some of the major battles of the Civil War. Following a short military career, he resigned in disgust over a lack of promotion and instead pursued a successful career in journalism. In his time, Bierce was a celebrity as a satirical columnist, but disappointment over a lack of acceptance of his fiction and a troubled personal life caused him to become increasingly bitter and withdrawn in his later years. In 1913, at the age of 71, he crossed the border into Mexico, "with a pretty definite purpose, which, however, is not at present disclosable." He was never heard from again.

BRANDON RAGNAR JOHNSON *(page 2)*

Illustrator Brandon Ragnar Johnson grew up under the sweltering sun and bright lights of Las Vegas. From there it was stints in Japan, Taiwan, Mexico and Hollywood before settling in Southern California with his wife and two children. He now works in advertising and as an animation development artist for Disney, MTV, Nickelodeon and other studios. Prints of Ragnar's illustrations of women and monsters, women and chimps, and women and women can be found in galleries, fine retail establishments and at www.littlecartoons.com.

H. P. LOVECRAFT *(page 4)*

Howard Phillips Lovecraft was born in Providence, Rhode Island in 1890. His father died in 1898, and his mother suffered from mental instability until her death in 1921. Poor health and his neurotic, overprotective mother combined to make something of a recluse of Lovecraft. He was obsessed with dreams, and wrote most of his stories and poems around a central theme of ancient gods who once ruled the earth and are merely awaiting a return to power. Since Lovecraft's death in 1937, his stories have grown in popularity and have spawned a huge cult of both fans and professional writers who continue to expand Lovecraft's themes through stories set in the "Cthulhu Mythos."

MICHAEL MANNING *(page 4)*

Michael is the creator of the erotic graphic novels *The Spider Garden, Hydrophidian, In A Metal Web I* and *II*, and *Tranceptor* (all NBM Publishing). He studied at the School of the Museum of Fine Arts in Boston, and began publishing comics in 1987 while working as an animator and director of short films and music videos. A move to San Francisco's Mission District in 1991 coincided with Michael's decision to focus on erotic illustration and gallery shows full-time. His admiration for the Symbolist and Pre-Raphaelite art movements as well as the classical ukiyo-e prints of Tsukioka Yoshitoshi and Unagawa Kuniyoshi has contributed to the formulation of Manning's distinct style. Michael's artwork can be seen online at www.thespidergarden.net and in the pages of *Graphic Classics: Bram Stoker* and *Graphic Classics: Robert Louis Stevenson*.

EDGAR ALLAN POE *(page 26)*

Edgar Allan Poe, the orphaned son of itinerant actors, led a tumultuous adolescence of drink and gambling, which resulted in the failure of both his university and military careers. Throughout his life he was plagued by poverty, poor health, insecurity, and depression, much by his own doing and a result of his continuing problems with alcohol. He struggled unsuccessfully as a writer until winning a short story contest in 1833. Today he is generally acknowledged as the inventor of both the gothic short story and the detective story, a pioneer of early science fiction and the founding father of the horror genre.

ROD LOTT *(page 26, 104)*

Based in Oklahoma City, Rod Lott is a freelance writer and graphic designer in the worlds of journalism, advertising and beyond. For the past ten years, he has served as editor and publisher of the more-or-less quarterly magazine *Hitch: The Journal of Pop Culture Absurdity*. Rod's humorous essays have been published in anthologies including *More Mirth of a Nation, 101 Damnations* and *May Contain Nuts*. You can learn more about his work online at www.rodlott.com and www.hitchmagazine.com.

KEVIN ATKINSON *(page 26)*

"I've lived in Texas my whole life with the exception of 1985–1988 when I went to New Jersey to study with [famed comics artist and teacher] Joe Kubert," says Kevin. Since then he has done short stories and full-length comics for various publishers. He wrote and drew two series, *Snarl* and *Planet 29* and collaborated on another, *Rogue Satellite Comics*. Lately he's inked *The Tick* comics, and illustrated Drew Edward's *Halloween Man* and *The Celebrated Jumping Frog* for *Graphic Classics: Mark Twain*. More of Kevin's art can be seen at www.meobeco.com/pulptoons/index.htm.

OLIVE SCHREINER (page 47)

Born in 1855 to South African missionaries, Olive Schreiner studied in England, where she published her first novel, *The Story of an African Farm*. The book was considered controversial for its feminist and anti-Christian sentiments. Her *Woman and Labour* (1911) is a key feminist work, and she was a leader in the British pacifist movement during World War I. Schreiner's 1897 book *Trooper Peter Halkett of Mashonaland* was an attack on imperialism and racism in South Africa, where she died in 1920.

JACKIE SMITH (page 47)

Jackie Smith comes from Sheffield, in northern England. She originally trained as an animator and has drawn comics since the late 1970s. She has been a T-shirt designer, graphic artist and Youth Arts Worker and a freelance cartoonist, writer and illustrator since 1980. Her work has appeared in *Knockabout Comics*, as well as *Graphic Classics: Ambrose Bierce* and *Graphic Classics: Mark Twain*. Other long-term contracts have been with *Big Mags* and *Myatt McFarlane*. She also takes comics and illustration into schools and has used *Graphic Classics* in her work with excluded teenagers. Jackie enjoys drawing caricatures and portraits at fairs and occasionally sneaks off to the wild peaks to paint landscapes. Present projects include a graphic novel and a series of portraits of scary teenagers.

HONORÉ DE BALZAC (page 52)

French novelist and journalist Balzac (1799–1850) is considered one of the creators of realism in literature. He studied law at the Sorbonne, but soon abandoned it in favor of a literary career. His prodigious output included his greatest work, a linked collection of nearly a hundred novels and short stories called *La Comédie Humaine*. It is a detailed record of French society at all levels, with a cast of over 2000 sometimes recurring characters.

MARK DANCEY (page 52)

Mark Dancey was born in Ann Arbor, Michigan in 1963. "For no good reason," Mark co-founded the satirical and highly influential *Motorbooty Magazine* in the late 1980s and filled its pages with his comics and illustrations. As a member of rock band Big Chief during the 1990s he got a lock on the position of band propagandist and subsequently produced all manner of CD covers, T-shirt designs, backdrops and posters for that outfit. Having extricated himself from the world of rock, Mark now lives in Detroit, where he produces painstaking works in oil and prints silk-screened posters under the aegis of his company, Illuminado.us.

W. W. JACOBS (page 53)

William Wymark Jacobs was a popular British writer of short humorous stories, often with surprise endings. Many were set on the London docks and the tramp steamers with which he was familiar. Today Jacobs is best known for his horror tales, especially his classic 1902 story *The Monkey's Paw*, which has been filmed, televised, adapted for the stage, and included in numerous anthologies.

JOHN W. PIERARD (page 53, back cover)

John Pierard has had a varied career in illustration. After leaving the bosom of his beloved Syracuse University for New York City, he immediately found work in publications such as *Screw* and *Velvet Touch Magazine*, where he illustrated stories like *Sex Junky*. In a major departure, he then graduated to illustrating children's fiction, including Mel Gilden's *P. S. 13* series, and various projects by noted children's author Bruce Coville. He has worked for Marvel Comics, *Asimov's Magazine* and Greenwich Press and has exhibited his art in New York galleries. John's comics adaptations also appear in *Graphic Classics: H.G. Wells*, *Graphic Classics: Jack London* and *Graphic Classics: Bram Stoker*.

SAKI (page 72)

Hector Hugh Munro was born in Burma in 1870. He was sent to Scotland to be raised and educated by two aunts he grew to despise. Hector briefly journeyed to Burma in his twenties as a police officer, but returned to England due to health problems. There he began to write for various periodicals and later as a correspondent in Paris, Russia and the Balkans. For his fiction he took the pen name "Saki" from the cupbearer in *The Rubaiyat* of Omar Khayyam. Munro enlisted in World War I, and was killed by a sniper's bullet in France in 1916.

GABRIELLE BELL (page 72)

Brooklyn artist Gabrielle Bell has contributed to anthologies including *Kramers Ergot*, *Bogus Dead*, *Scheherezade* and *Orchid*, for which she adapted another Saki story, *Tobermory*. Her book *When I'm Old and Other Stories*, a collection of her mini-comics, was published in 2003 by Alternative Press. Gabrielle is currently working on another series titled *Lucky*.

FITZ-JAMES O'BRIEN (page 76)

Born and educated in Ireland, O'Brien emigrated to the U.S. at age 24 in 1852. There he became a leader among the New York Bohemians as he began to publish fiction and poetry in various periodicals. He also wrote a number of plays which were very popular at the time, and was an accomplished short story writer who helped develop the American literary magazine, though today his work is little-known. O'Brien volunteered to fight with Union forces in the Civil War, and in 1862 he died of complications from a wound suffered in battle.

MILTON KNIGHT (page 76)

Milton Knight claims he started drawing, painting and creating his own attempts at comic books and animation at age two. "I've never formed a barrier between fine art and cartooning," says Milt. "Growing up, I treasured Chinese watercolors, Breughel, Charlie Brown and Terrytoons equally." His work has appeared in magazines including *Heavy Metal*, *High Times*, *National Lampoon* and *Nickelodeon Magazine*, and he has illustrated record covers, posters, candy packaging and T-shirts, and occasionally exhibited his paintings. Labor on *Ninja Turtles* comics allowed him to get up a grubstake to move to the West Coast in 1991, where he became an animator and director on *Felix the Cat* cartoons. Milt's comics titles include *Midnite the Rebel Skunk*, *Hinkley*, and *Slug and Ginger* and *Hugo*. Check for the latest news at www.miltonknight.net.

JACK LONDON (page 83)

As a sailor, petty thief, hobo, prospector, rancher, war correspondent and socialist spokesman, Jack London led a life that was as exciting, inspiring, and tragic as any of his many stories. London was born in San Francisco in 1876, an illegitimate child. His mother and stepfather were never far from poverty, and at the age of 13, Jack left school and began the life of a common laborer. But his appetite for reading allowed him to continue educating himself, and his talent for writing of the experiences of his life at sea, in the Klondike and around the world eventually made him, by the time of his premature death in 1916, the most popular author in America.

RYAN INZANA (page 83)

Ryan Inzana is an illustrator and cartoonist from Brooklyn, New York. His illustrations can be seen in publications including *The New York Times*, *The Wall Street Journal*, *The Nation* and *The Progressive*. Ryan's comics work has been published in *World War 3 Illustrated*, *New York Waste* and online in *Slate Magazine*. His graphic novel, *Johnny Jihad*, has been chosen as one of *Booklist's* top ten graphic novels of 2003. He is currently at work on a semi-autobiographical graphic novel series entitled *God-less America*, a brutal memoir of the life and times of a footloose artist in the belly of the beast in Brooklyn, New York, to be published by NBM.

HOWARD R. GARIS (page 94)

Howard R. Garis was a reporter for the *Newark Evening News* and a prolific author of children's books, best known for his *Uncle Wiggly* series about a gentlemanly rheumatic rabbit, which spawned the board game still produced today. He also wrote a vast number of books under various pseudonyms for the Stratemeyer Syndicate from 1910 to 1933. These included *The Bobbsey Twins* (as Laura Lee Hope), *The Great Marvel* (as Roy Rockwood), *Baseball Joe* (as Lester Chadwick) and the first 36 volumes of *Tom Swift* under the name Victor Appleton.

ONSMITH JEREMI (page 94)

Onsmith Jeremi (aka Jeremy Smith) grew up in a couple of small towns in central Oklahoma, putting in his factory and fast food time while nurturing an interest in small press comics, cartoons, and "zines." He then moved to Chicago, where he started a small press anthology, *Bomb Time for Bonzo*, with fellow artists Ben Chandler and Henry Ng (of the early *Non* anthology). With no formal art education, Onsmith has been producing comics for the past four years. His work has appeared in anthologies including *Expo 2002*, *Studygroup 12* and *Proper Gander*, as well as *Graphic Classics: H.P. Lovecraft*, *Graphic Classics: Jack London* and *Graphic Classics: Bram Stoker*. To see more of his work, visit www.onsmithcomics.com.

CLARK ASHTON SMITH (page 104)

A self-educated Californian, Clark Ashton Smith began writing fiction at age eleven, though most of his early writings were poetry. On the publication of his first poems in 1911, he was hailed as "the new Keats" by the San Francisco press, and became friends with Ambrose Bierce, Jack London and George Sterling. Despite the early success, and due to ill health, Smith chose to maintain a quiet, solitary life in rural California. Smith's first horror story was published in *The Overland Monthly* in 1925, and during the 1930s he produced about a hundred fantasy stories for the pulp magazines, especially *Weird Tales*. His work drew the attention of H.P. Lovecraft, with whom Smith corresponded until Lovecraft's death in 1937. After that date, Smith wrote little weird fiction, but concentrated on his poetry and artwork until his death in 1961. He is now considered one of the greatest fantasy poets of the 20th century.

RICHARD JENKINS *(page 104)*
Oklahoma artist Richard Jenkins is the illustrator and co-creator of the *Sky Ape* comic book series praised by *Entertainment Weekly* and featured in *Spin Magazine*. Jenkins also travels the country as an artist-in-residence teaching kids how to create their own comics. Check out his website at www.studiohijinx.com.

BRET HARTE *(page 124)*
Francis Bret Harte was born in New York in 1839, and moved to California in 1854. There he worked as a miner, teacher, stagecoach driver and journalist and was eventually appointed Secretary of the San Francisco Branch Mint. His first writings were for *The Californian*, where he worked with Mark Twain. He became the editor of *The Overland Monthly* in 1868, which brought his fiction to national fame. The magazine also debuted the work of Jack London, Ambrose Bierce and Clark Ashton Smith. Harte's stories and poems set in the American West were extremely popular in the Eastern U.S., and in 1871 he moved to New York, then to Boston. In 1878 he was appointed U.S. Consul to Germany, and later Consul to Scotland and England, where he died in 1902.

ANTONELLA CAPUTO *(page 124)*
Antonella Caputo was born and educated in Rome, Italy, and is now living in England. She has been an architect, archaeologist, art restorer, photographer, calligrapher, interior designer, theater designer, actress and theater director. Antonella's first published work was *Casa Montesi*, a weekly comic strip that appeared in *Il Journalino*. She has since written comedies for children and scripts for comics in Europe and the U.S., before joining Nick Miller as a partner in Sputnik Studios. Nick and Antonella previously collaborated in *Graphic Classics: H.G. Wells, Graphic Classics: Jack London, Graphic Classics: Mark Twain* and *Graphic Classics: Ambrose Bierce.*

NICK MILLER *(page 124)*
The son of two artists, Nick Miller learned to draw at an early age. After leaving college, he worked as a graphic designer before a bout of chronic fatigue syndrome forced him to switch to cartooning full-time. Since then, his work has appeared in numerous adult and children's magazines as well as comics anthologies in Britain, Europe and the U.S. His weekly newspaper comics run in *The Planet on Sunday*. He shares his Lancaster, England house with two cats, a lodger and Antonella Caputo. See more of Nick's work at www.cat-box.net/sputnik.

TOM POMPLUN
The designer, editor and publisher of *Graphic Classics*, Tom also designed and produced *Rosebud*, a journal of fiction, poetry and illustration, from 1993 to 2003. He is currently working on the eleventh book in the *Graphic Classics* series, *Graphic Classics: O. Henry.* This collection of stories from the master of the surprise ending will feature *The Ransom of Red Chief* (the precursor to *Home Alone*), illustrated by Johnny Ryan. Plus *The Caballero's Way,* the original tale of The Cisco Kid, by Mark A. Nelson, and the famed Christmas classic *The Gift of the Magi,* illustrated by Lisa K. Weber. With seven more stories, including a new O. Henry "sequel" by Mort Castle, and art by Rick Geary, Gerry Alanguilan, Joe Ollman, Rico Schacherl, Pedro Lopez, Shary Flenniken and a great cover by Esao Andrews. The book is scheduled for release in January 2005. You can see previews, samples from the series' artists and much more at www.graphicclassics.com.

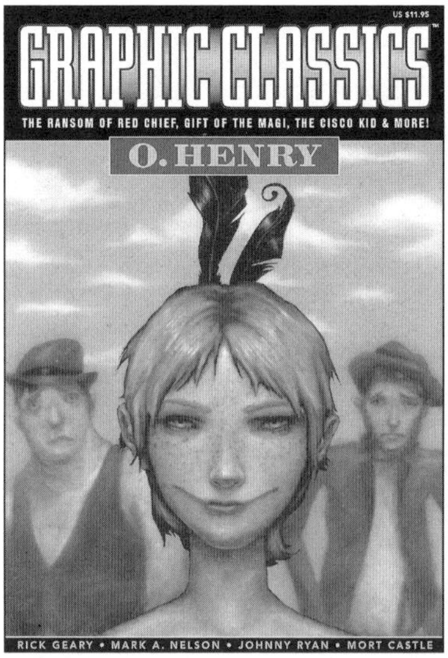
US $11.95
GRAPHIC CLASSICS™
THE RANSOM OF RED CHIEF, GIFT OF THE MAGI, THE CISCO KID & MORE!
O. HENRY
RICK GEARY • MARK A. NELSON • JOHNNY RYAN • MORT CASTLE